DATE DUE			
No. Independence Branch			
24 Hwy. & Spring			
Independence, MO 64050			
Phone: 252-0950			

NI

Teddy Bears Past & Present
A Collector's Identification Guide

by Linda Mullins

Photography by Scott Linnett and Myron Hemley.

Written in the "International Year of the Teddy Bear," designated by Good Bears of the World.

Published by HOBBY HOUSE PRESS, INC.
Cumberland, Maryland 21502

Additional Copies of this book may be purchased at $19.95
from
HOBBY HOUSE PRESS, INC.
900 Frederick Street
Cumberland, Maryland 21502
or from your favorite bookstore or dealer.
Please add $1.75 per copy postage.

ISBN: 0-87588-264-1

Table of Contents

Dedication

To my husband Wally with all my love and gratitude.

Personal Acknowledgements

I have so many people to thank for helping make my Teddy Bear book a reality. It was the enthusiasm and support of my family and friends that helped me accomplish this challenging project.

My husband Wally is at the top of the list. His understanding and encouragement throughout this past year has surpassed all the qualifications for a number one husband.

My very special new friend, Georgi Bohrod Rothe, deserves a very big thank you for all of her assistance, guidance and support. Her true personal interest and professional suggestions were of great importance to me.

Thanks also goes out to Flore Emory, for opening up her wonderful country home to enable the Teddy Bears to be photographed in natural settings; to my photographers Scott Linnett and Myron Hemley whose enthusiasm and patience never faltered during the hours and hours of taking pictures of hundreds of Teddy Bears; to Evelyn Gathings for her special artwork and Mr. A. Christian Revi, my patient and well advising editor. Finally, to my publisher Gary Ruddell, for having faith in me and this book.

Acknowledgements

My gratitude for the following companies and organizations for their assistance.

Applause, Woodland Hills, California (Katherine Galligan).

Bearly There Company, Westminster, California (Linda Spiegal).

C.B.S. Toys. New York, New York (Christopher Byrne).

R. Dakin and Company, San Francisco, California (Cathryn L. Sotir).

Dean's Childsplay Toys, Pontypool, Gwent, United Kingdom (Ian Scott).

Gebr. Hermann KG, West Germany (Margrit Drolshagen).

Geyer-McAllister Publications, *Playthings,* New York, New York (Harry J. Guckert, June Jones).

Good Bears of The World, Honolulu, Hawaii (Jim Ownby, Katherine Mitchell).

Gund, New York, New York (Ann Antonacci).

House of Nisbet, Winscombe, England (Jack Wilson).

Lasting Endearments, Costa Mesa, California (Pat Rypinski).

Merrythought, Shropshire, England (Oliver Holmes)

Pollock's Toy Museum, London, England (Mrs. M. Fawdry).

Theodore Roosevelt Collection, Harvard Library (Wallace F. Daily, curator).

Smithsonian Institution, Washington, D.C.

Margarete Steiff G.M.B.H., West Germany (Dr. H. Zimmermann, president) (Jörg Jünginger [Steiff]).

U.S.D.A. Forest Service, Smokey Bear Program, Washington, D.C. (Jo Baker).

Thank you to the following collectors for sharing their priceless collections with me.

Baldwin, Bob	Lauver, Barbara
Bowen, Sally and Warren	
Block, Elke	McNabb, Dick
Brewer, Kim	Madden, Sandra
Broder, Mark and Linda	Maxwell Jr., James S.
Burnett, Carl	Neble, Jeff and Karlene
Cain, Sally	Port, Beverly
Caputo, Virginia	Rohaly, Lillian
Carmen, Blossom	Runzo, Jim and Frankie
Cooney, Dan and Chris	Sawyer, Celia
Darter, Gale and Janice	Schoonmaker, Pat
Duncan, Jeri, Leslie	Sebestyen, Anita
Eldridge, Ernie	Sickler, Joan
Fernando, Barabra	Sieverling, Helen
Hebbs, Pam	Summit, Rol and Jo
Hiscox, Mimi	Volpp, Paul and Rosemary
Jorgensen, Fred	

And to the many others who were so generous with their precious bears.

4

Chapter One

What Teddy Bear Collecting Is All About

Teddy Bears have been popular for a long time, but their acceptance as a valuable collectible is remarkably recent. At the turn-of-the-century, children the world over fell in love with the soft, friendly stuffed animal. Now, men and women, young and old, novice collector and sophisticated dealer consider Teddy Bears from a different, more complex viewpoint. Because of this modern development, the study of bears became essential only in the past decade.

This book came to be because I, too, love Teddy Bears and everything about them. I intend to share a personal outlook of Teddy Bears from their historical roots to their actual construction. I have included personal memories, stories of bears and their original owners, thoughts from handmade bear artists and factual specifications of Teddy Bear identification. You'll also learn how to "play with" your bears through creative displays and how these special toys can help the less fortunate.

Bears satisfy many needs. They offer children the comfort and companionship of an always understanding, soft, furry friend. They provide a fullfilling hobby and profitable business to bear makers, ranging from large companies to single seamstresses. They intrigue adult collectors who spend delightful hours researching the origin of their own "grown-up" toys.

The more you know about bears, the more you'll enjoy their companionship. One look at a bear from years ago reinforces the evidence of the many levels and depth of their ongoing popularity.

Teddy Bears were not pampered, shined and polished by fastidious antique collectors. Sophisticated art connoiseurs did not exhibit the lovable creatures in well-lit protective glass cases in quiet art galleries. Libraries did not tag and catalog these toys, storing them in remote vaults for privileged scholars.

No.

Children loved Teddy Bears. They showed their affection by biting off their noses, dragging them through mud puddles, pulling off their arms and chewing on their ears. Children took care of their bears by feeding them strawberry jam, taking them swimming and generally destroying many of the most outstanding characteristics of this now valuable collectible.

Further compounding this ruthless destruction, were the mothers of these "thoughtless" children. In order to preserve the life of a bear, mothers, without consideration of those of us who want to know the "worth" of our priceless antique toy, actually restuffed, resewed and generally reconstructed ancient bears with materials and methods that are nearly impossible to trace.

Of course, it is this deep human involvement that makes us all love our bears so much. Yet, there is a desire to know from where our bear evolved, who made it and when.

Even with the lack of documentation standards and inconsistency in appearance, identifying the age and manufacturer of your Teddy Bears is, often possible. It does take practice, study and time.

So, please use this book as a guide and inspiration to enhance your understanding of these precious creatures who've taken a prominent spot in our hearts.

Chapter Two

Some Words About Me And How I Became A Collector

My birthplace, the County of Kent in England, is a storybook picture of old country homes, narrow winding lanes, endless green pastures and wonderful, intriguing "Flea Markets."

Some of my very first memories are vivid and frightening thoughts of World War II. Since we lived close to London, air raids were all too frequent. I can still remember the terrible howling of the warning sirens ringing in my ears. As soon as the horrible noise began, I'd cry "Quick, mum! Planes again!"

My mum would clutch me and together with my very first Teddy Bear, we'd hurry to the safety of the bomb shelter. Of course, there was no time to protect even our most precious, personal possessions. And there was always the fear that when the raid was over, our home may have been destroyed. Little did I realize that the comfort of hugging my dear Teddy Bear as a little girl would be a memory that influenced my whole life.

After I left school, my first job was in an office in London. Even though I enjoyed the daily commute (a walk across London Bridge) I soon changed employment to be closer to home. My new position was with a large department store where I stayed for eight years, eventually rising to the position of supervisor. After that I found myself managing a ladies apparel shop for two years.

Although there was a great deal of satisfaction in dealing with friendly customers and in my business achievements as a young woman, I must admit a deep yearning inside me gave birth to dreams of adventure, travel and excitement.

My aunt and uncle, who already had emigrated to California, wrote letters of warm, blissful sunshine, interesting people and new experiences. In June of 1968, with tearful goodbyes to my family and friends, I bravely set my sights on life in a new land.

To think that I embarked on my journey with just three suitcases and a couple of boxes amazes me. How my life has changed from that of the young English girl with nothing on her mind but sports, dancing and cricket matches.

Life in America surpassed my girlhood dreams. The bright California sun, in contrast to the dreary grayness of my homeland, was probably reason enough for this major move. The light of that sun nurtured a totally new outlook for me.

In 1971 I returned to England for a visit to introduce my husband Wally to my family, to show him where I was born and where I spent most of my childhood. However, even the most dutiful son-in-law, may find visiting in-laws tedious at times.

Always the collector, my husband was originally interested in antique cars. In fact, his old 1930 purple Packard Model 745 Roadster is part of Harrah's permanent museum collection in Reno, Nevada. Today, as a member of the Musical Box Society, Wally's main interests are hurdy-gurdies and merry-go-round organs. So I knew Wally would appreciate a day at the famous Portabello Antique Market in London.

It was there the collecting bug bit me. It's all Wally's fault. So the excursion we took ostensibly to please Wally, changed my life.

Every little shop displayed an entrancing array of beautiful objects. Delicate handmade laces, Victorian clothes adorned with dainty antique jewelry, handcrafted intricately carved furniture and elegant English silver created a fantasy world I never dreamed existed.

An elderly man strolled the streets. The sound of his hurdy-gurdy provided the sound track to the magical scene, while the colorful parrot perched upon his shoulder squawked greetings at the shoppers.

I couldn't get enough. Wally literally dragged me away as the stalls were closing.

It was then an awareness of the pleasures of collecting, that suspense of discovering hidden treasure and the satisfaction of preserving the wonders of the past began to grow within me.

Now my world is filled with many of the same kind of objects which so enthralled me during that day. And of all the beautiful and sentimental examples of human love, creativity and craft, the Teddy Bear is my favorite.

Illustration 1. Linda Mullins (age 4) with her first bear.

Illustration 2. The magical sound of the hurdy-gurdy man can be heard throughout the streets of the famous Portabello Road Antique Market.

Illustration 3. A "lucky find" during one of our visits to England.

Illustration 4. You can't mistake Linda and Wally's motorhome. The spare tire cover shows a cute hand-painted Teddy Bear with the words "The Bear Hunters" Wally and Linda.

Chapter Three

In The Beginning

History was not one of my better subjects in school. Yet, when it comes to the study of Teddy's evolution, the legends of this special creature's heritage never cease to intrigue me.

Even though most seasoned bear collectors are undoubtedly aware of the basic roots of their precious possessions, the special circumstances of Teddy's birth always deserve recalling. For those who are new to the fascinating world of bears, the unique settings, timing and love which brought Teddy to life will enhance your affection for Teddy Bears.

These chapters do not attempt to detail all the nuances, ins and outs, ups and downs and arounds of Teddy's development. They simply aim to highlight the very beginnings of our favorite subject, a creature born to capture the imagination of children and matured to become an all-time delight to young and old alike.

The social climate at the beginning of the twentieth century was ripe for Teddy's arrival. For the first time in history, even the "common" man found some time to relax and enjoy freedom from toil and drudgery. Not only did this post industrial revolution era forecast the possibilities of leisure time, it opened the door to modern communication.

So, in those early days of the 1900s, with a light-hearted gaiety pervading many levels of society and the means to share information with new ease, Teddy was born.

Actually, the bear itself has been a favorite with children and adults since the 1800s. Famous children's stories of real bears and the Victorian automated bears with fierce expressions and bodies realistically covered with fur were always quite popular in those turn-of-the-century days.

It appears until one of the first Steiff advertisements ran in 1906, bears were called Bruins or simply Bear. But, as we are well aware, today our bears are first and foremost known as Teddy.

The Father of the Teddy Bear

As a child, Theodore Roosevelt was frail and sickly. His first knowledge of the wonders of nature came to him vicariously from books. With maturity, his health and strength improved. The wealthy young man of Dutch heritage cut a rugged figure with the Rough Riders (the first U.S. volunteer cavalry). Yet the compassionate sensitivities developed in his youth never left. His love for animals and nature was commemorated on the side of Mt. Rushmore — and — on the bear that now carries his name.

It was in November 1902, that President Theodore Roosevelt journeyed south to settle a boundary dispute. His mission was to draw a line between the states of Mississippi and Louisiana.

During a break in political negotiations, the President accepted an invitation to join a hunting expedition in Smedes, Mississippi. Ten days of hunting and not a single bear was sighted. His hosts, in an effort to please their honored guest, wanted to make sure the President would have a trophy for his trouble. When no bears were evident, they frantically searched the woods. Finally, they found a small bear cub and drove the frightened animal in the President's direction. Brought out of his tent by the excited cry of "Bear!", Roosevelt was disgusted to see only a small cub tethered to a tree. He took one look at the little animal and turned away, saying he "drew the line" at killing anything so small.

The press capitalized on the event. Clifford K. Berryman, a well-known cartoonist with the *Washington Post,* illustrated Roosevelt, hand-upraised, refusing to shoot a bear cub. The caption read "Drawing the Line in Mississippi."

The cartoon, reprinted millions of times, attracted widescale attention from political commentators, humorists and toy makers world around. Bears of every shape and form flooded the stores.

Berryman, known to dislike personal publicity, could have made a fortune with his concept. But, at the time, he didn't realize how the political cartoon would set off a craze for the most lovable toy we know.

Four years later (in 1906) at a White House wedding reception for Roosevelt's daughter, guests were greeted by Steiff bears decorating the tables. As a tribute to Teddy Roosevelt's legendary outdoorsman prowess, the stuffed animals were dressed as hunters and fishermen. When the question was raised regarding the breed of the animals, a guest spoke up: "Why they're *Teddy* Bears, of course!"

And so they are.

Illustration 5. The November 10, 1902, historical event when President Roosevelt refused to shoot the helpless bear cub was satirized by Clifford Berryman in this famous cartoon. *Courtesy Harvard College Library.*

Chapter Four

History of Leading Bear Manufacturers Including A Guide To Identification

Companies manufacturing Teddy Bears abound throughout the world. Each possess a unique history. The following company histories will open the door to understanding some of the best in the field.

German Manufacturers

Germany was already renowned through Europe and America for its fine craftsmanship in early toys during the late 17th century. Many companies were family concerns beginning their businesses from their home and growing into recognized leading manufacturers by the early 1900s. The oldest and most well-known of these firms in the Teddy Bear world is Steiff.

Steiff

If Teddy Roosevelt was the father of the Teddy Bear, Margarete Steiff is certainly the mother.

Stricken by polio as a child, the young girl lived happily in a picturesque German village of Giengen-on-the-Brenz. A Hansel and Gretel-like village, with cobblestone streets and centuries-old quaint homes, it is just the setting for toyland to come alive.

Studying dressmaking as a young girl, Margarete was the first person in town to own a sewing machine. Her paralysis forced her to run the machine backwards. Although still a teenager, Margarete began to show her business acumen early. In 1877 she opened her own ladies' and children's clothing shop.

Children played a large part in the young dressmaker's life. Many a day children surrounded her at the door of her small home, intently listening to colorful stories woven by Margarete as she sat confined to a wheelchair. Her active mind was full of fantasies of the beautiful and fun things she would never fulfill because of her handicap.

In 1880, the imaginative seamstress conceived the idea of sewing an elephant into the form of a pincushion. She gave her little animal pincushion as gifts to her five nephews and two nieces.

Then Margarete had the idea to turn the pincushion into an elephant toy. The children were overjoyed. Soon, Margarete created a managerie of felt animals: pigs, monkeys, donkeys and camels. Her brother Fritz marketed the soft animals at local fairs.

At that time, felt was a new material with an elasticity which offered more versatility for Margarete's creation of animal designs.

Under Margarete's always watchful eye, the local factory produced Steiff soft animal toys in growing amounts. The "fraulein" herself set the superior quality stands still maintained by the company. She personally examined every toy animal before it left the floor.

Children throughout southern Germany sang her praises. By the turn-of-the-century, Margarete's nephews (Paul, Richard, Hugo, Otto and Ernest) joined her and turned the soft felt toys into a big business.

Margarete's nephew Richard entered the company in 1897. A graduate of art school, he was an important addition to the family team. While a student in Stuttgart, Richard Steiff spent many hours sketching at the Nills Animals Show. After working with these drawings, he designed a young bear toy.

It was not the first bear to be made. Bears standing on four legs, mechanical dancing bears already existed. But this one, with movable joints like a doll, could be dressed and cuddled and loved, Richard maintained. And he was right.

It is said Richard's aunt didn't think much of the prototype she created from his concept. Undaunted, Richard took the new movable bear to the Leipzig Trade Fair in 1903. Not too much attention was paid to the little toy displayed at the Steiff exhibit. By chance, an American buyer (from the George Borgfeldt Co.) saw the model bear and ordered 3,000 to be made. Quickly the order was increased to 6,000 and by the end of the year, Steiff had sold 12,000 of the soft, all-jointed fur bears.

The Steiff Company calls 1907 the Year of the Bear (in German, *Bärenjahre*). After the incident at the White House reception where Teddy received his name, (see Chapter Three, page 8), Steiff bears reached a record sale of nearly 1,000,000 units in that year.

In 1905, Margarete Steiff sent her customers a letter which stated: "From November 1, 1904 (on) each of my products without exception, shall have my trademark... elephant with S- shaped trunk, a small nickel button in left ear."

So, on May 13, 1905, the famous Steiff trademark,

created by Franz Steiff, was registered. The application for registration occurred on December 20, 1904. Since that date, the trademarks and buttons have somewhat changed. (For information on these changes please see the photo section of Steiff buttons and labels.)

The Steiff family built a new factory in 1903. The construction was way ahead of its time with a rather austere architectural style, constructed almost entirely of metal and glass. It offered workers a panoramic view of the majestic hills of the area. These extremely light, pleasant working conditions contributed to the generation of lovely toys that would be eventually produced by the thousands. Today, Giengen is still a company town with a larger percentage of its population employed by the Steiff Company.

Over the years, the Steiff company experienced many changes. New laws and regulations forced them to use new materials and institute new procedures.

I was fortunate enough to see some of these changes and the strict quality control enforced by the Steiff Company during an unforgettable visit to the enchanting village of Giengen and a fascinating tour through the Stieff factory personally conducted by Dieter Kaiser (Export Manager). It was one of the most special events of my many years of collecting.

The vast area of buildings, each one serving a special phase in the completion of the exquisite toys.

Jörg Jünginger heads the design department and is charged with the important and exciting role of responsibility for the Steiff creations.

The strict United States Product Safety Code requires soft toys to be filled with fire resistant and hygenic materials. The excelsior used for the early toys now can only be used for items specifically recommended for adult collectors, not children.

To replace the wearisome hand stuffing method (still performed in the collector series bears) new materials such as polyester fiber is blown into the toys by machine; then weighed to ensure uniformity. Sometimes polyurethane foam is poured into molds which are then baked, causing the material to rise and form the shape of the desired animals.

Dangerous shoe button and glass eyes have now been replaced with plastic eyes securely fastened with a machine called "Starlock" in an effort to protect against the possibilities of a small child swallowing these attached parts.

However, some methods remain the same. Over 80 percent of the cutting is still done by hand. This important phase is performed entirely in Tunisia, but the assembling and completion of the animals is still carried out in Germany and Austria.

One Steiff feature of particular note is the durability of their toys. Strength is added to their seams by the time consuming procedure of frequently reverse stitching and typing knots.

Animals that can now be posed in any position with new bendable wires replace joints in some of the toys. The use of modern day air brushes enables non-toxic color dyes to be artistically sprayed onto the animals' faces giving them character and realism.

The quality control department was extremely impressive. During my tour I saw conscientious Steiff employees reject flaws and mistakes so small that a magnifying glass was almost needed to detect them.

The last step — the stamp of quality and approval — is when the famous Steiff button is attached to the ear. Steiff prizes this procedure so much that only two machines in Giengen are allowed to apply the famous buttons.

Margarete Steiff died in 1909. But her love lives on in her toys. I remembered thinking to myself as I left the factory how happy she would be to know her motto "Only the best is good enough for our children" is still religiously maintained some 75 years later by her family.

Early 1900 Steiff bears are undoubtely one of the most collectible bears today. Their beautiful and distinguished characteristics, high quality of craftsmanship and unique features not only make them very desirable, but extremely difficult to locate. The elongated nose, arms, feet and hump give them a style that when studied is easier to recognize than most other bears.

The definite, identifiable trademark introduced in 1905, was the small metal button marked with the Steiff name that is affixed to the left ear. Unfortunately, many of these buttons were removed by protective mothers for fear that their child might swallow something that tiny.

Because of a large facility and inventory in Steiff warehouses, old stock was probably used throughout a number of different years. It is difficult to say that a certain button or label was used during any particular time. So the following photos should be used only as a guide.

However, we do approximately know the sequence in which buttons and labels were used and the photos will show you this ordering. The date assigned to the bears in the following illustrations is, to the best of my knowledge, when that particular design was introduced, unless I have reason to date them differently.

Steiff

LEFT: *Illustration 6.* Margarete Steiff. Her motto was "only the best is good enough for our children." *Courtesy Steiff.*

MIDDLE: *Illustration 7.* Margarete Steiff's first creation was a felt pincushion in the shape of an elephant. *Courtesy Steiff.*

BOTTOM: *Illustration 8.* Margarete Steiff (right) pauses from her sewing while she talks to her sister-in-law, Ana Steiff. *Courtesy Steiff.*

ABOVE: *Illustration 9.* Margarete's nephew, Richard Steiff. He designed the first Teddy Bear. *Courtesy Steiff.*

ABOVE RIGHT: *Illustration 10.* Drawings from Richard Steiff's sketch book. While studying in Stuttgart, one of his main occupation's was watching the bear acts at the Nills Animal Show. He spent many hours studying the animal's antics and filling his sketch book with renderings of the interesting creatures. It was from these drawings that he created the Teddy Bear. *Courtesy Steiff.*

RIGHT: *Illustration 11.* This original catalog page documents that Steiff was making bears as early as 1903. Note: the name *Bär* (Bear). The name Teddy was not yet being used. Also observe the shape of the bear and its resemblance to the illustrations of Steiff bears from that approximate period. *Courtesy Steiff.*

Neuheiten 1903-04.

Illustration 12. Bears, bears and more bears. 1906. *Courtesy Steiff.*

LEFT: *Illustration 13.* 1907 Steiff advertisement. *Courtesy Playthings.*

ABOVE: *Illustration 14.* The sewing department at the Steiff factory during the early 20th century. *Courtesy Steiff.*

LEFT: *Illustration 15.* After passing inspection, the final step is the Steiff mark of quality — the famous Steiff button affixed into the left ear. *Courtesy Steiff.*

BELOW: *Illustration 16.* Steiff Museum display of a collection of early Steiff dolls. *Courtesy Steiff.*

KNOPF IM OHR

Teddy

12 Teddy

Diese Steiff-Erfindung hat bis
heute von ihrer großen Beliebt-
heit nichts eingebüßt.
Der formenschöne Original-
Steiff-Teddy ist dem Kind ein
lieber Spielgefährte und ein
treuer Kamerad, der durch seine
Beweglichkeit hohen Spielwert
besitzt.

Gewicht kg	Nummer	Sitzhöhe cm	stehend cm	Packung
Teddy				
gegliedert				
Mohairplüsch weiß oder blond				
0.010	12/5307		10	36
mit Rassel				
0.040	5310		15	24
mit Drucksimme				
0.070	5313		18	12
weiß, blond oder dunkelbraun				
0.090	5315		22	12
mit Druckbrummstimme				
0.130	5317.2		25	12
0.210	5320.2		30	6
0.240	5322.2		32	6
0.360	5325.2		35	3
mit automat. Brummstimme				
0.620	5328.2		40	3
0.690	5332.2		46	2
0.950	5335.2		50	1
1.400	5343.2		60	1
2.270	5350.2		70	1
nur weiß oder blond				
0.600	5380.2		115	1
sehr weiß, langer, dichter **Mohairplüsch**				
rosa oder gelb				
Druckbrummstimme				
0.200	5323.2		33	6
0.280	5326.2		36	3
0.400	5330.2		44	2
0.660	5333.2		48	2

STEIFF-Bilderbuch
„Teddy und Verwandte reisen
durch die Lande"

28 Seiten Text, 12 farb. Bilder in
Vierfarben-Kunstdruck, Format
28 × 24 cm, Halbleinen.
Ein schönes Tierbilderbuch, in dem
Teddy, Bully und Molly die Haupt-
personen sind und viele STEIFF-
Tiere in die Handlung eingreifen.

Teddy als Gehänge Seite 30
Musik-Teddy 37

STEIFF-Bilderbuch

35 cm

12/5325.2

12/5307 10 13 5/15 5317.2 5320.2 5322.2 5325.2 5328.2

ABOVE: *Illustration 17.* Five generations of Teddy Bears. *Courtesy Steiff.*

LEFT: *Illustration 18.* Page from a c.1930 catalog advertising the wide variety of sizes in which Steiff made bears. Note the tag in the right hand corner depicts the design used during that period. *Courtesy Steiff.*

BELOW: *Illustration 19.* Steiff button. c.1930. 7/8in (2.2cm) in diameter. The design of this bear's head on this collectible advertising pin is the one used by Steiff on their identification label during the same period. *Author's collection.*

TRADE MARK
STEIFF
TOY ANIMALS
LOOK FOR
BUTTON
IN EAR

Wash day for the bears in the woods is always fun when everyone lends a helping paw. *Author's collection.*

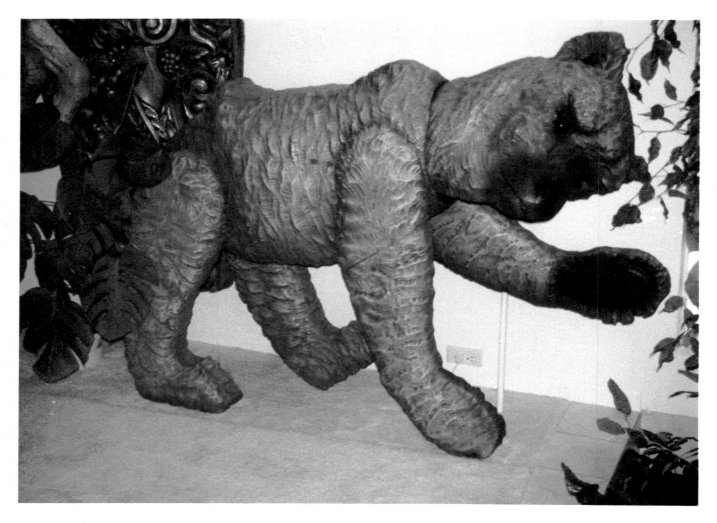

ABOVE: Carousel Bear. Charles I.D. Looff. c.1907. 43in (108.1cm) high x 60in (152.4cm) long; carved wooden bear with jointed head and glass eyes. Condition: Mint. Comments: The majority of carousel bears resemble a real bear; this is a magnificent example of a carousel Teddy Bear which is extremely rare. *Courtesy Summit Collection.*

OPPOSITE PAGE: The French bisque doll (Jumeau, 26in [66cm]) takes a group of early Steiff and other bears to the woods riding in an old wood wagon. *Author's collection.*

"Teddy Bears." Lithograph on cloth. c.1907. 24in (61cm) x 24in (61cm); rare political picture showing two bears returning from a hunt, carrying their game for the day. The bear on the left has "Washington D.C." written on his pouch. The bear on the right wears a Teddy Roosevelt style hat which states "I did it" on the brim. Copyright 1907. Schwab and Wolf, New York. *Author's collection.*

Out for a stroll on an Autumn day. This German bisque doll (Kestner #260, 29in [73.7cm]) pushes a 1910 wicker doll's buggy with Steiff Teddy Bears (c.1905) enjoying the ride. *Author's collection.*

OPPOSITE PAGE: Steiff Bears on wheels cross the old wooden bridge. *Author's collection.*

Left to right: Wally Mullins, Dr. Herbert Zimmermann (President, The Steiff Company), Linda Mullins. Shown at a dinner honoring Dr. Zimmermann held by the Glendale B.E.A.R. Club on May 10, 1984. *Photograph by Warren Bowen.*

OPPOSITE PAGE: Steiff Teddy Bears (c.1903-1905) have so much fun playing hide and seek in the hollowed-out tree stumps. *Author's collection.*

Portrait postcard. c.1917. Handpainted photograph postcard shows a little girl leaning against a huge Steiff Teddy Bear. Marked: "Philco Series. Printed in England." *Author's collection.*

OPPOSITE PAGE: Running through the woods hunting mushrooms is the favorite pastime of the beautiful French doll (Jumeau. 22in [55.9cm]). The Steiff bear (c.1907) would much rather climb tree stumps. *Author's collection.*

The Record Steiff Teddy enjoys riding his scooter watched by the French bisque doll (Jumeau, 18in [45.7cm]). *Author's collection.*

A group of early 1900s Steiff Teddy Bears play on the front porch of their home in the woods. *Author's collection.*

OPPOSITE PAGE: An early Steiff Teddy Bear rides a Steiff bear on wheels watched by a German pouty doll (Kämmer and Reinhardt #114, 20in [50.8cm]). *Author's collection.*

A Schuco Yes/No Monkey is seated in the wooden wagon. A tiny Steiff bear rides the horse, while the large Steiff bear (c.1907) sits watching. *Author's collection.*

OPPOSITE PAGE: Taken for a ride in an early 1900s Joel Ellis buggy is this c.1907 Steiff Teddy Bear and a German baby doll (Kämmer and Reinhardt #121, 16in [40.6cm]). The beautiful French bisque doll (Jumeau, 29in [73.7cm]) takes the papier mâché French bull dog (c.1900) along for a walk. *Author's collection.*

OPPOSITE PAGE: Teddy receives a gift. It is a bisque Kewpie doll from the beautiful German bisque doll (Kämmer and Reinhardt #117, 28in [71.1cm]). *Author's collection.*

The hurdy-gurdy is pulled by a Steiff Bear (c.1908), surrounded by Steiff Monkeys. *Author's collection.*

12 5310 15   20   28   25,2   30,2   32,2   .35,2

12 Teddy

Der schöne Orig.-Steiff-Teddy ist unübertroffen in Ausdruck und Qualität und eine Leistung an Preiswürdigkeit.

Die beiden letzten Ziffern jeder Nummer = ganze Länge in cm

gegliedert, Moharplüsch weiß, blond oder dunkelbraun

| 0,010 | 12 5310 | — 75 |

weiß oder blond

0,040	12 5315	1.—
0,070	5320	1.40
0,090	5323	1.80

weiß, blond oder dunkelbraun
mit Doppel-Druckstimme

0,130	12 5325,2	2.50
0,210	5330,2	3.30
0,240	5332,2	4.—
0,360	5335,2	5.—

mit automatischer Brummstimme

0,620	12 5343,2	6.50
0,690	5345,2	8.—
0,950	5350,2	11.—
1,400	5365,2	16.—
2,270	5375,2	24.—

5343,2   5345,2   5350,2

7309   7315   7322   7330,2   7338,2   7340,2

12 G Teddy Baby

gegliedert, freistehend Moharplüsch mais oder dunkelbraun

0,030 12 G 7309	1.20
0,070	7315	2.—
0,110	7322	3.50

mit Doppel-Druckstimme

0,270	7330,2	5.50
0,480	7338,2	8.50
0,630	7340,2	10.—
0,800	7345,2	12.50

LEFT: *Illustration 20.* Page from a c.1930 catalog. The now rare Teddy Baby is shown at the bottom of the page. *Courtesy Steiff.*

BELOW: *Illustration 21. Teddy Bear's Tea Party*, by Lucy Leffingwell Cable tells the story of three little girls who give a tea party for their Teddy Bears. A marvelous representation of Steiff Teddy Bears ranging in approximate size from 14in (35.6cm) to 48in (121.9cm). *The Ladies' Home Journal 1907. Author's collection.*

The Teddy Bears' Tea-Party

By Lucy Leffingwell Cable

Photographs by Mrs. H. Nettour

OPPOSITE PAGE: The composition Dopey doll (20in [50.8cm]) takes a Schuco Yes/No (14in [35.6cm]) Teddy for a walk. *Author's collection.*

Steiff Tag Identification Guide

TOP LEFT: *Illustration 22.* 1892. Steiff's first trademark was the figure of a camel with the words "Schutz" (protected) and "Marke" (mark) on either side of the camel. This is evident in the bottom of this illustration. The picture was taken from the cover of an original Steiff catalog. The two young boys mistreating the camel on wheels represents that quality and durability were one of the main features of even Steiff's first toys. *Courtesy Steiff.*

TOP RIGHT: *Illustration 23.* 1898. The figure of an elephant on wheels with upraised curved trunk circling Margarete Steiff's initials replaced the camel. It was used through the early 1900s, until the introduction and success of the Teddy Bear. Then the tag changed, portraying the head of a bear.

BOTTOM LEFT: *Illustration 24.* 1905. "Knopf im Ohr" (Button in Ear). This was Steiff's registered trademark (registered May 13, 1905) and is still used today. *Courtesy Steiff.*

BOTTOM RIGHT: *Illustration 25* & **OPPOSITE PAGE TOP LEFT:** *Illustration 26.* 1921-1927. Due to the success of the Teddy Bear, a variety of realistic looking bears' heads was introduced on the Steiff tags and many printed matters. *Courtesy Steiff.*

TOP RIGHT: *Illustration 27.* c. 1927. A white paper tag with a realistic looking gold bear with square head design and "U" shape smiling mouth. The border is in red with the words "STEIFF-ORIGINAL-MARKE" encircling the top of the label in white print.

BOTTOM LEFT: *Illustration 28.* c.1950. White paper tag. Gold bear now has cuter features; rounded head with "W" shaped mouth outlined in blue. The words "STEIFF-ORIGINAL-MARKE" circle the top of the label in a red border with white writing.

BOTTOM RIGHT: *Illustration 29.* c.1972-present day. Red and yellow tag. The top half of the label is in yellow with the word "Original" written in red. The bottom half of the label is in red with the outlined bear's head and the words "Steiff" and "Knopf im Ohr" written in yellow.

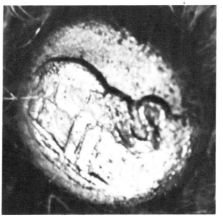

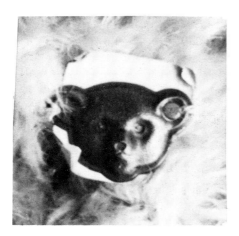
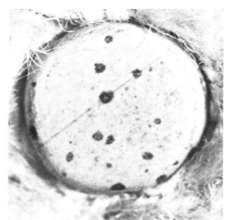

OPPOSITE PAGE TOP ROW LEFT: *Illustration 30.* Blank button. c.1903-1904. Small metal blank button; two prong attachment. Note the buttons were attached to the left ear fastening the white identification label. The smaller buttons appear to be the earliest.

MIDDLE: *Illustration 31.* Elephant button. c.1903-1904. An elephant with curved trunk was embossed on a metal button with two prong attachment. The exact date the elephant button was used is as yet unknown. We do now know, however, it was only used for a very short period, and Teddy Bears found with this identification are of a very early unusual design and extremely rare. (For more information see chapter on Steiff Bears with Metal Rods connecting the joints.)

RIGHT: *Illustration 32.* Printed "STEIFF" button. c.1905-1950. The famous Steiff trademark. Raised "STEIFF" name in block capital letters with the "F" underscored on metal button; resembles pewter. A two year transition of changing from the printed "Steiff" to the script button in *Illustration 36.* Note: the smaller buttons appear to be the earliest.

MIDDLE ROW LEFT: *Illustration 33.* Bear's head button. c.1936. Extremely rare. *Courtesy Margaret Francis.*

MIDDLE: *Illustration 34.* Grey painted button. c.1940. Used only for a short period during World War II. Found mainly on cotton plush animals.

RIGHT: Illustration 35. Printed "Steiff" button. c.1940. Without "F" underscored; Steiff name is raised in block capital letters on a shiny metal button with two prong attachment; limited number used. Note: the shiny nickel sometimes tarnishes, giving the buttons a pewter effect.

BOTTOM ROW LEFT: *Illustration 36.* Steiff in script. c.1950. Steiff name is raised in script on shiny (nickel) metal button; two prong attachment.

MIDDLE: *Illustration 37.* Incised script on chrome button. c.1965. Steiff name is incised in script on shiny chrome button; two prong attachment; also came riveted into ear.

RIGHT: *Illustration 38.* Brass button with raised Steiff in script. c.1975. Steiff name is raised in script on brass type button; two prong attachment; also was riveted into ear.

ABOVE: *Illustration 39.* Brass button with incised Steiff in script. c.1980-present day. Steiff name is incised in script on shiny brass type button. Riveted into ear. Note the button is now a little larger.

Due to strict quality control on their products even today, there are only two machines in Giegen that affix the famous Steiff "Knopf Im Ohr" (Button in Ear) — the ultimate mark of quality.

Explanation of Numbers on Steiff Labels

The numbers show the exact look of the animals as to posture, covering, height in cm and outfit.

Before the line = series (kind of animal) **12**/5328,2

After the line
Thousands = Posture

1 |.|.|.| standing	**1**343,2
2 |.|.|.| lying	**2**312
3 |.|.|.| sitting	**3**317
4 |.|.|.| begging	**4**322
5 |.|.|.| jointed	**5**322
6 |.|.|.| young	**6**522
7 |.|.|.| grotesque	**7**314

Hundreds = Covering

.|1|.|.| felt	**1**17
.|3|.|.| mohair	3**3**17
.|4|.|.| velvet	6**4**12,0
.|5|.|.| wool plush	6**5**22
.|6|.|.| DRALON Plush	6**6**20
.|8|.|.| wood	**8**95
.|9|.|.| steel	3**9**80

Tens and Singles = Height in cm

.|.|2|2| 22cm high incl. head	13**22**,0

After the Comma = Outfit

.|.|.|.|,0	without wheels	1328,**02**
.|.|.|.|,1	cuddly voice	6328,**1**
.|.|.|.|,2	strong squeeze voice	
	or pull voice of	
	riding animals	1328,**20**
.|.|.|.|,3	with music box	
.|.|.|.|,ST	steering	
.|.|.|.|,ex	on excentric wheels	

cm = inches
03 = 1¼
04 = 1½
06 = 2½
07 = 3
08 = 3¼
09 = 3½
10 = 4
12 = 5
14 = 5½
15 = 6
17 = 6½
18 = 6½
19 = 6½
22 = 8½
23 = 8½
25 = 10
28 = 11
35 = 13½
40 = 16
43 = 17
50 = 20
60 = 24
65 = 25½
75 = 29½
80 = 31½
100 = 40

Courtesy Steiff.

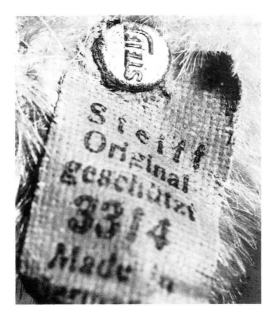

TOP LEFT: *Illustration 40.* White label. c.1903-1904. One of the earliest labels used; white with black writing; numbers indicate the exact look of the animal as to posture, covering and height (in centimeters); most often found in conjunction with blank button (see Explanation of Numbers on Steiff labels chart).

TOP RIGHT: *Illustration 41.* White label. c.1905-1926. More information added to label: "geschutzt" (protected by law); Germany Importe d' Allemagne (made in Germany); most often found in conjunction with "printed" Steiff button.

BOTTOM LEFT: *Illustration 42.* Red label. c.1926-1934. Same information as white label. This label may sometimes appear orange due to discoloration over the years; used in conjunction with printed Steiff button.

BOTTOM RIGHT: *Illustration 43.* Yellow label. c.1934-1950. Same information as red label. Used in conjunction with printed Steiff button. Note: a separate label normally attached to the side seam of the bear reading "Made in U. S. Zone Germany" can occasionally be found on bears made for a short time after World War II in Western Germany.

ABOVE LEFT: *Illustration 44.* Yellow label. c.1950-1970. Note style of information has changed. Place is now designated for the price. Also used in conjunction with the chrome button with raised Steiff in script.

ABOVE RIGHT: *Illustration 45.* Yellow label. c1970. Style of information is the same but a slash is now used instead of the comma. Also used in conjunction with the brass type button with raised Steiff in script.

LEFT: *Illustration 46.* White and yellow woven label. 1980-present day. (A black and white woven label is used for all Limited Editions and Collector series.) Used in conjunction with shiny brass-type button with Steiff incised in script. Note change in material used for labels.

Glossary of Materials Used for Making Teddy Bears

The following is a list of materials manufacturers used for the making of early Teddy Bears. For more recent information please refer to Chapter Seven (Colleen Tipton's Bearmaking Method).

Felt: Derived from the Anglo-Saxon word meaning to fit or filter, felt is a non-woven sheet of matted material made from wool, fur or certain man-made fibers. Felting is similar to fiber array which takes place by a combination of heat, moisture and pressure. No bonding adhesive is used. Some felts are made with cotton or other fibers held together with adhesives or plastics. Felt is commonly a woven fabric made of cotton or wool which is heavily fulled and shrunk so that yarns become closely interlocked.

Mohair: A long white lustrous hair obtained from the angora goat that is native to Asia Minor and derives its name from the province of Angora in Turkey. Although it has been raised for thousands of years in that area, it is also raised today in Texas and South Africa. Turkey still remains a world center for angora along with Texas and South Africa. The arabic word "mukhayyar" is a goat's hair fabric and during medieval times the fabric was called "mockaire." Length of angora hair ranges from 4in (10.2cm) to 12in (30.5cm), growing in uniform locks. It ranges from relatively coarse to quite fine in kid mohair. It lacks any natural crimp and has no felting properties. It often contains a good deal of kemp. Dirt resistant, it is an ideal fabric for manufacturing soft toys.

Burlap: A coarse, plain weave cloth made with single jute yarns. It may be natural-colored, dyed or printed. In Great Britain and Europe the terms burlap and hessian are interchangeable.

Nettle Fiber: Steiff used nettle fiber during World War I when materials were scarce. This is a woven material from a plant called *die brennessel* (nettle) and a paper plush. The result is a fine, short stem fiber resembling linen, which is not very durable and in very short supply.

Velveteen: A cotton fabric with a short close pile like velvet.

Draylon: Produced by Bayer, A.G., West Germany, this acrylic staple and tow is made in a wide range of deniers for all types of knitting.

Plush: The word is derived from the French *peluche* (taken from the Latin pilus, meaning hair). Plushes are referred to as one-, two- or three-frame fabrics, according to the number of different kinds of yarns used in the pile warp. Plush itself is a warp pile fabric with cut pile surface longer than velvet pile and less closely woven. The weave is a variation of the plain weave. The ground is generally cotton, and the pile may be mohair, wool, cotton or man-made fiber. Plushes may be crushed or embossed to imitate fur.

Stuffing Materials

Excelsior: Excelsior is long fine wood shavings. Sometimes referred to as straw stuffing, this was the first material used for stuffing Teddy Bears. Early versions were shaved quite finely, but the thickness of the shavings increased over the years, giving bears a firmer feeling.

Kapok: Kapok is a cottony or silky fiber which covers the seeds of the tropical Kapok tree which grows in Africa, the East Indies and tropical parts of America. It was sometimes used around the voice boxes of the early bears along with the traditional excelsior. Later it totally replaced excelsior in some manufacturer's Teddy Bears.

The following illustrations represent some of the voice boxes Steiff used throughout the years. (Stuffing and voice boxes are taken from bears in the corresponding picture.)

ABOVE: *Illustration 47.* c.1908. Stuffing includes fine excelsior and kapok. Very often Kapok was used to surround the voice box. Voice box shown is one of the earliest versions. Sound is produced by tilting the bear back and forth causing a weight to fall onto bellows.

LEFT: *Illustration 48.* Bear. 15in (38.1cm); honey colored mohair; shoe button eyes; jointed arms and legs; swivel head.

ABOVE: *Illustration 49.* c.1908. Stuffing includes excelsior (with wood shaving a little thicker than previously), kapok, tissue paper, pieces of thread. Very often scraps were not wasted but used to stuff the early bears. Voice box is a large spring held together by two oval shaped wooden disks, encased by a type of oilcloth material. Sound is produced by squeezing the spring causing air to escape through a hole covered by a small piece of metal with enough space left for the air to be released to make the sound. This "squeeker" type cry box was used for many years, only the exterior material was changed to cardboard disks encased with soft kid leather.

RIGHT: *Illustration 50.* Bear. 20in (50.8cm); cinnamon mohair; shoe button eyes; jointed arms and legs; swivel head; printed Steiff button.

ABOVE: *Illustration 51.* c.1950. Stuffing is excelsior (with much thicker wood shavings than earlier). Bears from this era on were stuffed extremely tightly. Voice box is slightly heavier duty spring and is held together by two oval shaped cardboard disks; encased by oilcloth type material; sound is produced by squeezing air through the large applied dowel.

LEFT: *Illustration 52.* Bear. 14in (35.6cm); beige mohair; glass eyes; jointed arms and legs; swivel head; Steiff button with raised script.

ABOVE: *Illustration 53.* c.1970. Voice box is tilt type. Now the casement is plastic; sound is produced the same way as in early versions; metal weight falls onto bellows as bear is tilted back and forth.

RIGHT: *Illustration 54.* Bear. 20in (50.8cm); long silky caramel mohair; glass eyes; jointed arms and legs; swivel head; Steiff button incised script on shiny chrome. Today Steiff use tilt- and squeeze-type voice boxes for their Teddy Bears.

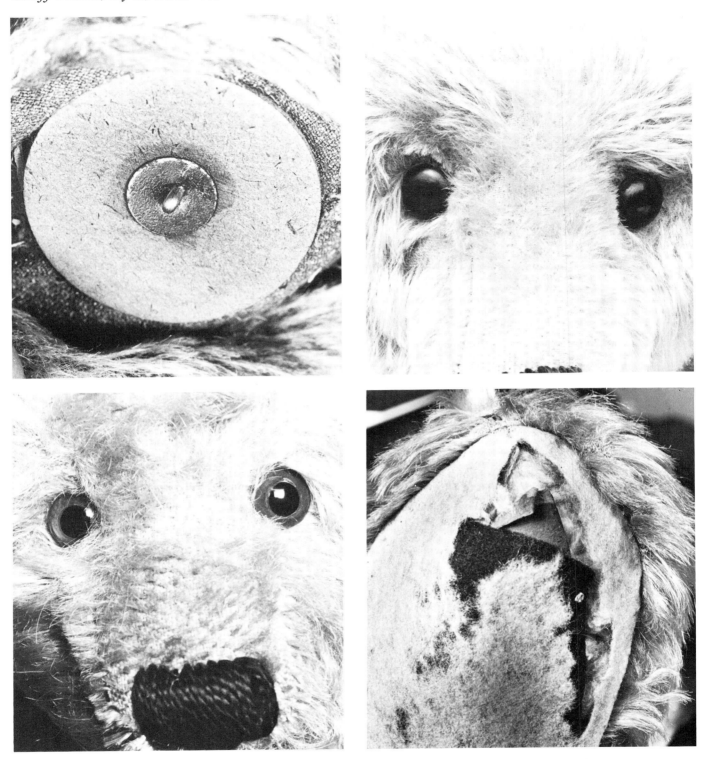

TOP LEFT: *Illustration 55.* Jointing method. Steiff's *main* method for assembling the jointed bears has not changed from the first bears. A wooden disk and metal washer are secured by a bent-over metal pin. Each limb including the head is attached in this manner.

TOP RIGHT: *Illustration 56.* Eyes. Initially, black shoe button eyes were used. As the bears' size increased, larger black buttons were used.

BOTTOM LEFT: *Illustration 57.* Blown glass eyes were introduced on Teddy Bears approximately World War I and later on completely replaced shoe button eyes. (Note: Glass eyes appear to have been used earlier on bears on wheels and the very large Teddy Bears [see *Illustration 102*].) Due to American safety laws plastic eyes are now required for bears made for children.

BOTTOM RIGHT: *Illustration 58.* Pads. Felt has been used for the pads throughout the years. The early versions reinforced the felt on the feet with cardboard and black or colored felt.

Nose

Steiff's designs of stitching for the nose has basically stayed the same over the years. The early versions were reinforced with felt underneath the stitching. Guttapercha (an early hard plastic) has been found only on bears with metal rods connecting the joints, like the bear in *Illustration 84*.

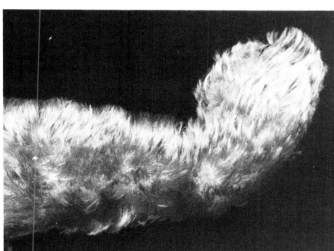

Steiff's Identifying Body Styles Through The Years

Due to the fact that Steiff buttons are very often removed or lost, also old stock of buttons could have originally been used on later bears, the following photos will enable you to recognize some of the body styles and approximate period when they were introduced.

TOP LEFT: *Illustration 59*. c.1903-1904. One of the earliest versions of a Steiff Bear. 30in (76.2cm); honey colored mohair; large button eyes; jointed arms and legs; swivel head; excelsior stuffing; felt pads; squeeze-type cry box; blank button. Especially note the very wide head. Arms and legs are plump at the joints tapering down to large paws and feet.

TOP RIGHT: *Illustration 60*. c.1903-1904. The elongated characteristics of the early Steiff is easy to recognize. Note the especially large hump on back; long nose; big feet; long arms; when sitting, the arms will extend over the feet.

BOTTOM LEFT: *Illustration 61*. c.1903-1904. The arms of the earlier Steiff bear were long with an upward curve to the paw.

BOTTOM RIGHT: *Illustration 62*. c.1903-1904. Long tapered legs and extra large feet were in proportion to the other over emphasized features.

 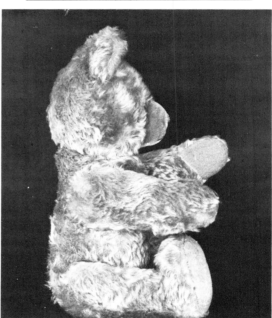

Although the wonderful characteristics of Steiff were still prominent through the early 1900s we start to see the features on some of their bears beginning to be less exaggerated. The nose is getting a little shorter; the hump is still there but less pronounced; the body is not quite so fat. The arm is still long and will extend over the foot, but it is losing the deep curve as it comes down to the paw. The leg is tapered but the foot is smaller. By 1930 many other Teddy Bear designs were introduced including the popular Zotty and Teddy Baby (see illustrations in Steiff's 1930-1950 section). The following illustrations show the style of the basic design of their Teddy Bear line during those years.

TOP LEFT: *Illustration 63.* c.1950. 15in (31.1cm); gold mohair; glass eyes; jointed arms and legs; swivel head; excelsior stuffing; felt pads; squeeze-type cry box. The realistic looking bear shape is starting to be replaced by a more tailored bear. Characteristics still similar; stuffing packed extremely tightly.

TOP RIGHT: *Illustration 64.* c.1950. A very neat and trim bear; the hump is almost gone; body is straight and narrow. Although the arm still extends over the feet, it is much shorter and almost straight in comparison to the earlier bears. The legs and feet still have nice shape, but are much shorter.

BOTTOM LEFT: *Illustration 65.* c.1970. 15in (38.1cm); honey colored silky mohair; glass eyes; jointed arms and legs; swivel head; excelsior stuffing; synthetic pads; tilt type cry box, incised script chrome button; muzzle now shaved; stuffing extremely tightly packed. You can really notice the change in the design of the Steiff bears from this era.

BOTTOM RIGHT: *Illustration 66.* c.1970. The bear now has developed a chunky appearance. Head is fatter and nose is much shorter. Hardly any hump is visible. A shorter fat arm with less shape is now used along with a similarly shaped leg.

ABOVE LEFT & ABOVE RIGHT: *Illustrations 67 & 68.* c.1903-1904. 30in (76.2cm); long silky honey colored mohair; large button eyes; jointed arms and legs; swivel head; excelsior stuffing; blank button. Condition: Mint. Comments: Rare size; note elongated features; fine example in unplayed with condition. *Author's collection.*

RIGHT: *Illustration 69.* Steiff. c.1903-1904. 16in (40.6cm); white mohair; shoe button eyes; jointed arms and legs; swivel head; excelsior stuffing; blank button. Condition: Excellent. Comments: Nose, mouth and claws embroidered with brown waxed twine. *Author's collection.*

ABOVE LEFT: *Illustration 70.* Steiff. c.1903-1904. 21in (53.3cm); gray curly mohair; large button eyes; jointed arms and legs; swivel head; excelsior stuffing; blank button. Condition: Excellent. Comments: Rare. Wonderful example of an early Steiff. Beautiful wide shaped head and facial features. Brown embroidered nose, mouth and claws. *Courtesy Beverly Port.*

ABOVE RIGHT: *Illustration 71.* Steiff. c.1903-1904. 24in (61cm); white mohair; large shoe button eyes; jointed arms and legs; swivel head; excelsior stuffing; blank button. Condition: Excellent. Comments: Rare size and color. *Courtesy Helen Sieverling.*

LEFT: *Illustration 72.* Steiff. c.1903-1904. 15in (38.1cm); honey colored mohair; shoe button eyes; jointed arms and legs; swivel head; excelsior stuffing; blank button. Condition: Mint. Comments: Rare. Label attached to back of bear reads "Gretchen's favorite Teddy and I believe her first." *Author's collection.*

LEFT: *Illustration 73*. Steiff. c.1903-1904. 15in (38.1cm); honey colored mohair; shoe button eyes; jointed arms and legs; swivel head; excelsior stuffing; blank button. Condition: Good. Note that as the size decreases some of the bear starts to lose the wide look in the head. *Author's colllection.*

RIGHT: *Illustration 74*. Steiff. c.1903-1904. 13in (33cm); white mohair; shoe button eyes; jointed arms and legs; swivel head; excelsior stuffing; blank button. Condition: Mint. Comments: Rare. White mohair appears to be one of the hardest colors to find in Steiff bears. Blank button with original Steiff identifying white label (#5322) still intact (see *Illustration 40*.) Brown embroidered nose, mouth and claws. This color thread was very often used on white bears. *Author's collection.*

Illustration 75. (Left) Steiff Bear. c.1903-1904. 10in (25.4cm); light beige mohair; shoe button eyes; jointed arms and legs; swivel head; excelsior stuffing, blank button. Condition: Excellent. (Center) Early 1900s mechanical key-wind rabbit. (Right) Steiff Bear. c.1905. 13in (25.4cm); light beige mohair; shoe button eyes; jointed arms and legs; swivel head; excelsior stuffing. Condition: Excellent. *Courtesy Volpp Collection.*

LEFT: *Illustration 78*. Steiff Bear. c.1903-1904. 10in (25.4cm); beige mohair; shoe button eyes; jointed arms and legs; swivel head; excelsior stuffing; blank button. Condition: Fair. *Author's collection*. Steiff elephant. c.1940. 11in (27.9cm); cotton plush; glass eyes; unjointed; gray painted button. Condition: Good. *Courtesy Joan Sickler*.

RIGHT: *Illustration 79*. (Left) Steiff. c.1903-1904. 10in (25.4cm); white mohair; shoe button eyes; jointed arms and legs; swivel head; excelsior stuffing; brown embroidered nose, mouth and claws. Condition: Mint. Comments: Rare size and color. (Right) Steiff. c.1903-1904. 14in (35.6cm); white mohair; shoe button eyes; jointd arms and legs; swivel head; excelsior stuffing; blank button with early white label attached; brown embroidered nose, mouth and claws. Condition: Mint. Comments: Rare. Highly collectible color and facial expression. Especially desirable with original Steiff identifying white label. Number on label 5325. (See *Illustration 40*.) *Author's collection*.

OPPOSITE PAGE ABOVE: *Illustration 76*. (Left) Steiff Bear. c.1903-1904. 13in (33cm); honey colored mohair; shoe button eyes; jointed arms and legs; swivel head; excelsior stuffing; blank button. Condition: Fair. Comments: Note narrow feet and paws characteristic of this size of the first Teddy Bears. (Center) Steiff Dog. c.1905. 9in (22.9cm); beige mohair; shoe button eyes; excelsior stuffing; iron wheels. *Courtesy Joan Sickler*. (Right) Steiff Bear. c.1904. 10in (25.4cm); light beige mohair; shoe button eyes; jointed arms and legs; swivel head; excelsior stuffing; blank button. Condition: Mint. *Courtesy Joan Sickler*.

BELOW: *Illustration 77*. Steiff Bear. c.1903-1904. 12in (30.5cm); white mohair; shoe button eyes; jointed arms and legs; swivel head; excelsior stuffing; blank button. Condition: Excellent. Comments: Nose and claws stitched with brown thread. *Author's collection*. Steiff Cat. c.1910. 8in (20.3cm) by 6in (15.2cm); white mohair; green glass eyes; jointed arms and legs; swivel head; excelsior stuffing; printed Steiff button; red stitched nose and mouth. Condition: Excellent. Comments: Rare. *Courtesy Joan Sickler*.

Illustration 80. When I first acquired this magnificent bear as a Christmas gift from my husband, I knew that he was in a class all his own. He has become one of my favorite bears. His unusual features fascinated me as I had never seen any like them before. As I examined his hard leather nose and firm excelsior body, I saw that his head, arms and legs appeared to be on metal rods and swiveled completely differently from those of my other bears. His arms were extremely long and curved. Although he had all the elongated characteristics of Steiff, I'd never seen such a bear, or even read about one before.

Then one day, a friend of mine told me about a bear she had purchased that sounded just like mine. We were both excited and got together and compared their similarities. Her bear's nose had been replaced, but the body and construction were the same as mine. My friend told me of one other bear like ours that was owned by Blossom Karmen. We phoned back east and discovered Blossom's was the same — but *her's* still had its original "elephant" Steiff button!

Steiff Bears With Metal Rods Connecting The Joints

The following illustrations are of Steiff bears jointed by metal rods connecting the joints. These bears are extremely rare, and appear to have only been made by Steiff for a very short period of time. As far as I have been able to discover, they have so far only appeared with an elephant button in the ear. A straight metal rod attaches each arm and leg, the head is attached to the rod which connects the arms. Each joint is held together by a disc and small metal pin to allow the swivel motion. Stuffed with excelsior. The body is extremely hard. The nose originally was gutta percha (hard early plastic).

Note the body features of these bears in the following illustrations and how much they resemble the bears (bar) in the Steiff 1903-1904 advertisement in *Illustration 11*.

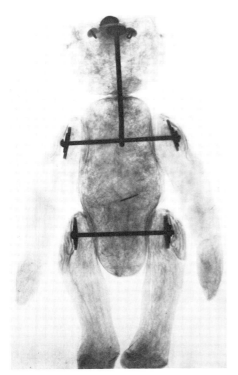

LEFT: *Illustration 81*. The x-ray shows the rare jointing method of the Steiff bears with metal rods connecting joints.

BELOW LEFT: *Illustration 82*. Steiff. c.1903-1904. 20in (50.8cm); long, silky apricot colored mohair; large button eyes; jointed arms and legs; swivel head; metal rods connecting joints; excelsior stuffing; body extremely hard; new stitched nose; "elephant" button in ear. Condition: Excellent. Comments: Magnificent example of this extremely rare bear, especially scarce with an elephant button (see button in *Illustration 31*). *Courtesy Blossom Karmen*.

BELOW RIGHT: *Illustration 83*. Steiff. c.1903-1904. 15in (38.1cm); long silky medium beige mohair; large button eyes; jointed arms and legs; swivel head; metal rods connecting joints; excelsior stuffing; body extremely hard; gutta percha (hard early plastic) nose. Condition: Mint. Comments: Extremely rare. Unusual body shape and long curved arms. Note the resemblance to the bear in the top right hand corner of *Illustration 11*. *Author's collection*.

LEFT: *Illustration 84.* This very rare gutta percha nose has only been found on bears with metal rods connecting the joints. Nose from the bear in *Illustration 83.*

Steiff Bears With Metal Rods

BELOW LEFT: *Illustration 85.* Steiff. c.1903-1904. 16in (40.6cm); beige mohair; large shoe button eyes; jointed arms and legs; swivel head; metal rods connecting joints; excelsior stuffing; body very firm; hard early "plastic" nose; "elephant" button in ear. Condition: Good. Comments: Extremely rare, especially scarce to find with elephant button and hard plastic nose still intact. *Courtesy Virginia Caputo.*

BELOW RIGHT: *Illustration 86.* Steiff. c.1903-1904. 17in (43.2cm); long silky white mohair; large button eyes; jointed arms and legs; swivel head; metal rods connecting joints; excelsior stuffing; body extremely hard; new stitched nose. Condition: Good. Comments: Rare. Note the wide head, low ears and body shape very closely resemble the bear (bär) standing with the monkey in the Steiff 1903-1904 advertisement in *Illustration 11. Courtesy Sally Cain.*

Steiff Bears With Center Seam In Head

The Steiff Bears in the following illustrations have a seam running down the center of their head. Unfortunately we haven't been able to find the exact date these were manufactured but they have appeared only in bears with blank and printed Steiff buttons. Their body style is always the early 1900s design. They must have been made only for a short period as they appear to be very rare and a highly collectible bear.

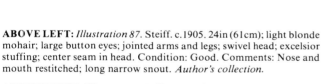

ABOVE LEFT: *Illustration 87.* Steiff. c.1905. 24in (61cm); light blonde mohair; large button eyes; jointed arms and legs; swivel head; excelsior stuffing; center seam in head. Condition: Good. Comments: Nose and mouth restitched; long narrow snout. *Author's collection.*

ABOVE RIGHT: *Illustration 88.* Close up of bears head in *Illustration 87,* showing the rare center seam.

MIDDLE RIGHT: *Illustration 89.* Steiff. c.1905. 20in (50.8cm); dark gold mohair; large button eyes; jointed arms and legs; swivel head; excelsior stuffing; printed button; center seam in head. Condition: Excellent. Comments: This bear was a dark gray until I cleaned him and he came up a beautiful deep golden brown color. *Author's collection.*

BOTTOM RIGHT: *Illustration 90.* Steiff. c.1904. 15in (38.1cm); white mohair; shoe button eyes; jointed arms and legs; swivel head; excelsior stuffing; blank button; center seam in head. Condition: Mint. Comments: Beautiful example of rare early Steiff. Steiff elephant. c.1907. 5½in (14cm); white mohair; shoe button eyes; jointed arms and legs; swivel head; excelsior stuffing; printed Steiff button. Condition: Mint. *Courtesy Sally Cain.*

Illustration 91. Steiff. c.1905. 21in (38.1cm); long beige silky mohair; large button eyes; jointed arms and legs; swivel head; excelsior stuffing; printed button; center seam in head. Condition: Excellent. Comments: Magnificent expression on this rare early bear. *Courtesy Sally Cain.*

Illustration 92. Steiff. c.1904. 24in (61cm); long silky cinnamon mohair; large button eyes; jointed arms and legs; swivel head; excelsior stuffing; center seam in head. Condition: Mint. Comments: Rare size and color; wonderful specimen. *Courtesy Volpp Collection.*

ABOVE LEFT: *Illustration 93.* Steiff. c.1915. 17in (43.2cm); bright gold mohair; glass eyes; jointed arms and legs; swivel head; excelsior stuffing; printed button. Condition: Mint. *Author's collection.*

ABOVE RIGHT: *Illustration 94.* Steiff. c.1905. 28in (71.1cm); deep gold mohair; large button eyes; jointed arms and legs; swivel head; excelsior stuffing; printed button. Condition: Very good. Comments: Rare. Magnificent facial expression. The smaller 13in (33cm) Steiff is used to show size comparison. *Courtesy Virginia Caputo.*

RIGHT: *Illustration 95.* Side view of the 28in (71.1cm) Steiff in *Illustration 94* really displays the wonderful elongated features only characteristic of early Steiff Teddy Bears. Note how similar the body and head style is to that of the bears with the blank button. It appears Steiff continued to use this design for several years.

ABOVE LEFT: *Illustration 96.* Steiff. c.1905. 3½in (8.9cm); white mohair; small button eyes; jointed arms and legs; swivel head; excelsior stuffing; brown embroidered nose, mouth and claws. Condition: Mint. Comments: Extremely rare size and color; especially rare to find four identical bears, all still with original early white labels (#5307). (See *Illustration 41.*) *Courtesy Beverly Port.*

MIDDLE LEFT: *Illustration 97.* Steiff "Roly Poly." c.1905. 13in (33cm); brown burlap; shoe button eyes; unjointed head and body; excelsior stuffing; small remaining part of white label attached to printed button. Bear permanently stands on wooden base. Condition: Excellent. Comments: Rare version of this desirable roly poly toy. *Courtesy Celia Sawyer. Photography Ronald Sawyer.*

BOTTOM LEFT: *Illustration 98.* Steiff. c.1905. 21in (53.3cm); light honey colored mohair; large button eyes; jointed arms and legs; swivel head; excelsior stuffing; printed button. Condition: Mint. Comments: Beautiful round wide head; rare. *Courtesy Sally Cain.*

ABOVE RIGHT: *Illustration 99.* Steiff "Teddy Baby." c.1940. 20in (50.8cm); bright cinnamon mohair; short beige mohair snout and feet; glass eyes; jointed arms and legs; swivel head; excelsior stuffing; printed button without the "F" underscored; yellow tag. (See *Illustration 35.*) Condition: Mint. Comments: Rare. Fine example of this highly collectible bear. Collar and bell original. *Courtesy Celia Sawyer. Photography Ronald Sawyer.*

ABOVE LEFT: *Illustration 100.* Steiff. c.1935. 7in (17.8cm); short gold mohair; glass eyes; jointed arms and legs; swivel head; excelsior stuffing; printed button with original yellow Steiff label. Condition: Mint. Tricycle made by Chad Valley. *Author's collection.*

ABOVE RIGHT: *Illustration 101.* (Left) Steiff. c.1905. 24in (61cm); white mohair; large shoe button eyes; jointed arms and legs; swivel head; printed button; excelsior stuffing. Condition: Mint. Comments: Rare size and color. Brown embroidered nose and mouth. Early tin medal hangs around bear's neck with the words "Won't you be my Teddy Bear" embossed around a figure of a Teddy Bear. (Right) Steiff. c.1905. 13in (33cm); honey colored mohair; shoe button eyes; jointed arms and legs; swivel head; excelsior stuffing. Condition: Good. *Courtesy Virginia Caputo.*

MIDDLE RIGHT: *Illustration 102.* Steiff. c.1910. 46in (121.9cm); honey colored mohair; large glass eyes; jointed arms and legs; swivel head; excelsior stuffing; printed button. Condition: Excellent. Comments: Extremely rare size. Wonderful elongated features; 23in (58.4cm) length of arm; 18in (45.7cm) length of leg; size of foot 11in (27.9cm); waist is 38in (152.4cm). *Courtesy Barbara Lauver.*

BOTTOM RIGHT: *Illustration 103.* Barbara Lauver stands beside her magnificent 46in (121.9cm) Steiff bear to demonstrate his enormous size.

ABOVE LEFT: *Illustration 104.* Steiff. c.1907. 26in (66cm); gold silky mohair; large button eyes; jointed arms and legs; swivel head; printed button; excelsior stuffing. Condition: Mint. Comments: Rare. *Courtesy Helen Sieverling.*

MIDDLE LEFT: *Illustration 105.* Steiff. c.1913. 13in (33cm); light beige mohair; shoe button eyes; jointed arms and legs; swivel head; excelsior stuffing; printed button. Condition: Good: Comments: Rare. Original Steiff muzzle. *Courtesy Volpp Collection.*

BOTTOM LEFT: *Illustration 106.* Steiff. c.1930. 25in (63.5cm); long white silky mohair; glass eyes; jointed arms and legs; swivel head; excelsior stuffing; printed button with "red Steiff label." Condition: Good. Comments: Very early features to be found on a bear of this era. *Author's collection.*

ABOVE RIGHT: *Illustration 107.* Steiff. c.1907. 3½in (8.9cm); gold worn mohair; shoe button eyes; jointed arms and legs; swivel head; printed button; excelsior stuffing. Condition: Worn. Comments: Desirable size with early elongated features. *Author's collection.*

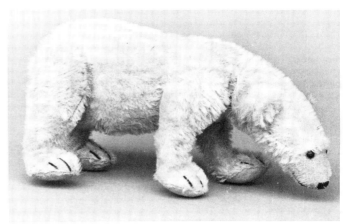

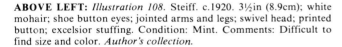

ABOVE LEFT: *Illustration 108.* Steiff. c.1920. 3½in (8.9cm); white mohair; shoe button eyes; jointed arms and legs; swivel head; printed button; excelsior stuffing. Condition: Mint. Comments: Difficult to find size and color. *Author's collection.*

ABOVE RIGHT: *Illustration 109.* Steiff Polar Bear. c.1913. 10in (25.4cm) long, 5in (12.7cm) tall; white mohair; shoe button eyes; jointed arms and legs; swivel head; printed button; excelsior stuffing. Condition: Mint. Comments: Rare. *Courtesy Joan Sickler.*

MIDDLE RIGHT: *Illustration 110.* Steiff "Movable Tail." c.1930. 13in (33cm) long x 8in (20.3cm) high; rich dark brown mohair; short beige mohair muzzle; glass eyes; unjointed body; excelsior stuffing; small remaining part of red label attached to printed button. Condition: Mint. Comments: Rare. Action: When tail is turned head will move in circular motion. *Courtesy Celia Sawyer. Photography Ronald Sawyer.*

BOTTOM RIGHT: *Illustration 111.* Steiff Teddy Bear "Movable Tail." c.1930. 7in (17.8cm); white mohair; white velveteen pads on hands and feet; glass eyes; jointed arms and legs; swivel head; excelsior stuffing. Condition: Excellent. Comments: Rare. Action: When tail is turned head will move in circular motion.
Steiff Dog "Movable Tail." c.1930. 4in (10.2cm); short cinnamon mohair; glass eyes; swivel head; unjointed body; printed button with rare original "red" tag. Condition: Mint. Comments: Rare. Action: When tail is turned head will move in ciruclar motion. *Courtesy Celia Sawyer. Photography Ronald Sawyer.*

The following bears have either lost their button or cautious mothers have removed the button for safety reasons. So, in order to date them, I have carefully studied their characteristics and compared them to the bears that still have their buttons intact. Taking into consideration that different designs were manufactured for several years after the original creation, I have assigned an approximate date of when the bear was introduced to the best of my knowledge.

ABOVE LEFT: *Illustration 112.* Steiff. c.1905. 24in (61cm); light gold long silky mohair; large button eyes; jointed arms and legs; swivel head; excelsior stuffing. Condition: Excellent. Comments: Rare. *Author's collection.*

ABOVE RIGHT: *Illustration 113.* Steiff. c.1904. 20in (50.8cm); cinnamon mohair; large button eyes; jointed arms and legs; swivel head; excelsior stuffing. Condition: Mint. Comments: Rare. *Author's collection.*

LEFT: *Illustration 114.* (Left) Steiff. c.1910. 10in (25.4cm); gold mohair; shoe button eyes; jointed arms and legs; swivel head; excelsior stuffing. Condition: Excellent. (Center) Steiff. c.1907. 10in (25.4cm); light beige mohair; shoe button eyes; jointed arms and legs; swivel head; excelsior stuffing. Condition: Mint. (Right) Steiff. c.1907. 10in (25.4cm); white mohair; shoe button eyes; jointed arms and legs; swivel head; excelsior stuffing. Condition: Excellent. Comments: All three bears are easily recognized as Steiff, but because they were handmade and manufactured at different times, their facial features differ somewhat. *Author's collection.*

Illustration 115. Steiff. c.1910. 12in (30.5cm); black mohair; shoe button eyes; jointed arms and legs; swivel head; excelsior stuffing. Condition: Good; new pads and restitched nose. Comments: Very rare color. *Author's collection.*

Illustration 116. Steiff. c.1907. 24in (61cm); long silky beige mohair; large button eyes; jointed arms and legs; swivel head; excelsior stuffing. Condition: Excellent. *Author's collection.*

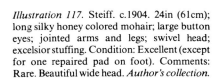

Illustration 117. Steiff. c.1904. 24in (61cm); long silky honey colored mohair; large button eyes; jointed arms and legs; swivel head; excelsior stuffing. Condition: Excellent (except for one repaired pad on foot). Comments: Rare. Beautiful wide head. *Author's collection.*

ABOVE LEFT: *Illustration 118.* Steiff. c.1908. 30in (76.2cm); long silky honey colored mohair; large button eyes; jointed arms and legs; swivel head; excelsior stuffing. Condition: Excellent. Comments: Rare size. Wonderful elongated features. This beautiful bear has been passed down to three generations of granddaughters. The last of which received it from England where the bear was used as packing in a crate of china. *Courtesy Sally Cain.*

ABOVE RIGHT: *Illustration 119.* Steiff "Glove Puppet." c.1913. 15in (38.1cm); gold mohair; shoe button eyes; swivel head; jointed arms. Condition: Mint. Comments: Rare. *Courtesy Celia Sawyer. Photography Ronald Sawyer.*

LEFT: *Illustration 120.* Steiff. c.1910. 14in (35.6cm); light brown mohair; shoe button eyes; jointed arms and legs; swivel head; excelsior stuffing. Condition: Excellent. Comments: Rare color. *Courtesy Helen Sieverling.*

ABOVE LEFT: *Illustration 121.* Steiff Bear. c.1910. 7in (17.8cm); short honey colored mohair; tiny black shoe button eyes; jointed arms and legs; swivel head; excelsior stuffing. Condition: Good. Comments: No paw pads. Unusual size. *Author's collection.* Steiff Dog. c.1913. 8in (20.3cm) long and 7in (17.8cm) tall; brown felt; shoe button eyes; unjointed; excelsior stuffing; wooden wheels. Condition: Good; replaced ears. Comments: Incised on wheels "Steiff made in Germany Imported D'Allemagne." *Courtesy Joan Sickler.*

ABOVE RIGHT: *Illustration 122.* A group of beautiful rare Steiffs. c.1905-1907. Ranging in size from 22-25in (55.9-63.5cm). Their long silky mohair is the desirable deep cinnamon color. *Courtesy Kim Brewer.*

RIGHT: *Illustration 123.* Steiff. c.1910. 12in (30.5cm); white mohair; shoe button eyes; jointed arms and legs; swivel head; excelsior stuffing. Condition: Excellent. Schoenhut piano. Schuco clockwork clown. *Author's collection.*

LEFT: *Illustration 124.* Steiff "Roly Poly." c.1897. 9in (22.9cm). Brown burlap; excelsior stuffing; wooden base; shoe button eyes; unjointed. Wooden stick with chain. Condition: Excellent. Comments: Extremely rare. *Courtesy Steiff Museum.*

BELOW LEFT: *Illustration 125.* Steiff. c.1907. 17in (43.2cm); silky white mohair; shoe button eyes; jointed arms and legs; swivel head; excelsior stuffing. Condition: Mint. Comments: Rare. Original "Teddy B" outfit. (See Kahn and Mossbacher advertisement, *Illustration 205.*) *Author's collection.*

BELOW RIGHT: *Illustration 126.* Steiff. c.1907. 14in (35.6cm); beige mohair; shoe button eyes; jointed arms and legs; swivel head; excelsior stuffing. Condition: Excellent. Comments: Outfit could have been made by D.W. Shoyer & Co (see *Illustration 206*). *Author's collection.*

OPPOSITE PAGE ABOVE LEFT: *Illustration 127.* Steiff. c.1905. 25in (63.5cm); deep rust mohair; large button eyes; jointed arms and legs; swivel head; excelsior stuffing. Condition: Excellent. Comments: Rare. *Courtesy Sally Cain.*

ABOVE RIGHT: *Illustration 128.* Steiff. c.1907. 15in (38.1cm); white mohair; shoe button eyes; jointed arms and legs; swivel head; excelsior stuffing. Condition: Mint. *Author's collection.*

BELOW: *Illustration 129.* Steiff. c.1907. 10in (25.4cm); gray mohair; shoe button eyes; jointed arms and legs; swivel head; excelsior stuffing. Condition: Fair. Mutt and Jeff Dolls. Made in Switzerland. *Author's collection.*

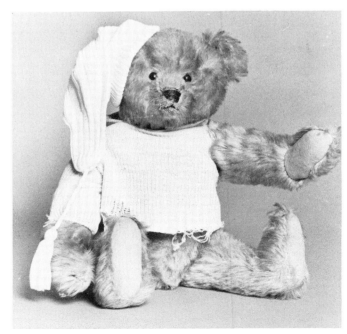

ABOVE: *Illustration 130.* Magnificent collection of rare Steiff and American Teddy Bears, c.1903-1940, in an array of beautiful colors of mohair, ranging in size from 30in (76.2cm) to 18in (45.7cm). *Courtesy Kim Brewer.*

BELOW LEFT: *Illustration 131.* Steiff Bear. c.1910. 15in (38.1cm); light beige mohair; shoe button eyes; jointed arms and legs; swivel head; excelsior stuffing. Condition: Fair. *Author's collection.* Steiff (Zeppelin Mascot) Dog. c.1928. 11in (27.9cm) tall, 14in (35.6cm) long; white mohair, glass eyes; unjointed body and head; excelsior stuffing; printed button. Condition: Excellent. *Courtesy Joan Sickler.*

BELOW RIGHT: *Illustration 132.* Steiff Bear. c.1910. 3½in (8.9cm); short honey colored mohair; black shoe button eyes; jointed arms and legs; swivel head; excelsior stuffing. Condition: Excellent. *Author's collection.*

70

ABOVE LEFT: *Illustration 133.* Steiff Muff. c.1910. 10in (25.4cm) high, 7in (17.8cm) wide; white mohair; shoe button eyes; swivel head; arms, legs and head filled with excelsior. Condition: Mint. Comments: Rare. Completely original. *Author's collection.*

ABOVE RIGHT: *Illustration 134.* Steiff (Tumbling) Bear. c.1908. 12in (30.5cm); brown mohair; shoe button eyes; jointed arms and legs; swivel head; excelsior stuffing; mechanical mechanism concealed in body. Condition: Excellent; replaced paw pads. Comments: Rare. Arms wind clockwork mechanism to activate tumbling motion. *Author's collection.*

RIGHT: *Illustration 135.* Steiff "Teddy Baby." c.1930. 14in (35.6cm); gold mohair; glass eyes; jointed arms and legs; swivel head; excelsior stuffing. Condition: Mint. Comments: Rare. Closed mouth Teddy Baby. Note: paws turned down to resemble a cub. *Courtesy Helen Sieverling.*

Steiff 1950-1960

LEFT: *Illustration 136.* Steiff "Teddy Baby." c.1950. 3½in (8.9cm); brown mohair; beige velveteen snout and feet; glass eyes; jointed arms and legs; swivel head; excelsior stuffing; nickel raised script Steiff button. Condition: Mint. Comments. Rare size. *Courtesy Jeri Leslie Duncan.*

BELOW LEFT: *Illustration 137.* (Left) Steiff "Teddy Baby." c.1950. 15in (38.1cm); light beige mohair; glass eyes; jointed arms and legs; swivel head; excelsior stuffing; nickel raised script Steiff button. Condition: Mint. Comments: Rare. (Right) Steiff "Teddy Baby." c.1950. 11in (27.9cm); brown mohair with beige mohair snout and feet; glass eyes; jointed arms and legs; swivel head; excelsior stuffing; chrome raised script Steiff button. Condition: Mint. Comments: Rare. *Courtesy Volpp Collection.*

BELOW RIGHT: *Illustration 138.* Steiff. c.1950. (Left to right) 14in (35.6cm), 14in (35.6cm), 8in (20.3cm), 3½in (8.9cm); all bears are mohair with jointed arms and legs; swivel heads, glass eyes; excelsior stuffing; nickel buttons with raised Steiff in script. *Author's collection.*

RIGHT: *Illustration 139.* c.1953. 8in (20.3cm); short white mohair; glass eyes; jointed arms and legs; swivel head; excelsior stuffing; nickel raised script Steiff button. Condition: Mint. Comments: Original hunting outfit. Accompanying Steiff booklet shows picture of Roosevelt on horse surrounded by bears in hunting attire. *Courtesy Joan Sickler.*

BELOW: *Illustration 140.* Steiff "Musical Bear." c.1950(?) 13in (33cm); beige mohair; glass eyes; jointed arms and legs; swivel head; excelsior stuffing. Condition: Excellent. Comments: Rare. Music is produced by squeezing bellows encased inside body. Made only for a limited period of time. Mickey and Minnie Mouse. c.1930. (Left to Right) 7in (17.8cm), 5in (12.7cm), 10in (25.4cm); unjointed velvet body and head with felt ears; velvet clothes. *Courtesy Joan Sickler.*

ABOVE: *Illustration 141.* Steiff (Zotty). c.1950. 17in (43.2cm); long curly caramel mohair; glass eyes; jointed arms and legs; swivel head; excelsior stuffing; nickel button with raised Steiff in script. Condition: Mint. *Courtesy Harriett Early.*

BELOW: *Illustration 142.* Steiff. c.1950. 5in (12.7cm), 8in (20.3cm) long; beige mohair; glass eyes; unjointed; excelsior stuffing; nickel raised script Steiff button. Condition: Excellent. Comments: This style also came with a swivel head. *Author's collection.*

OPPOSITE PAGE ABOVE: *Illustration 143.* Steiff Bear. c.1960. 15in (38.1cm); gold silky mohair; glass eyes; jointed arms and legs; swivel head; excelsior stuffing. Condition: Mint. *Courtesy Harriett Early.* Steiff Monkey (Jacko). c.1950. 6in (15.2cm); brown mohair; felt face, hands and feet; glass eyes; jointed arms and legs; swivel head; excelsior stuffing. Condition: Mint. Comments: Rare. Specially designed shoe measuring ruler with monkey attached. Ruler markings: "The Scholl Mfg Co Inc. Chicago, New York, Toronto, London." *Courtesy Joan Sickler.*

BELOW LEFT: *Illustration 144.* Steiff. c.1950. 3½in (8.9cm); short light beige mohair; glass eyes; jointed arms and legs; swivel head; excelsior stuffing; nickel raised script Steiff button. Condition: Mint. *Author's collection.*

BELOW RIGHT: *Illustration 145.* Steiff. c.1950. 5½in (14cm); gold mohair; black button type eyes; nickel raised script button; wire armature throughout unjointed body; swivel head; body stuffed with excelsior; head stuffed with kapok; felt hands and bottom of feet. Condition: Excellent. Comments: Felt outfit. *Courtesy Beverly Port.*

Jackie — The Jubilee Bear

In 1953, the Steiff factory commemorated their fifty years of manufacturing Teddy Bears with Jackie, the Jubilee Bear.

Designed to be a baby bear, his short fat back legs and chunky body gave him the appearance of a little cub. His most identifiable features are a pink stitch on the top of the dark thread of his nose and a small dark-shaded area in the mohair on his tummy which represents a navel.

He was offered for sale in three sizes: 6½in (16.5cm), 9in (22.9cm) and 13in (33cm) in either beige or brown mohair. My research shows that the brown Jackie is the rarest color.

A little booklet accompanied the bear with a cute picture of the cub on the front. The booklet is full of historical facts about the Steiff company, from Margarete's dream of making the children of the world happy by creating her beautiful toy animals, to the evolution of the Teddy Bear designed by her nephew Richard.

Jackie, the Jubilee Bear is highly sought after by collectors today.

Illustration 146. Steiff (Jackie Baby). c.1953. (Left) 13½in (34.3cm), (Right) 9in (22.9cm); beige mohair; glass eyes; jointed arms and legs; swivel head; excelsior stuffing. Condition: Mint. Comments: Rare. Made to commemorate Steiff's 50 years of making Teddy Bears. Identifying features are pink silk thread across nose, dark shaded area for navel. *Courtesy Volpp Collection.*

Illustration 147. This little booklet accompanied the Jackie Baby Bears, telling the history of Margarete Steiff and how Richard Steiff created the Teddy Bear in 1903.

Illustration 148. The author with her two pet life-sized Steiff bears. The polar bear is 62in (157.5cm) tall. c.1960. White long curly mohair; short mohair muzzle; jointed arms; stationary legs; swivel head; glass eyes; excelsior stuffing; leather claws. The bear standing on all fours is 38in (96.5cm) tall; 66in (167.7cm) long. c.1970. Long beige mohair; short cream colored mohair face; leather nose; glass eyes; excelsior stuffing.

Illustration 149. Steiff Teddy Roosevelt on Horse. c.1953. Horse size 8ft 2in (245.8cm) tall; 6ft (182.8cm) long; horse is beige mohair; glass eyes; excelsior stuffing covering metal frame; horsehair mane; leather reins. Teddy is 5ft 5in (152.9cm) tall; felt body; glass eyes; excelsior stuffing; uniform is cotton; hat is wool. Condition: Excellent, except for tear on horse's thigh. Comments: Extremely rare. Produced for Bloomingdale's Department Store, New York, New York. *Courtesy Ernie Eldridge and Anita Sebestyen. Photograph by Thomas E. Malloy.*

LEFT: *Illustration 150.* Steiff St. Bernard Dog. c.1950. 52in (131.1cm) long; white and brown mohair; glass eyes; unjointed body; excelsior stuffing. Condition: Excellent. Comments: Rare. *Courtesy Joan Sickler.*

MIDDLE LEFT: *Illustration 151.* Steiff Alligator. c.1950. 72in (182.9cm) long; beige and green mohair; green felt ridge on back; wooden eyes; unjointed body; excelsior stuffing. Condition: Mint. Comments: Rare. *Courtesy Joan Sickler.*

BOTTOM LEFT: *Illustration 152.* Steiff Monkey. c.1950. 32in (81.3cm) tall; brown mohair; beige felt face with white mohair around chin; beige felt hands and feet; jointed arms and legs; swivel head; glass eyes; excelsior stuffing; nickel raised script Steiff button. Condition: Mint. Comments: Rare. *Courtesy Joan Sickler.*

BELOW: *Illustration 153.* Steiff Beagle Dog. c.1950. 28in (71.1cm) tall; beige and brown mohair; wooden eyes; unjointed body; swivel head; excelsior stuffing; nickel raised script Steiff button. Condition: Excellent. Comments: Rare. *Courtesy Joan Sickler.*

ABOVE LEFT: *Illustration 154.* Steiff Rabbit. c.1950. 30in (76.2cm) tall; white and brown mohair; pink felt lined ears; glass eyes; unjointed body; swivel head; excelsior stuffing; nickel raised Steiff script button. Condition: Mint. Comments: Rare. *Courtesy Joan Sickler.*

ABOVE RIGHT: *Illustration 155.* Steiff Kangaroo. c.1950. 21in (53.3cm) tall; white and brown mohair; felt lined ears; unjointed legs; jointed head and arms; glass eyes; excelsior stuffing; tiny kangaroo in pouch. Condition: Mint. Comments: Rare. *Courtesy Joan Sickler.*

Illustration 156. Steiff Leopard. c.1950. 28in (71.1cm) long; white and gold mohair with black spots; green glass eyes; unjointed body; excelsior stuffing.

TOP LEFT: *Illustration 157.* Similar designs to this strong metal frame reinforces all Steiff animals on wheels.

TOP RIGHT: *Illustration 158.* Steiff. c.1908. 36in (91.4cm) long, 30in (76.2cm) tall; short brown mohair (resembles burlap); glass eyes; unjointed head; excelsior stuffing; deep growler activated by pull ring on bear's back; printed Steiff button. Condition: Excellent. Comments: Extremely rare size. Muzzle not original. *Author's collection.*

BOTTOM: *Illustration 159.* Each wheel is marked Steiff. 7in (17.8cm) metal wheels. Taken from bear in *Illustration 158.*

Illustration 160. Steiff. c.1910. 17in (43.2cm) long, 13in (33cm) high; worn cinnamon mohair; glass eyes; unjointed head; pull ring on back activates growler; excelsior stuffing; metal wheels. Condition: Fair. *Author's collection.*

Illustration 161. Steiff. c.1908. 30in (76.2cm) long, 21in (53.3cm) high; brown burlap; large button eyes; swivel head; excelsior stuffing; metal wheels. Condition: Good. Comments: Note head shaped more like a Teddy Bear. This seems to be a characteristic of bears on wheels with swivel heads. *Author's collection.* (I purchased this bear at the London Toy Show and brought him back to our hotel room via the underground [subway].)

Illustration 162. Steiff. c.1907. 41in (104.1cm) long x 33in (83.8cm) tall; short brown mohair (resembles burlap); large glass eyes; deep growler activated by pull ring on bear's back; printed Steiff button; large metal wheels. Condition: Good. Comments: Extremely rare size. Small 14½in (36.9cm) bear gives size comparison. *Courtesy James S. Maxwell, Jr.*

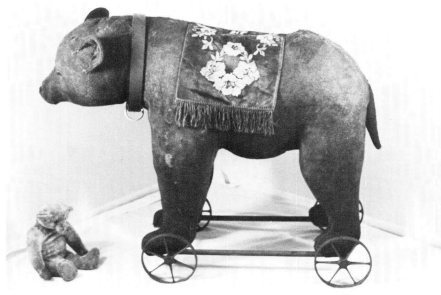

ABOVE LEFT: *Illustration 164.* Steiff. c.1958. 30in (76.2cm) long x 24in (61cm) high; beige mohair; glass eyes; unjointed head; excelsior stuffing; red painted steel frame and disc wheels; white rubber tires; pull ring on back activates growler. Condition: Mint. *Author's collection.*

ABOVE RIGHT: *Illustration 165.* Steiff "Record Teddy." c.1910. 9in (22.9cm) long, 11in (27.9cm) high; gold mohair; shoe button eyes; jointed arms and legs; swivel head; excelsior stuffing; wooden wheels marked Steiff; metal frame. Condition: Excellent. Comments: Rare. As toy is pulled, bear moves back and forth. *Author's collection.*

OPPOSITE PAGE ABOVE: *Illustration 163.* Steiff. c.1907. 24in (61cm) long, 16in (40.6cm) high; white mohair; large button eyes; unjointed head; pull ring on back activates growler; excelsior stuffing; metal wheels. Condition: Excellent. *Author's collection.*

RIGHT: *Illustration 166.* Wooden wheel marked Steiff. Taken from the bear in *Illustration 165.*

BELOW: *Illustration 167.* Steiff Bear Pull Toy. c.1926. 9in (22.9cm) tall x 9in (22.9cm) long; (Left) purple mohair; (Right) gold mohair; removable ruffs; shoe button eyes; excelsior stuffing; red wooden wheels; metal frame. Condition: Excellent. Comments: Rare. As toy is pulled, bears move back and forth simultaneously. *Courtesy Volpp Collection.*

Steiff Dolls

Illustration 168. Three rare early Steiff dolls. c.1910-1912. (Left) The Musician, 16in (40.6cm), is adorned with sixteen printed Steiff buttons. Also note the center seam on his face is horizontal instead of the usual vertical seam found on the majority of Steiff dolls. (Center) Peasant, 20in (50.8cm), has the most beautiful facial coloring and expression. (Right) Proud looking Gendarme, 9in (22.9cm), completely original in his navy and bright red felt jacket and hat, with black felt molded trousers. All three dolls are in excellent condition. *Courtesy Kim Brewer.*

Gebrüder Hermann KG

"Gebr." is the abbreviation for the German word *Gebrüder*, which means brother. The story of the German toy manufacturer is best told in the words of a member of the Hermann family herself, Margit Grolshagen-Hermann.

"The history of the Gebr. Hermann KG, Teddy-Plüschspielwarenfabrik, began in 1907 when Johann Hermann (1854-1920) decided to manufacture Teddy Bears. Assisted by members of his family, he started his trade and business in a small workshop at Neufang near Sonneberg in Thuringia, in today's German Democratic Republic (GDR). He had three sons and three daughters who all energetically helped him to establish his newly founded firm.

"In 1903 he sent his oldest son, Bernhard, to Meiningen for his apprenticeship in trade and business. His second son, Artur, stayed at home to work in his father's factory. He mainly was occupied with designing toys, but was also in charge of production. After Bernhard had completed his apprenticeship, he returned home and worked in his father's toy business for several years. In 1911 he established his own business and became independent from his father.

"In 1912, Bernhard Hermann was married to Ida Jaeger who was the daughter of a mason and builder.

Then he moved to Sonneberg where he founded a small factory. He employed several men and women who were specialized in manufacturing Teddy Bears and dolls. At that time, Sonneberg was the world's center of toy manufacturing. It was the place where numerous toy factories were established. But also many important American purchasers, such as Woolworth, S.S. Kresge, G.O.A. Borgfeldt, Louis Wolf & Sons, etc., maintained their export houses in this little town. At that time, these firms were buying Teddy Bears and dolls from Bernhard Hermann for importation into the United States.

"Bernhard Hermann had four sons, Hellmuth, Artur, Werner and Horst. His oldest son, Hellmuth, was trained in his father's business. Later, he established his own business. Artur and Werner attended a commercial and industrial business school. Their studies included designing, modeling, and pattern making. After graduation, they assisted their father in managing the manufacture and the sale of Teddy Bears and other plush animals that were added to their line of merchandise.

"In 1948, Bernhard Hermann and his three sons relocated the business and the factory from the GDR to Hirschaid near Bamberg, in the American Zone of Germany, which is now in the Federal Republic of Germany, and the firm was re-established.

Gebrüder Hermann KG

ABOVE LEFT: *Illustration 169.* Hermann Cat "Oskar." c.1930. 7½in (19.1cm); composition head with grey flocked hair; hard rubber pipe; painted features; cloth body; grey mohair feet and tail; jointed arms and legs; swivel head; original clothes; original Hermann tag. Condition: Mint. Comments: Rare. *Courtesy Jeri Leslie Duncan.*

ABOVE RIGHT: *Illustration 170.* Hermann. c.1920. (Left) 15in (38.1cm), (Right) 17in (43.2cm); beige mohair; glass eyes; jointed arms and legs; swivel head; excelsior stuffing. Condition: Mint. Comments: Note short moahir on muzzle, characteristic of Hermann. *Courtesy Sally Bowen. Photograph by Warren Bowen.*

"Since that time, the success and prosperity of the Hermann toy factory continued to grow and Hermann became one of the most famous manufacturers in their industry. While the firm was established in Sonneberg, its name was Bernhard Hermann. In Hirschaid, it continued as the Teddy-Plüschspielwarenfabrik Gebr. Hermann KG. (Hermann Brothers Company, Manufacturers of Teddy Bears and plush toy animals). The three sons of the original founder became partners in this business.

"When Bernhard Hermann died in 1959, his legacy to his sons included a successful and prosperous business that was a famous worldwide factory for fine Teddy Bears and other plush toy animals.

"Teddy Bears have always been number one of all the animals made by Hermann. Thousands of handmade "Teddies" leave Hirschaid every year and are shipped to destinations all over the world. Skilled employees ensure the manufacture of well-designed and highly-finished toys. Many of these workers have been employed by the Gebr. Hermann KG for more than one or two decades. Currently, Artur and Werner Hermann manage the firm. Artur is responsible for the finances and the sales. Werner, as the product manager, makes the designs and assures the highest quality of workmanship. Hellmuth, the director of operations, retired in 1980.

"The Gebr. Hermann KG continues the high ideals of the old firm in manufacturing only the finest quality handmade Teddy Bears and other soft toy animals and pursue its rich traditions."

Unfortunately, as far as we know, no identifying mark was attached to the early Hermann Teddy Bear, other than a tag. So, without this positive marking, identification is quite difficult.

Some Hermann bears have a very similar resemblance to that of the 1930s-1950s Steiff. Their features, however, weren't quite as accentuated. As with Steiff, they were completely jointed. They were made of the finest quality of mohair.

Early bears were stuffed with excelsior and came with shoe button and glass eyes. One distinctive characteristic of some of the earlier versions is the short mohair muzzle. Two-tone (varigated) mohair was also used with solid colored muzzles. An early Hermann bear is a true collector's item.

Many of the currently-made collectibles are distributed in the United States by Kathy Ann Dolls, Imports of Northwood, Ohio, and Jesco Inc., of Los Angeles, California.

Illustration 171. Hermann. c.1940. (Left) 7in (17.8cm), (Right) 8in (20.3cm); gold mohair; glass eyes; jointed arms and legs; swivel head; excelsior stuffing. Condition: Excellent. Comments: Note the similarity to the Steiff bears of the same era. *Courtesy Sally Bowen. Photograph by Warren Bowen.*

Illustration 172. Hermann. c.1980. (Left to right) 27in (68.6cm), 20in (50.8cm), 14in (35.6cm), 16in (40.6cm), 12in (30.5cm), 9in (22.9cm); long silky varigated mohair; short mohair muzzle; glass eyes; jointed arms and legs; swivel head; open mouth lined with felt. Condition: Mint. Comments: This design of Teddy Bear has been manufactured by Hermann for many years. Note the resemblance to the Steiff Zotty bear in *Illustration 141. Courtesy Sally Bowen. Photograph by Warren Bowen.*

Schuco Toy Company

It was the complimentary skills of the creative genius of Heinrich Müller and the management skills of Adolf Kahn that allowed Schuco to rise to world fame.

According to Schuco's 50th anniversary catalogue, the company was founded by Heinrich Müller. At 17, young Müller decided he needed more experience as a technician and designer. He halted production at his own company and went to work for Gebrüder Bing, another Nurnberg toy manufacture of great repute.

The time came when the ambitious Müller was ready to go back into business for himself. So, on November 16, 1912, Müller, along with his new partner, Heinrich Schreyer founded the Schreyer u. Co. on the Roorstrasse in Nürnberg. They abbreviated Schreyer u. Co. to the name with which we are so familiar today — Schuco. They began in 1600 square feet of space with ten employees.

Their success quickly demanded a move to larger quarters. After a time in new facilities, the partners were drafted into military service for World War I. The factory closed.

When the war ended, Schreyer left the company, seeing no future in making toys. Müller felt differently. He was determined to keep Schreyer and Company in operation. He found a new partner, Adolf Kahn, and together they opened another factory on the Singerstrasse in Nürnberg.

Schuco

Illustration 173. Schuco (Yes/No). (Left) c.1924. 14in (35.6cm); bright gold short mohair; glass eyes; jointed arms and legs; swivel head; excelsior stuffing. Condition: Mint. Comments: Note the earlier design of straighter arms and smaller feet. Head nods "yes" and "no" when tail is moved. (Right) c.1920. 11in (27.9cm); light gold mohair; shoe button eyes; jointed arms and legs; swivel head; excelsior stuffing. Condition: Good. Comments: The small facial features and feet are characteristic of the earlier Yes/No Schuco Teddy Bears. Head nods "yes" and "no" when tail is moved. *Author's collection.*

Kahn, born in a small German village in 1882, had moved to Nürnberg at the age of 18. He was in the textile business and constantly heard in his travels of the fame of Nurnberg *toys*. So, when at the end of his military service he returned to Nurnberg, he ran a newspaper ad looking for a partner in a toy company. Müller responded and Schuco was on its way to worldwide fame.

The renown of their mechanical toys propelled them to well respected heights in their industry. A mechanical bird called "Pecking Bird," was highly touted in 1929.

My personal collection contains a number of Schuco's fascinating bears. One of my favorites is the "Bell Hop" (c. 1923) *(Illustration 177)*. Made of gold mohair, he proudly wears a red felt jacket and hat with black felt pants. The rare bear nods his head "yes" or "no" when his tail is moved.

I also enjoy three other c.1948 Schuco yes/no bears in my collection. The largest bear in this family (17in [43.2cm]) is also musical, wound by a key in the front of his beige mohair chest. An attached red tag shows his name "Tricky." *(Illustration 175.)* During the c.1920-c.1970 Schuco also created wonderful miniature bears. Uniquely constructed with patented metal bodies. The early versions measured 2⅜in (6cm) in height with tiny attached felt paws. By c.1930 the paws were discontinued and the bears size slightly increased with a sturdier body. Schuco continued to use this basic model for their future miniature bears. The company also used this clever construction in many novelty adaptations.

For instance, my tiny (3½in [8.9cm]) perfume bottle bear has a removable head which covers a glass perfume bottle *(Illustration 179)*. Another variation is a compact bear whose jointed body contains an oval mirror on one side and a powder puff and tray on the other. *(Illustration 180)*.

Schuco is also remembered for their walking, tumbling and somersaulting bears including one which pushes a stick back and forth while moving forward on roller skates *(Illustration 185)*.

With the rise to power of Hitler, Müller and Kahn (who was Jewish) dissolved their partnership in 1936. Their relationship had been good, but the pressures of the political climate and Nazism forced Kahn and his wife to escape to England, leaving behind most of their possessions. Their son Eric had already left for the United States where he served in the U.S. Army for 4½ years.

When Eric returned to civilian life, he and his father re-established a business relationship with Herr Müller. The father and son travelled to West Germany and created a business alliance with Schuco. Operating under an exclusive contract, the new independent Schuco Toy Co. retained "import rights to all Schuco products" in the U.S. and Canada. The new company was legally formed in 1947.

According to Eric Kahn, at first "the German Schuco company had no interest in this firm. Eventually the American Schuco had sales representatives in the 48 states and Canada and Schuco products became a well-known brand in this part of the world."

Muller died in 1958, and his only son Werner, along with Schreyer and Co. manager Alexander Girz, continued business operations. Schuco's strong lead was challenged heavily by the up and coming Japanese toy industry and the company was sold.

From then on, the company struggled to survive. Eventually, Schreyer and Company declared bankruptcy in 1970.

During their 50 years in business, they created and manufactured diminutive and larger-scale toy animals which are highly prized today by collectors the world over.

ABOVE: *Illustration 174.* Schuco (Yes/No) Bear on Wheels. c.1920. 9in (22.9cm) high x 14in (35.6cm) long; short rich brown mohair; glass eyes; unjointed body; swivel head; excelsior stuffing; iron frame and wheels. (Schuco-Patent embossed on wheels.) Condition: Excellent. Comments: Rare. Head nods "yes" and "no" when tail is moved. *Courtesy Kathy George.*

Illustration 175 & 176. Schuco (Yes/No). c.1948. (Left to right) 17in (43.2cm), 12in (30.5cm), 8in (20.3cm); beige mohair; glass eyes; jointed arms and legs; swivel head; excelsior stuffing. Condition: Mint. Comments: Rare; heads nod "yes" or "no" when tail is moved. The 17in (43.2cm) bear is also musical, wound by a key in front of chest. Red plastic tag reads: "Schuco 'Tricky' Patent ANG." Reverse of tag: "D.B. Pat. ang. IND. PATENTS pending. Made in U.S. Zone Germany." *Author's collection.*

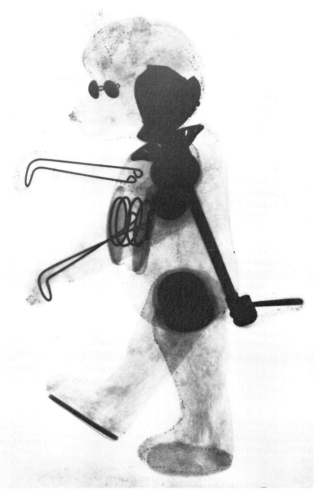

ABOVE LEFT: *Illustration 177.* Schuco "Bell Hop" (Yes/No). c.1923. 14in (35.6cm); gold mohair; red felt jacket and hat; black felt pants; replaced shoe button eyes; jointed arms and legs; swivel head; excelsior stuffing. Condition: Excellent. Comments: Rare. Head nods "yes" or "no" when tail is moved. *Author's collection.*

ABOVE RIGHT: *Illustration 178.* The x-ray shows the mechanism for the Schuco Yes/No Teddy Bears. When the tail is moved, the head nods "yes" or "no."

RIGHT: *Illustration 179.* Schuco (Perfume Bottle). c.1930. 3½in (8.9cm); gold mohair; black metal eyes; jointed arms and legs; swivel head; metal frame. Condition: Mint. Comments: Rare. Removable head discloses glass perfume bottle. *Author's collection.*

OPPOSITE PAGE TOP LEFT: *Illustration 180.* Schuco (Compact). c.1930. 3½in (8.9cm); gold mohair; black metal eyes; jointed arms and legs; swivel head; metal frame. Condition: Mint. Comments: Rare. Removing head discloses compact. *Author's collection.*

BOTTOM LEFT: *Illustration 181.* Removing head on bear in *Illustration 180* discloses compact.

TOP RIGHT & BOTTOM RIGHT: *Illustration 182 & 183.* Schuco (Two Face). c.1950. 3½in (8.9cm); gold mohair; black metal eyes; jointed arms and legs; swivel head; metal frame. Condition: Mint. Comments: Rare. Faces change by twisting brass knob at base of body. *Author's collection.*

ABOVE RIGHT: *Illustration 184.* Schuco (Panda Yes/No). c.1948. 8in (20.3cm); black and white mohair; glass eyes; jointed arms and legs; swivel head; excelsior stuffing. Condition: Mint. Comments: Rare. Head nods "yes" or "no" when tail is moved. *Author's collection.*

BELOW RIGHT: *Illustration 185.* Schuco (Mechanical). c.1950. 10in (25.4cm); short beige mohair; glass eyes; jointed arms and legs; swivel head; excelsior stuffing. Condition: Mint. Comments: Rare. Key wind mechanism. Bear pushes back and forth on stick as he moves forward on roller skates. *Author's collection.*

BELOW: *Illustration 186.* Schuco key for mechanical bears.

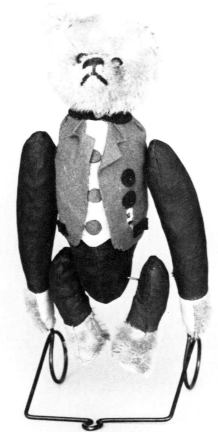

RIGHT: *Illustration 190.* Schuco (Yes/No). c.1950. 7in (17.8cm); short beige mohair; glass eyes; jointed arms and legs; excelsior stuffing. Condition: Mint. Comments: Very rare. Head nods "yes" or "no" when tail is moved. Three bees are trying to get to the papier mâché hive. The bear has honey on his nose and paw. Purchased in Broadway Department Store, he was displayed among the jewelry. *Courtesy Harriett Early.*

BELOW LEFT: *Illustration 191.* Schuco (Pandas). c.1930-1960. (Left) 3½in (8.9cm), (Right) 2½in (6.4cm); black and white mohair; black metal eyes; jointed arms and legs; stationary head; metal frame for entire body. Condition: Good. *Author's collection.*

BELOW RIGHT: *Illustration 192.* Schuco. c.1950. 3½in (8.9cm); short gold mohair; black metal eyes; jointed arms and legs; stationary head; metal frame for entire body. Condition: Mint. Comments: The earlier versions of these miniature Teddy Bears were smaller with tiny attached felt paws. *Author's collection.*

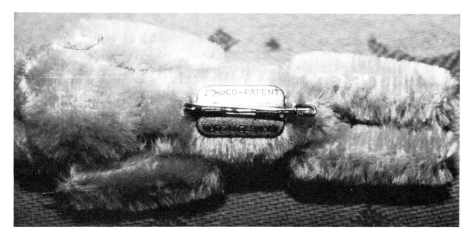

ABOVE: *Illustration 193.* A Group of Rare c.1920-1930 Schuco Monkeys. Range in size from 3½in (8.9cm) to 5in (12.7cm). Yes/No, perfume and compact versions. Note: The little felt hands and feet. This was how the Teddy Bears and monkeys were made in this era. Later discontinued, the design changed to look like the bear in *Illustration 192. Author's collection.*

MIDDLE LEFT: *Illustration 194.* Schuco "Teddy Bear Pin." c.1920(?). 3½in (8.9cm); short gold mohair; black metal eyes; jointed arms and legs; swivel head; metal body. Condition: Excellent. Comments: Rare. Metal plate on back of bear reads "Schuco-Patent//Made in Germany." Pin is attached so bear may be worn as ornament. See picture of bear in *Illustration 196* (far left). *Courtesy Beverly Port.*

BELOW LEFT: *Illustration 195.* (Left) Schuco "Felix Perfume." c.1920. 5in (12.7cm); short black mohair; black and white metal face with round nose; jointed arms and legs; swivel head; metal body. Condition: Excellent. Comments: Very rare. (Center) Schuco Teddy Bear. c.1950. 3½in (8.9cm); short gold mohair; black metal eyes; jointed arms and legs; swivel head; metal body. Condition: Excellent. (Right) Schuco Elephant "Yes/No." c.1920. 5in (12.7cm) tall; gray mohair; jointed arms and legs; swivel head; metal body. Condition: Excellent. Comments: Rare. Head nods "yes" or "no" when tail is moved. *Courtesy Beverly Port.*

ABOVE: *Illustration 196.* A group of rare Schuco Teddy Bears. *Courtesy Beverly Port.*

RIGHT: *Illustration 197.* Schuco Ducks (Yes/No). c.1926. 11in (27.9cm); white mohair; glass eyes; unjointed bodies; swivel heads; orange felt beaks and orange felt covered metal feet; original Schuco tag. *Courtesy Jeri Leslie Duncan.*

Gebrüder Bing

The Nuremberg company of Gebrüder Bing was founded in 1865 by Ignaz Bing and his brother Adolf.

This well-known toy manufacturer started out by making tin and kitchenware. Then in 1890 they began to produce enamelled toys. Today, they are most recognized by bear collectors for their fine work in manufacturing clockwork bears and toys in the early 1900s. They also produced soft toys in fur fabric, felt and velvet.

The name of the company originally was Nürnberger Spielwarenfabrik Gebrüder Bing (Bing Brother's Nuremberg Toy Factory). The factory was situated in Karolinestrasse.

In 1890, a factory at Grünhain in Saxony was opened to manufacture enamelled toys, including boats and ships. Other warehouses and administrative office centered around the Nuremberg building.

Then in 1895, the firm became a limited company and the name was changed to Nürnberger Metall und Lackierwarenfabrik vorm, Bing A.G. (Nuremberg Metal and Enamelware Works). Differences occurred between the brothers Ignaz and Adolf. Ignaz took over as Chairman of the Board.

Over the years a large percentage of the company's production was assembled by cottage industry workers. The costumes of the bears were most probably made in this manner.

The success of the company is proved by the high honors bestowed on them for their beautiful toys including boats, cars and key wound figures. Walking, climbing tumbling bears made by Bing are prized collector's items today. Many of the bears were dressed in colorful outfits made of felt and silk.

A distribution firm known as Concentra was organized to market Bing's complete line in 1917 under various brand names.

"G.B.N." (Gebrüder Bing Nürnberg) was still the identifying mark on toys until approximately 1919. This was changed to "B.W." (Bing Werke) by 1920.

In 1918 Ignaz Bing died and Stefen Bing took over as Director General in 1919. Due to differences with the supervisory board, Stefen severed all family connections in 1927.

With the worldwide depression and internal company problems, the firm went into receivership in 1932 causing the business to split. The ship department was taken over by Fleischmann.

Gebruder Bing

Illustration 198. Bing-Walking Bear. c.1915. 10in (25.4cm); short cinnamon mohair; shoe button eyes; excelsior stuffed head and arms; metal frame body encases key wind mechanism; heavy metal legs and feet. Action: Bear rocks from side to side as it moves slowly forward. Comments: Rare. Small features (note ears and nose) are an identifying factor of some of the mechanical Bing Bears. *Author's collection.*

Illustration 199. Bing. c.1910. 16in (40.6cm); white mohair; shoe button eyes; jointed arms and legs; swivel head; excelsior stuffing. Condition: Excellent. Comments: Rare. Metal tag affixed to ear reads "G.B.N." (Gebrüder Bing Nurnberg). *Courtesy Pam Hebbs.*

OPPOSITE PAGE: The Steiff Teddy Bear family find the ideal spot in the woods for their picnic lunch. *Author's collection.*

The googlie-eyed German bisque doll (Kestner #172, 18in [45.7cm]) steadies the little Steiff Teddy Bear as he rides the early toy horse. *Author's collection.*

OPPOSITE PAGE: Steiff Teddy Bears play with the cute little French bisque doll (Steiner A-9, 16in [40.6cm]). *Author's collection.*

OPPOSITE PAGE: A huge 62in (157.5cm) Steiff Polar Bear raises up on his haunches on the big rock. *Author's collection.*

The big Steiff Teddy Bears enjoy the afternoon sun as they play amongst the old tree stumps. *Author's collection.*

Taking a sleigh ride is a bisque French doll
(Jumeau, 29in [73.7cm]), a German bisque doll
(Kestner #260, 29in [13.7cm]) and group of Steiff
Teddy Bears. *Author's collection.*

OPPOSITE PAGE: An old express wagon is a
fun place for these Steiff Teddy Bears to play with
the bisque German doll made by Kestner. *Author's
collection.*

These tiny 3in (7.6cm) Steiff Teddy Bears enjoy the attention of the 12in (30.5cm) French Belton dolls. *Author's collection.*

OPPOSITE PAGE: A Teddy Bears' Family Reunion. *Author's collection.*

The big Steiff Bear (c.1970; 66in [167.7cm] long) stalks the woods. *Author's collection.*

OPPOSITE PAGE: The cute bisque little girl doll (S.F.B.J. #247) makes a pet of the Steiff bear on wheels (c.1907). *Author's collection.*

OPPOSITE PAGE: The cute little bisque googlie-eyed doll (Heubach #318. 14in [35.6cm]) discovers the Steiff rabbits playing with the Teddy Doll (13in [33cm]) in the woods. *Author's collection.*

This German bisque googlie doll (Kestner #165. 20in [50.8cm]) plays with the Steiff baby goose while the gosling's mother observes. *Author's collection.*

Marie, a German bisque doll (Kämmer and Reinhardt #101, 18in [45.7cm]) enjoys watching the Stieff Teddy Bears (c.1907) ride in the wagon pulled by a Schuco Yes/No Bear on all fours. *Author's collection.*

ABOVE LEFT: *Illustration 200.* Bing. c.1910. 10in (25.4cm); light gray mohair; shoe button eyes; jointed arms and legs; swivel head; excelsior stuffing. Condition: Excellent. Comments: Metal button affixed to left side of bear reads "G.B.N." (Gebrüder Bing, Nurnberg). *Author's collection.*

ABOVE RIGHT: *Illustration 201.* Bing. c.1920. 18in (45.7cm); long beige mohair; shaved muzzle; glass eyes; jointed arms and legs; swivel head; excelsior stuffing. Condition: Excellent. Comments: Rare, metal tag affixed to right arm. "German B.W." (Bing Werke). *Courtesy Debbie Ratliff.*

RIGHT: *Illustration 202.* Bing "Tumbling Bear." c.1920. 9in (22.9cm); gold mohair; shoe button eyes; jointed arms and legs; swivel head; excelsior stuffing. Condition: Excellent. Comments: Rare. Arms wind clockwork mechanism to activate tumbling motion. Metal tag on arm "B.W." (Bing Werke). *Courtesy Beverly Port.*

Grisly

When you hear the name Grisly, bears immediately come to mind. I am sure this is what Karl Unfricht had in mind when he founded the Grisly Spielwaren Fabrik in 1954. Karl Unfricht died in 1980 and the family business is now owned by his son, Hans-Georg Unfricht and daughter, Hannelore Wirth.

As with many German firms, the Grisly company was originally conducted in the private family dwelling. Located in the lovely village of Kircheimbolanden, West Germany, the company has now enlarged and employs close to forty people, and manufactures a large range of plush Teddy Bears and animals.

The company originally produced bears in mohair, one of the most luxurious, dirt resistant fabrics in the world. But now, due to the rising costs of mohair, the Grizly company also uses dralon and acrylic plush for their animals.

Until approximately 1974, the company identified their products with a metal button securely fastened to the chest of the animal. Their trademark was a bear on all fours with what appears to be a needle and thread encircling part of the bear. The name Grisly is also printed on the button. Without this button some of their animals could be mistaken for Steiff or Hermann.

A 1984 "Original Grisly Teddy" with a limited edition of 1,000 has been manufactured bearing the Grisly button. Mostly made by hand, the animals are produced under the strict control of the family.

Grisly

Illustration 203. (Left) Grisly. c.1960. 21in (53.3cm). Beige mohair; glass eyes; jointed arms and legs; swivel head; excelsior stuffing. Condition: Mint. (Right) Grisly Panda. c.1960. 12in (30.5cm). Black and white mohair; glass eyes; jointed arms and legs; swivel head; excelsior stuffing. Condition: Mint. Comments: The name Grisly is printed in red on a small metal button fastened to the bear's chest. *Courtesy Brigitte Nohrudi.*

More German Teddy Bear Manufacturers

It is interesting to note many of the German Teddy Bear manufacturers were originally doll and toy companies. With the tremendous demand for the new popular toy, it was an easy article for them to produce as no extra equipment was necessary. As long as a company had a good seamstress, a pattern and a sewing machine, they were in business.

Many of the following companies are new to us in the Teddy Bear world. This only makes us realize that numerous amounts of Teddy Bears were manufactured by all these different manufacturers. Unfortunately, with no identification found on the Teddy Bear, or old catalogs available, positive identification is nearly impossible on many Teddy Bears. With the thirst for knowledge and the evergrowing popularity of our most-loved toy, we hope further research may shed light on so many of our unanswered questions.

Oskar Büchner, Ebersdorf, Germany: Manufactured dolls, dummies and cloth toys. In 1925 their trademark pictured the silhouette of a Teddy Bear sitting holding the initials "O" in his right arm and "B" in the left. The design of a triangle surrounds the bear.

Cresco-Spielwarenfabrik GmbH., Schweinfurt, Bavaria, Germany: Advertised dancing Teddy Bears in 1920.

E. Dehler, Coburg, Germany: Advertised plush animals in 1906. A 1911 sample card pictured beautiful, jointed mohair Teddy Bears.

Josef Deuerlein, Nachf. (Successors to Kohler and Rosenwald), Nuremberg, Germany: "Hercules" was their trademark registered in 1907 for "Toy of felt and leather." One trademark design was a smiling, jointed Teddy Bear within a circle holding the name "Hercules." Another showed a jointed Teddy Bear holding a flag advertising the name "Kolundro," while his other hand pulled an elephant on wheels with a monkey seated on its back.

Deutsche Kolonial-Kapok-Werke, Berlin, Potsdam and Ergenzingen, Germany: In 1925 the company advertised their name as "DeKawe" — softly stuffed play animals and toys, can swim. Only genuine with monkey head on neck!" Their trademark pictured a diamond design with the head of a Bulldog surrounded by the words "Dekawe" "Spieltiere and Puppen." The tag of a monkey's head hangs around the dog's neck."

Dressel and Pietschmann, Coburg, Germany: In 1923, the company advertised "Toys with double-joints." Their trademark explicitly shows this with a jointed Teddy Bear in a sitting position, a standing circus type bear, Santa Claus holding a Christmas tree and a jointed doll. Below are the initials: D.D.C.

Julius Engelhardt, Sonneberg and Rodach, Germany: Founded in 1823 by Julius Engelhardt at Rodach, the company manufactured dolls. In 1911, an advertisement showed the company produced plush animals and dolls made of felt and plush with celluloid and *papier-mâché* heads.

Fleischmann and Bloedel, Sonneberg, Germany; Paris, France; and London, England: Founded by Salomon Fleischmann and Jean Bloedel in 1873, the company manufactured dolls with walking movements. After the death of Jean Bloedel, in 1905, the company expanded and was taken over by Josef Berlin who introduced plush animals and Teddy Bears to their line. "Michu" was his trademark. Also a doll dancing with a Teddy Bear was used in 1914. The company prospered and a new factory was built in 1920, supplying the whole world with their products. The toy industry suffered during the inflationary times of the 1920s which caused the firm to go into bankruptcy. It closed its doors in 1926.

Adolf Fleischmann and Craemer, Sonneberg, Germany: Founded in 1844, the company was owned by Adolf Fleischmann and Messrs. Hetzel and Sachsenwäger. It produced toys, figures, animals and dolls.

Albert Förster, Neustadt, Germany: In 1929, the company manufactured dolls and knock-about dolls. Their trademark, however, shows a jointed Teddy Bear in walking position, within a triangle. The initials "AF" are below the bear.

Gustav Förster, Neustadt, Germany: Founded in 1905 by August Förster, the company produced dolls and toys. In 1925, their catalog offered 2,000 items. Their trademark was a bearded gentleman smoking a pipe with a gun over one shoulder. A sack of toys hung from the other shoulder. The initial "G" was on the right of the man and "F" appeared on the left. "Neustadt b Coburg" was printed at the bottom of the figure.

Otto Gans, Waltershausen, Germany: The doll factory Gans and Seyfarth, Waltershausen, was founded by Otto Gans and Mr. Seyfarth in 1908. In 1922, Otto Gans opened his own factory. The trademark "*Kindertraum* (a child's dream) for dolls and animal figures as cloth toys" was registered in 1930. It pictured a child standing beside a dog with the name "Kindertraum" encircled with the letter "G."

Hahn and Company, Nuremberg, Germany: "Hanco" was the company's registered trademark in 1921 for "plush bears, cloth animals, knock-about dolls." It pictured a Teddy Bear waving the "Hanco" flag from the center of a world globe with "Nurenberg, Germany," across the top and "*Schutz-Marke*" at the base.

Carl Harmus, Jr., Sonneberg, Germany: Incorporated into the commercial register in 1887, the factory's first owner (Carl Harmus, Jr.) died in 1896. Georg Neugebauer became the new owner, manufacturing "felt-like elastic doll faces." A topsy-turvy doll in combination with an animal figure was created in 1907. The registered trademark in 1909 was "Bear with doll" for "Dolls, dolls' trousseaux and softly stuffed animals." The shape of a triangle with a jointed Teddy Bear sitting on a box holding a doll was pictured. Below the bear were the words "*Schutz-Marke.*

Johann Heinrich Kletzin and Company, Leipzig, Germany: The factory was founded in Neustadt, near Coburg, in 1920. They exhibited their dolls and stuffed animals at the Leipzig Fair in 1921. A 1925 advertisement in *Games and Toys* shows a dressed "Mew Puss" (cat) that walked, talked and laughed.

Henze and Steinhäuser, Erfurt and Gehren, Germany: The company was started by the two unmarried Wacker sisters at Erfurt. The two women eventually became Ann Steinhäuser and Laura Henze. They specialized in woolen toys. In 1907, Mrs. Steinhäuser's son, Kurt, became sole owner and later advertised dolls made of plush with full and half-celluloid heads. Plush and woolen animals with the new soft Kapok stuffing were advertised in 1925 bearing the "Henza" trademark (a monkey on all fours with words "Henza original").

Walter Jügelt, Coburg, Germany: In 1923, the company produced dolls and toys. Their trademark was an unrealistic looking bear on all fours looking towards a kneeling lady doll. The name and location of the company surrounded this design.

Kohler and Rosenwald (succeeded by Josef Deuerlein), Nuremberg, Germany: In 1927 they registered the trademark "Kolundro" (standing for Kohler und Rosewald) for "Toys, especially for figures stuffed by cloths and felt." Their trademark design was a realistic looking marching bear carrying a flag.

Werner Krauth, Leipzig, Germany: Manufacturing toys and dolls, their trademark depicted this by showing dolls and a Teddy Bear dancing around a globe of the world. The company's initials "WR" are separated by a ship at full-sail at the top of the design.

Leven and Sprenger, Sonneberg, Germany: Founded in 1891 by Hubert Josef Leven and Theodor Sprenger, this company manufactured toys exclusively for export. A 1910 sample card advertised a wide range of beautiful dolls, toy animals and a jointed plush Teddy Bear.

Louis Philipp Luthard, Neustadt, Germany: The company, founded in 1909, advertised "cloth animals, bears, eskimos, softly stuffed dolls of all kinds" in 1921.

Andreas Müller, Sonneberg, Germany: The company, owned by Andreas Müller, manufactured toys. It was incorporated into the commercial register in 1887. One of their trademark's was a detailed picture of a jointed Teddy Bear and doll turning a windmill. Seated on top is a jester. The initials "A.M.N." are printed at the base of the windmill.

Gustav Schmey, Sonneberg, Germany: Founded in 1853, the company changed the name to G. Schmey Nachf. In 1896, it advertised "dolls, fun articles, drawing figures and animals of fur." A 1911 sample card showed the wide variety of dolls, toys and plush animals including a fierce looking bear on all fours with a chain attached to its nose.

Edvard Schmidt, Coburg, Germany: Founded in 1904 by Edvard Schmidt, the doll factory manufactured in 1924: " 'Sicora' dolls and 'Sicora' Teddies that walk with the registered 'Sicora' walking shoe even on the slickest linoleum floor. 'Sicora' wonder dolls and 'Sicora'

Teddies attract attention, especially with the 'Sicora' walking stick." A picture of a little girl walking and holding a stick attached to a doll demonstrates the toy's action.

Herman Steiner, Neustadt, Germany: The factory was founded in Tann/Rhön and produced plush animals. A 1929 advertisement showed the latest novelty in their line of cloth animals: "Rolf, the favorite Teddy Bear opening his mouth when grumbling (with the living Steiner eye)."

Wilhelm Strunz, Nuremberg, Germany: The factory for cloth toys was founded in 1902, manufacturing cloth dolls, In 1905, it manufactured "a connecting device for stuffed dolls parts consisting of a wire rod with movable discs jointed at its ends." Court proceedings were taken up against Wilhelm Strunz in 1905 by Margarete Steiff who claimed his company was using the same "button in the ear" trademark as Steiff. An agreement was made between the two companies the same year. Wilhelm Strunz henceforth would "fix the labels of his products" by a wire clamp. In 1911 he advertised "cloth and felt toys" and "animals with voice boxes and genuine hair."

Otto Wohlmann, Nuremberg, Germany: Founded in 1908, the company specialized in dolls and caricatures. Registered trademark was "OWN" for "softly stuffed toys of felt and plush." The silhouette of a real looking bear standing sideways with the initials OWN are within the shape of a diamond.

Gottlieb Zinner and Sohne, Schalkau, Germany: Gottlieb Zinner founded the company in 1845. It participated in the arts and trade exhibition at Sonneberg in 1879 with "mechanical toys with music." In 1925, the company advertised "mechanical music toys of best quality with Swiss music work."

American Companies

Since 1903, America imported German Teddy Bears by the thousands.

With the Teddy Bear market growing by leaps and bounds, and German manufacturers barely able to fill expanding orders, America started to manufacture bears domestically. By 1907, factories had opened up in almost every major city throughout the states.

This lovable, furry creature captured the hearts of little people everywhere. It swept the toy industry off its feet. Never before had anythings compared to the craze of the Teddy Bear. Teddy Bears practically drove all the other soft toys out of the market, as there wasn't enough time to manufacture other animals.

American manufacturers had the tremendously high standards of imported fine quality Steiff products to compete with.

The History of American Bears

Domestic manufacturers — such as The American Doll and Toy Manufacturers, Bruin Manufacturing Company of New York, Hecla Bears, Harman Manufacturing Company of New York City and Aetna Bears — each advertised their Teddy Bears as made from the highest grade mohair "With the style and workmanship that equalled the finest imported bears." (*Playthings,* 1907).

In 1908, The Ideal Novelty Company advertised as the "Largest Bear Manufacturers in the country" in *Playthings.*

Europe was supplying America with mohair, but large quantities of the bear fabric was manufactured in the United States.

Tingue Manufacturing Company in Seymour, Connecticut, was said to be using 4,000 Angora goats per week to make the material used for making Teddy Bears.

Mohair looms were extremely expensive and had limited production capabilities. At the height of Teddy Bear season America, too, suffered difficulty in meeting the demands for mohair. The Teddy Bear boom also affected other industries depending on mohair. The needs of the upholstery business, garment industry and, of course, the increase in Teddy Bear companies caused great anxiety among those producing the soft mohair so greatly desired.

Equally as important to the bears construction were cry boxes. When these also became scarce, America tried to replace the German imports with their own verison. They quickly found them too expensive and time consuming, to make and continued to import them from Germany.

Teddy Bears were proving to be truly the most loved toy of all time.

Enterprising manufacturers produced complete outfits for the bears. As early as 1906, Kahn and Mossbacher and D.W. Shoyer designed a full line of clothes for Teddy Bears. Overalls, coats, pajamas, underwear, clown outfits, sailor and rough rider suits complete with trunks and wardrobes became the rage by 1908. *(Illustrations 205 and 206).*

Patterns for ambitious mothers to use in sewing Teddy Bear clothes for their children were available as well. The popularity of Teddy Bear apparel also saw patterns for knitting sweaters, toques and suits.

Evidence of the influence of Seymour Eaton's Roosevelt Bears can be found not only in ads referring to the bears as Teddy B and Teddy G, but these names were also embroidered on Teddy Bear clothes. The monogrammed clothes and bears found in their original outfits are the only positive method of identifying actual Teddy Bear clothes. Usually, early clothing found these days is accepted as really belonging to dolls, rather than Teddy Bears.

Like dolls, Teddies enjoyed having their own toys in which to ride. The Lloyd Manufacturing Company (Menominee, Michigan) announced "The Best Selling Novelty Line of the Year," which were cute Teddy wagons, circus-type carts and cages. Pedal cars for lifesize Teddies to drive were advertised by Hamburger and Co.

Our wonderful jointed Teddy Bear could now be dressed in all different outfits and taken for rides, but toy manufacturers (always looking to the future) felt if they made bears actually do something to amuse children, it would further increase their popularity (and, of course, increase sales).

The Strauss Manufacturing Company, of New York City invented a musical Teddy Bear made in brown or white plush. It came in sizes 10in (24.5cm), 12in (30.5cm), 14in (40.6cm) and 18in (45.7cm). The musical toy was completely American-made except for the concealed German music box that could be played by turning a small crank at the back of the bear's body. (*Playthings,* 1907).

Strauss also made a fascinating self-whistling Teddy Bear. An advertisement in the 1907 *Playthings* featured a bear who whistled as he was turned upside down and right side up again. The whistling mechanism was hidden in the body of the bear.

Another extremely popular bear which is highly collectible today is the Electric Eyes Teddy Bear. Several versions of this truly electrifying addition to the Teddy Bear market were made by different companies.

The eyes were tiny glass bulbs. A dry battery, camouflaged in the body of the bear, controlled the lighting of the eyes. A seam at the back of the bear could be opened to replace the batteries. Manufacturers urged stores to order in limited amounts on a regular basis, rather than in large quantities, to ensure the freshness of the batteries at time of sale. *(Illustration 215.)*

Methods to light up Teddy's eyes varied. Fast Black Skirt Company of New York City showed their version in a 1907 *Playthings.* Shaking the right paw would activate the eyes which lit up by means of connecting wires from the eyes and paw to the battery. Their sizes were 15in (38.1cm), 18in (47.5cm), 24in (61cm) and 36in (91.4cm).

Other interesting electric models have found their way into lucky collectors' hands over the years.

An electric cord with a push button on the end attached to the bear is one sort. Other versions used a switch at the back of the body or the head. Some bears' eyes twinkled with a squeeze of their tummies. As well as with jointed bodies, these bears also came with stationary heads and legs. Their mohair fur colors included gold and black. A patriotic red, white and blue variety was very unusual.

The Columbia Teddy Bear Manufacturer, already producing large quantities of jointed bears, added to their line with the Laughing Roosevelt Teddy Bear. He was a jointed bear with an addition of two rows of shining white teeth between the bear's jaws, giving the toy a very lifelike bear appearance. *(Illustration 212.)*

With dolls still in mind, "Teddy Dolls" were created. They had all the features of a jointed Teddy Bear body, but the doll face was either celluloid, composition or bisque. Usually, a little hood made of the same material as the body surrounded the head.

A rare acquisition to any collection is the two-faced bear. This is a regular Teddy Bear body, but the head is a Teddy Bear on one side and a doll's face on the other. The two faces could be swiveled back and forth. *(Illustrations 208, 209 and 210).*

Hahn and Amberg, New York City, advertised in *Playthings* "The Teddy Dolls were the novelty sensation of

1908." They came in eight colors of beautiful mohair in 12in (30.5cm), 13½in (30.6cm), 15in (38.1cm) and 18in (45.7cm).

Harman Manufacturing Company, made an Eskimo Doll. The darling doll's body was designed just like a Teddy Bear's, but was covered with real fur. The bisque head had sleep eyes, a wig and matching fur hat. The bisque heads and cry boxes were imported from Germany. Their hands were felt pads or little felt-formed gloves.

A "Billiken" doll was manufactured by E.I. Horsman in 1909. It had a composition head with a very unusual elflike expression (broad smile, little black slant lines for eyes, pointed ears and hair coming to a peak at the top of his head). The body came in plush and later changed to pink sateen, Horsman bought the sole rights to manufacture Billiken dolls from the Billiken Sales Company. This was one of the first dolls to be copyrighted. In the first six months, 200,000 Billikens were sold. At the peak of their popularity over half a million were sold in a year. Their price was approximately $1.00. *(Illustration 211.)*

Ladies and children's fashion showed signs of being influenced by the Teddy Bear bonanza. Bearskin coats were very much in vogue. Teddy Bear decorated muffs, hats, even a complete Teddy Bear suit could be purchased for the child who wished to pretend he was a real bear.

Dreamland Doll Company offered a Topsy Turvy toy, which had a cloth doll at one end and a Teddy Bear at the other. A reversible skirt separated the two.

Tumbling bears were another delightful variation on the Teddy Bear theme. Mrs. G.C. Gillespie hid a heavy weight in the bear's stomach which caused the acrobatic action (*Playthings* 1907).

But it appears as though the finest intricate mechanical bears were still being imported from Europe.

By 1908, the toy industry began to question the future or the fate of the Teddy Bear. Could this incredible fad continue at this pace?

Today many people ask the same question. However, in 1907, Teddy Bears were purchased for children and women bought them for fashion and sheer enjoyment. 1984 surveys reveal approximately 40 percent of all bears are being purchased by adults, not just because they are in style, but because knowledgeable collectors consider these toys a good investment.

Teddy Bears have proven themselves the most consistently popular toy ever. 1985 was designated as The International Year of the Teddy Bear. So, even if the enthusiasm subsides, the ongoing importance of our faithful little friend insures that he will always remain the King of the Toy World.

America manufactured such a wide variety of Teddy Bear designs in the early 1900s that it is difficult to attribute a definite style to the American Bear. However, research shows several features were used more commonly on domestic bears.

Bodies, for example, were longer and narrower than their English and German counterparts. The long arms and curved paws were changed to short arms with less, or in some cases, hardly any curve to the paw at all. Feet were also smaller by comparison, and the legs were very straight.

In actual fact, all features, including the head and nose, were not accentuated like that of the German examples. Their construction and jointed method was not changed. Mohair and excelsior were primarily used. One feature seems prominent — the stuffing was extra firm.

These identifying features will be more clear with the following chapters and photos.

Since the Teddy Bear evolved from President Roosevelt's historical hunting expedition, it is only natural for Americans to claim the first Teddy Bear as their very own.

American Bears

Illustration 204. "Equal to the Imported" was the sales point of many American Teddy Bear manufacturers. Here "Helca Bears" advertise in *Playthings* (1907). Note the resemblance in the picture to that of the Steiff bears. *Courtesy Playthings (1907).*

RIGHT: *Illustration 205.* Kahn and Mossbacher of New York advertised Teddy Bear outfits in a 1907 *Playthings.* Note the embroidered "Teddy G" on sleeve. This original outfit can be seen worn by an early Steiff Teddy Bear in *Illustration 125. Courtesy Playthings (1907).*

MIDDLE RIGHT: *Illustration 206.* Knitted sweaters and toques for bears were advertised in a 1907 *Playthings.* An outfit resembling this ad can be seen in *Illustration 126. Courtesy Playthings (1907).*

BELOW: *Illustration 207.* The Harman Mfg. Co. advertised making Teddy Bears from 10in (25.4cm) to 36in (91.4cm). *Courtesy Playthings (1907).*

Illustrations 208, 209 & 210. Manufacturer unknown. "Two Face." c.1915. 10in (25.4cm); dark brown mohair; jointed arms and legs; swivel head; excelsior stuffing; Teddy Bear has glass eyes; doll face is celluloid with painted features. Condition: Excellent. Comments: Rare. Head swivels to change faces. *Author's collection.*

OPPOSITE PAGE ABOVE LEFT: *Illustration 211.* "Billiken." c.1909. 12in (30.5cm); short white mohair; composition head; painted features; jointed arms and legs; swivel head; excelsior stuffing. Condition: Body, mint; head, crazing in composition. Comments: Unusual elf-like features, later came with pink satin body. Label reads: "Copyright 1909 by The Billiken Doll Company." Billiken was one of the first dolls to be copyrighted. *Author's collection.*

ABOVE RIGHT: *Illustration 212.* Columbia Teddy Bear Manufacturers. "Laughing Roosevelt Teddy Bear." c.1907. 22in (55.9cm); short reddish gold mohair; glass eyes; jointed arms and legs; swivel head; excelsior stuffing. Condition: Excellent. Comments: Rare. Squeezing mechanism in stomach causes mouth to open and shut by adjoining cord, revealing fierce looking white glass teeth. When mouth closes, teeth fit into holes in upper wooden jaw. *Author's collection.*

BELOW LEFT: *Illustration 213.* Manufacturer unknown. "Laughing Bear." c.1908. 14in (35.6cm); pale gold mohair; glass eyes; jointed arms and legs; swivel head; excelsior stuffed body; hollow molded papier mâché head; hard material nose, mouth and teeth. Condition: Very good. Comments: Extremely rare. May possibly be one of the early Roosevelt Laughing Teddy Bears. *Courtesy Beverly Port.*

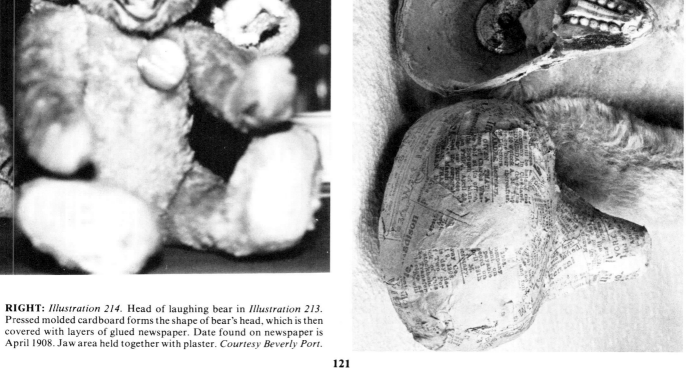

RIGHT: *Illustration 214.* Head of laughing bear in *Illustration 213*. Pressed molded cardboard forms the shape of bear's head, which is then covered with layers of glued newspaper. Date found on newspaper is April 1908. Jaw area held together with plaster. *Courtesy Beverly Port.*

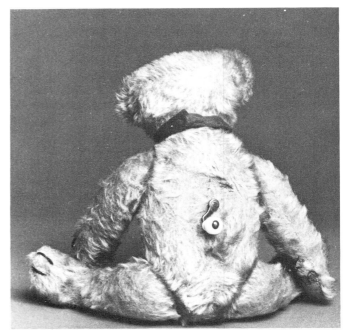

TOP LEFT: *Illustration 215.* Manufacturer unknown. "Electric Eye Bear." c.1915. Dark gold mohair; eyes are small flat bulbs; jointed arms and legs; swivel head; excelsior stuffing. Condition: Excellent. Comments: Rare. Round wood box concealed in stomach stores batteries. Wires connect batteries to light bulbs causing eyes to light up when stomach is squeezed. *Courtesy Beverly Port.*

TOP RIGHT: *Illustration 216.* A fascinating "self-whistling" Teddy Bear was created by Strauss Mfg. Co. of New York, New York. *Courtesy Playthings (1907).*

BOTTOM LEFT & RIGHT: *Illustrations 217 & 218.* "Musical Bear." c.1910. 19in (48.3cm); light beige mohair; glass eyes; jointed arms and legs; swivel head; excelsior stuffing; leather pads; crank type music box. Condition: Excellent. Comments: Rare. Action: Porcelain knob is turned at back of bear to produce music. Possibly manufactured by Strauss Mfg. Co. *Author's collection.*

122

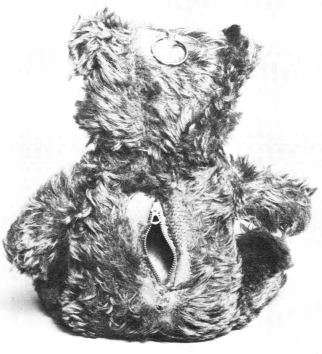

TOP LEFT: *Illustration 219.* The B.M.C. (Bruin Mfg. Co.) label is just visible on the large Teddy Bear advertised in *Playthings* 1907 magazine. *Illustration 220* shows an original B.M.C. bear with label. *Courtesy Playthings (1907).*

TOP RIGHT: *Illustration 220.* Bruin Mfg. Co. c.1907. 13in (33cm); gold mohair; shoe button eyes; jointed arms and legs; swivel head; excelsior stuffing. Condition: Excellent. Comments: Rare. Label on foot shows B.M.C. in gold letters. It is difficult to find American marked bears. *Courtesy Helen Sieverling.*

BOTTOM LEFT & RIGHT: *Illustrations 221 & 222.* Commonwealth Toy and Novelty Co., "Feed Me" Bear. c.1937. 16in (40.6cm); cinnamon mohair; glass eyes; unjointed head and body; kapok stuffing. Condition: Fair. Comments: Rare. When the ring located at top of the head is pulled, the mouth opens and dry foods and candy are swallowed by this ingenious Teddy Bear. The food can then be removed by opening a zipper at the back of the bear, disclosing a metal compartment where the food is stored, without harming the bear. Bears like this originally came with a bib and carried a lunch box. The National Biscuit Co. used the bears to advertise their animal crackers. *Author's collection.*

Illustration 223. (Left) Manufacturer unknown. "Teddy Doll." c.1908. 8in (20.3cm); short light beige mohair; celluloid face; painted features; jointed arms and legs; swivel head; excelsior stuffing; beige felt hands and feet. Condition: Good. (Right) Manufacturer unknown. "Teddy Doll." c.1908. 13in (33cm); bright purple mohair; celluloid face; painted features; jointed arms and legs; swivel head; excelsior stuffing; beige felt hands and feet. Condition: Excellent. Comments: Rare. These Teddy dolls were produced by American and German companies. Unfortunately, no markings have been found to link them to their manufacturer. The American versions imported the head and voice boxes from Germany. They also came with bisque and composition faces. Real fur was also used for their bodies. These were called Eskimo Dolls. *Author's collection.*

LEFT: *Illustration 224.* Manufacturer unknown. "Teddy Doll Muff." c.1908. 14in (35.6cm); dark red and beige mohair; celluloid face; painted features; unjointed arms and legs; swivel head. Condition: Excellent. Comments: Rare. Body is padded and lined throughout for hands to be warmed inside. With the close resemblance to the Teddy Doll, the muff was probably produced by the same companies with the face manufactured in Germany. *Courtesy Joan Sickler.*

Some of the following bears resemble the features credited to American Bears: long narrow bodies, fairly straight arms and legs, small feet, short bristle type mohair.

MIDDLE: *Illustration 225.* Manufacturer unknown. c.1915. 16in (40.6cm); short cinnamon mohair; glass eyes; jointed arms and legs; swivel head; excelsior stuffing. Condition: Excellent (replaced pads). *Courtesy Harriett Early.*

RIGHT: *Illustration 226.* (Left) Manufacturer unknown. c.1928. 10in (25.4cm); gold mohair; replaced shoe button eyes; jointed arms and legs; swivel head; excelsior stuffing. Condition: Good. (Right) Manufacturer unknown. c.1928. 12in (30.5cm); white mohair, replaced shoe button eyes; jointed arms and legs; swivel head; excelsior stuffing. Condition: Good, replaced pads. *Courtesy Colleen Tipton.* (Belonged to her father-in-law, Donald Tipton.)

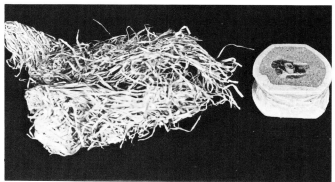

LEFT: *Illustration 227*. Manufacturer unknown. c.1910. 19in (48.3cm); short gold mohair; shoe button eyes; jointed arms and legs; swivel head; excelsior stuffing; squeeze type voice box. Condition: Mint. *Author's collection.*

ABOVE: *Illustration 228*. Squeeze type voice box used in many American bears. Excelsior stuffing and cry box taken from bear in *Illustration 229*.

BELOW LEFT: *Illustration 229*. Manufacturer unknown. c.1915. 12in (30.5cm); short gold mohair; glass eyes; jointed arms and legs; swivel head; excelsior stuffing; squeeze type voice box. Condition: Mint. *Author's collection.*

MIDDLE: *Illustration 230*. Manufacturer unknown. c.1940. 18in (45.7cm); gold mohair; glass eyes; jointed arms and legs; swivel head; kapok stuffing; velveteen pads; "metal nose." Condition: Good. *Courtesy Volpp Collection.*

RIGHT: *Illustration 231*. Manufacturer unknown. c.1927. 18in (45.7cm); gold mohair; glass eyes; jointed arms and legs; swivel head; excelsior stuffing. Condition: Good. *Courtesy Paul Volpp.* (Was purchased for him in May Company in 1927 by his aunt).

TOP LEFT: *Illustration 232.* (Left and Center) Knickerbocker. c.1930. 18in (45.7cm); long dark brown mohair; glass eyes; jointed arms and legs; swivel head; kapok stuffing. Condition: Good. (Right) Knickerbocker. c.1930. 12in (30.5cm); long brown mohair; replaced eyes; jointed arms and legs; swivel head. Condition: Good. *Courtesy Harriett Early.*

TOP RIGHT: *Illustration 233.* Knickerbocker. c.1940. 20in (50.8cm); white mohair; glass eyes; jointed arms and legs; swivel head; kapok stuffing. Condition: Good. Comments: Original tag "Knickerbocker Toy Co. Inc., New York." *Private Collection.*

BOTTOM LEFT: *Illustration 234.* Character. c.1948. 19in (48.3cm); gold mohair; black button eyes; jointed arms and legs; swivel head; kapok stuffing. Condition: Good. Comments: Original label in left ear reads "Character." *Courtesy Volpp Collection.*

BOTTOM RIGHT: *Illustration 235.* (Left) Character on all fours. c.1960. 4in (10.2cm) high, 7in (17.8cm) long; white mohair; black button eyes; unjointed arms and legs; swivel head; kapok stuffing. Condition: Good. Comments: Original Character label. (Right) Character. c.1960. 9in (22.9cm); white mohair; black button eyes; unjointed head and body; kapok stuffing. Condition: Good. Comments: Original Character label. *Courtesy Volpp Collection.*

The Ideal Toy Company

The most famous legend comes from the Ideal Toy Company, one of America's largest toy manufacturers, and first known to make an American Teddy Bear.

It is said that Morris Mitchom, a Russian immigrant, was inspired to make a little jointed bear after he saw the famous cartoon by Clifford Berryman. His wife was a seamstress and sewed the little bear by hand. The couple displayed the bear in their small novelty and stationary store on Thompson Avenue in Brooklyn, New York. The toy was an instant success.

Mitchom, it has been claimed, wrote the President and requested permission to christen the new toy "Teddy." (Unfortunately, this letter has never been found to document the story). Roosevelt gave his OK, but added he didn't know how his name would ever help the stuffed animal business.

The Mitchoms presented their newly-created bear to the Butler Brothers, a large wholesaler. The company recognized the bear's potential and in 1903 is said to have bought the Mitchom's entire stock of toy bears. Butler Brothers backed Mitchom's credit with plush producing mills and in a year mass production for The Ideal Novelty Toy Company became a reality. The company shortened its name to The Ideal Toy Company in 1938.

Throughout the past three-quarters of a century, Ideal has literally played Santa Claus to countless numbers of children, creating hundreds of dolls and toys such as the familiar Shirley Temple, Sparkle Plenty, Patty Playpal, Robert the Talking Robot, and Evel Knievel.

The major figures primarily responsible for the company's success were Abraham Katz, Benjamin Mitchom and Lionel Weintraub.

Katz joined the company in 1912 "to help out." He served as co-chairman of the board and has a long list of accomplishments to his credit, especially in the areas of production and design.

Benjamin Mitchom, Morris Mitchom's son, was one of the great inspirational marketers within the toy industry since he joined Ideal in 1923, in the position of co-chairman.

In 1962, Lionel A. Weintraub, who joined Ideal in 1941, was elected president. Under his supervision, Ideal became a publicly-owned company in 1968. Its stock was traded on the New York Stock Exchange.

From the first Teddy Bear, hand-stuffed with excelsior, Ideal's production capabilities grew to the company's 600,000 square foot Hollis headquarters and a new ultra-modern, one million square foot facility in the Newark (New Jersey) Meadowlands. Its international division coordinated the manufacturing and sales activities of wholly- and partially-owned companies in Canada, the United Kingdom, Germany, Australia, New Zealand and Japan, with more than 4,000 persons employed.

But as Ideal progressed it did not lose sight of it's humble beginnings. It paid homage to its heritage by using the motto: "Excellence in Toy Making Since the Teddy Bear."

In 1982 Ideal was acquired by C.B.S. Inc. The president of the company is Boyd Browne. Morris Mitchom's son, Benjamin, is no longer involved in the business, and sad as it may seem, neither is the Teddy Bear. The C.B.S. range of toys no longer includes the Mitchom's historic little bear.

Ideal

Illustrations 236 & 237. Ideal. c.1908. 13in (33cm); short gold mohair; shoe button eyes; jointed arms and legs; swivel head; excelsior stuffing. Condition: Excellent, replaced pads. Comments: Rare. Note wide head shape, low larger ears. This design of Teddy Bear is known to have been distributed in a small size as a promotional bear during Theodore Roosevelt's campaign. *Author's collection.*

Unfortunately my research hasn't been too successful in finding early 1900s Teddy Bears with any form of identification that would document them as being a bear made by the Ideal Toy Company. However, many collectors, including myself, feel there appears to be some definite features with particular bears that we recognize as possibly being attributed to the Ideal Toy Co. The following photos show this representation.

TOP LEFT & RIGHT: *Illustrations 238 & 239.* Ideal. c.1908. 24in (61cm); light gray mohair; large button eyes; jointed arms and legs; swivel head; excelsior stuffing. Condition: Mint. Comments: Rare. Note the wide head shaping (resembles the shape of an eggplant); large low ears; feet come to a point. *Author's collection.*

BOTTOM LEFT: *Illustration 240.* Kim Brewer proudly stands her rare mint condition 26in (66cm) Ideal Teddy Bear to display his marvelous shape.

BOTTOM RIGHT: *Illustration 241.* The Smithsonian Institution exhibits this beautiful gold mohair jointed Teddy Bear as representing one of the first examples made by the Ideal Novelty Toy Company. *Photograph courtesy of the Smithsonian National Museum of History and Technology.*

Gund

The company was founded by Adolf Gund of Germany in 1898, and he worked out of a small shop in Norwalk, Connecticut.

A partnership was formed with Jacob Swedlin in 1910 and the operation moved to New York City. Mr. Swedlin took over the company in 1922 when Mr. Gund retired.

The actual date when the Teddy Bear was introduced in the Gund line is unknown, however bears were in production as early as 1927-1928, when the line featured several varieties of "silk plush" bears.

Today Gund is larger than ever. The company is renowned worldwide for its exceptional quality soft plush animals.

The current owners are descendants of Jacob Swedlin.

GUND ANIMALS ARE SOLD THROUGHOUT THE WORLD

BEAR ON WHEELS

A PRACTICAL, indestructible wheel toy. Made of plush with a steel frame on substantial, solid rubber-tired wheels that can easily sustain a weight of 150 lbs. 14 inches in height. The sales magnet of the "bear" back ride for baby will make friends and sales for the merchant.

Gund

ABOVE: *Illustration 242.* Gund Bear on wheels. 14in (35.6cm) tall; made of plush with a steel frame. Advertised in Gund's 1927-1928 catalog.

RIGHT: *Illustration 243.* The front cover of Gund's 1942 catalog states they have been manufacturing stuffed toys since 1898.

The Leading Line

Panda Bears   Teddy Bears   Honey Bears
Scotties   Terriers   Pekes
"Honey Lou" Soft Dolls   Easter Novelties
Infant Novelties

Since 1898 ---

Gund
MEANS REAL VALUE IN
STUFFED TOYS

FALL · 1942

GUND Manufacturing Co.

J. SWEDLIN, Inc., Succ. . . . 200 Fifth Ave., N. Y. City

718 Mission Street
SAN FRANCISCO

Merchandise Mart
CHICAGO

2018 Condon Way
SEATTLE

Applause

The Wallace Berrie company was founded in 1966. Wallace Berrie began as a supplier with a limited product line of novelty gifts. The company continued to expand over the next few years and in 1979 plush products represented a large percentage of their business.

In 1981, Larry Elins and Harris Toibb purchased the Wallace Berrie Co., and in August of the following year introduced a beautiful new line of realistic looking animals.

The design and development of this new Avanti line dates back to 1980 when Larry Elins, president of Wallace Berrie and Garry Trumbo, vice president of marketing, first noticed these beautifully crafted animals at the Milan Toy Show. They were particularly impressed with the fine attention to detail, the quality construction, and careful finishing. The animals had an unprecedented realism, from a natural sparkle in their eyes to the softness of their fur. It was almost as if the animals lived and breathed.

Upon inquiry, Elins and Trumbo learned that the animals, then marketed throughout Europe under the "Jockline label," were created by Riccardo Chiavetta, formerly of the renowned plush manufacturing company, Aux Nations.

Wallace Berrie contacted Chiavetta and through an arrangement with Jockline, acquired the worldwide marketing rights. Thus, the Avanti line began.

Wallace Berrie and Company's intent from the onset was to manufacture the Avanti line in the Orient. This would achieve a vital marketing objective.

First materials had to be found that matched the European standards for softness and texture. Hand-stitching and hand-finishing had to be taught until they were an art form — skills that took over a year to develop. The designs had to faithfully replicate the detail of their real-life counterparts.

In order to duplicate the structure of real-life animals, photographs and behavior patterns of each animal were carefully studied, characteristics identified, and fur coloring and textures matched. Even today, after all the research and development, producing the lifelike Avanti line animals takes a third more of the time than that of the more conventional plush line.

Patience paid off. By August of 1982, Wallace Berrie & Company introduced fourteen Avanti animals. By December, these products were completely sold out. At the 1983 New York Toy Fair, seven more animals were added to the line. Now (1985), Wallace Berrie & Company totals one hundred beautiful animals in the Avanti collection.

Riccardo Chiavetta continues to design the popular animals for the company.

In 1983, Applause (once a division of Knickerbocker) was acquired by Wallace Berrie & Company. The Applause toys include long time favorites Raggedy Ann and Andy, Disney characters Mickey and Minnie Mouse and many more child and adult favorites.

Applause and Wallace Berrie & Company merged to form the Applause Division in 1984.

Applause

RIGHT: *Illustration 244.* (Left) Larry Elins; (Right) Harris Toibb — owners of Applause. *Courtesy Applause.*

BELOW: *Illustration 245.* Avanti Classic Teddy Bears. 1982. (Left to right) 19in (48.3cm), 22in (55.9cm), 32in (81.3cm), 20in (50.8cm); brown and white soft acrylic fur; realistic looking eyes and features; unjointed head and body; soft stuffing. *Courtesy Applause.*

R. Dakin and Company

"I can see a world without lots of things," says Harry Nizamain, President and Chief Executive Officer of R. Dakin and Company, "but I can't see a world without a Teddy Bear."

It wasn't always this way for the world's largest maker of quality plush animals. R. Dakin and Company came to the industry through a lucky fluke.

In 1955, the company was founded by the now late Richard Y. Dakin to import expensive hand-crafted goods from Italy and Spain. Two years later, R. Dakin added a general line of merchandise to its inventory. The expansion included the manufacture of a battery-operated replica of the Southern Pacific Railroad's Silver Zephyr locomotive and train.

In 1957, while developing the new toy, a shipment of sample toy trains arrived. The packing material turned out to be a small velveteen stuffed toys. The attractiveness of the velveteen toys prompted Roger Dakin (son of the founder) to order a small sample and test market them in northern California. Originally, Dakin ordered 25 dozen from the Japanese manufacturer.

When a buyer for the San Francisco department store, The Emporium, saw the samples, he was very impressed. His immediate order for 300 dozen officially put R. Dakin in the soft toy business.

Phasing out the sporting goods division in 1963, R. Dakin and Company reached the one million dollar sales mark. The next spring, it acquired the assets of a Lindsay, California, manufacturer of infant plush toys, the Dardenelle Company. Now known as the Domestic Production Division, this part of the firm alone has grown from 5 to 135 employees.

The next four years marked the expansion of R. Dakin and Company to production bases in Japan, Hong Kong and Mexico.

In 1966 tragedy struck. A plane crash took the lives of Mr. and Mrs. Roger Dakin, four of their children and Dakin's parents. In spite of the terrible loss, the company pulled together. In 1970, with Harold A. Nizamian at the helm, the toy company reached an excess of six million dollars in sales.

A particular point of pride for this giant firm are high safety standards. No toxic materials are ever used in any phase of production. Stress tests (a 15 pound pull by a machine) ensure that eyes, noses and other attached parts are secure. The company often sets safety standards higher than government regulations demand.

During the years 1976-1982, the company grew dramatically. Now with more than 350 full-time employees, Dakin contracts 10,000 people around the world who exclusively make R. Dakin products.

Of course, the most popular Dakin product is the Teddy Bear, with fifty varieties. Every size, type and color of bear imaginable comes from this company. A 6in (15.2cm) bean bag bear, a 3ft (91.4cm) tall "Super Cuddles," "Smokey Bear," "Bentley Bear," and a bear reproducing the sound of a mother's womb called "Rock-A-Bye Bear" are among their many products. "Pooky," the Teddy Bear owned by Garfield is a Dakin favorite of many. Dakin bears are both proprietary and produced under license.

Chief designer Virginia Kemp and her six-person staff study books and magazines in their efforts to create new bears. Every new bear is so carefully analyzed for marketing possibilities, sales and safety that its development evaluations result in near perfection at the first try.

About 40 percent of the company's bears are purchased by adults. Frequently at the forefront of Teddy Bear creativity, the company pays close attention to fashion trends, color and fabrics.

"We believe an animal must be true to nature," says its president, "But, also be true to fantasy."

"Americans are longing for security," philosophized Nazamian. "There is nothing secure about clutching a video disk, but it is a good feeling to hold a Teddy Bear. The Teddy loves you best of all."

Even though Dakin employs many people, the company remains privately held by family members who have entrusted management to a talented team of executives.

R. Dakin and Company

Illustration 246. Harold A. Nizamian, President of R. Dakin and Company. *Courtesy Dakin Co.*

Illustration 247. (Left) Dakin "Bently Bear." 21in (53.3cm); silky brown acrylic fur; natural brown eyes; jointed arms and legs; swivel head; soft stuffing. (Center) Dakin "Wee Woolie Bear." 10in (25.4cm); white woolen type material; natural brown eyes; unjointed body; swivel head; soft stuffing. Dressed in red and white striped scarf. The bear also comes in gold with green and beige striped scarf. (Right) Dakin "Woolie Bear." 14in (35.6cm); white woolen type material; natural brown eyes; unjointed body; swivel head; soft stuffing. Dressed in red and white striped scarf and socks. The bear also comes in gold with green and beige striped scarf. *Courtesy Dakin Co.*

Smokey Bear: The All-American Hero

An extremely important contribution to the world of Teddy Bears is our all-American hero, Smokey Bear.

Nationally recognized by young and old alike, Smokey is synonomous with forest fire prevention. The "guardian of the forest" is phenomenally popular. His achievements as "spokesbear" for the Cooperative Forest Fire Prevention advertising campaign are unbeatable.

Smokey did not arrive on the scene as the furry friend we know today. He first appeared in a poster.

Due to the temendous fires that destroyed unbelievable amounts of forest land, the Cooperative Forest Fire Prevention Campaign joined forces with a newly formed Wartime Advertising Council to launch a 1940s fire prevention campaign that remains one of the most powerful and famous efforts in history.

Prior to Smokey, the Advertsing Council designed many eye-catching ads. Walt Disney's Bambi was Smokey's forerunner, proving to be very successful. The well-known baby fawn appeared in posters with the plea: "Please Mister, Don't be Careless."

The Advertising Council realized its need to find an animal to solely represent the Cooperative Forest Fire Prevention Campaign. This animal would project an image of power and courage. Of course, a bear fit this mental conception and was soon voted as the animal best suited for the part.

So, in 1944, Albert Staehle, cover artist for *The Saturday Evening Post* was chosen to depict this bear. His first work showed the bear (*au natural*) pouring a bucket of water over a campfire. Shortley afterwards, the bear began to wear blue jeans, giving him a more human identity.

The bear is said to have been named after an assistant chief of the New York City Fire Department, "Smokey Joe" Martin, who served in that post during the years 1919 to 1930.

Smokey Bear was an unbelievable success. His popular image reached out to everyone, carrying his first message on a poster "Smokey says: Care will prevent 9 out of 10 forest fires." During the next two years, Staehle created two more posters. The one that gained enduring memorability was done in 1947. Remember? "Only You Can Prevent Forest Fires."

These early posters showed Smokey looking rather austere, unlike the warm friendly bear that we know, love and respect today.

Rudy Wendelin took over the position of Smokey's offical artist in 1946. Wendelin gave his Smokey a more humanized look by shortening his nose, which made him seem cuddlier. Wendelin drew Smokey posters and ads for thirty years.

The tragedy of a forest fire in New Mexico's Lincoln National Forest in the early spring of 1950 gave us an actual bear to act as the live counterpart of the pictorial creation. Starting as a small fire following an extremely hot, dry spell, and fanned by warm winds, the flames grew and grew, until the blaze was totally out of control.

A little brown bear cub fought for his life amongst the billowing smoke and gigantic flames that ate their way through the forest. Firefighters found the bear who was separated from his mother. The tiny, terrified creature clung to a charred tree. Badly burned and dazed, the cub was taken back to camp and later transported to Dr. E. J. Smith, a Santa Fe (New Mexico) veterinarian who kindly tended the orphaned bear's wounds.

Being a living example of what the fire prevention campaign stood for, it seemed only natural for the cub to be christened Smokey.

Little Smokey did not respond too well to hospitalization and refused to eat his food. Ray Bell of the New Mexico Department of Fish and Game had watched over Smokey from the beginning. He took Smokey home where the animal could benefit from the love and personal attention of Bell's wife Ruth and four-year old daughter Judy.

The watchful eye of Ruth Bell combined with her miracle food mixture (instant baby food and honey), and the motherly care fostered by Judy was just the prescription Smokey needed. It wasn't long before he regained his strength and was up to all sorts of mischief.

Ray Bell, however, didn't make such a big hit with his furry brown charge. It was Bell's duty to change the cub's bandages, causing the bear considerable agony. Smokey reminded his keeper of his dislike with the procedure by biting him on the leg when Ray least expected it.

On June 9, 1950, a decision was made to present Smokey to the National Zoological Park in Washington, D.C. as a gift to the Forest Service. He was dedicated to them as a publicity program for fire prevention and preservation of wildlife.

Smokey became an immediate star attraction. Millions of children and adults flocked to see the national celebrity. Since he was now a living, breathing creature, his popularity increased even more.

So famous was this advertising character, that he had to be protected from unauthorized use and exploitation. In May 1952 the 82nd Congress passed Public Law 359, better known as the "Smokey Bear Act." This law gave the Secretary of Agriculture authority to grant permission for the reproduction, manufacture and other use of the Smokey Bear Bear character only after consultation with the Association of State Foresters and the Advertising Council. All fees collected are to be deposited in a special forest fire prevention account.

In 1953 the Ideal Toy Company of New York created one of the first licensed Smokey toys offered on the market.

Now children could own a Smokey Bear of their very own.

A Teddy with the true likeness and appeal of the poster, he had a vinyl head, hands and feet stuffed with cotton. His body was brown plush. He carried his blue plastic shovel, ready to help fight forest fires at a moment's notice. His removable silver badge reads "Smokey/Ranger/Prevent Forest Fires." As in the poster, he wears blue jeans, a Smokey silver belt buckle and a hat reading Smokey.

Just a few months later, in 1954, the second version was released. This time only his head was vinyl, the remainder of his body was brown plush. A large Ideal Smokey Bear was presented to President Dwight D. Eisenhower for his five-year old grandson in 1953.

Ideal had the marvelous inspiration to enclose an application card in the box with the bear. Once filled out by the new Smokey owner and mailed to the Forest Service the child then became a "Junior Forest Ranger." This proved to be such a tremendous success that the mail pouring in for Smokey was given its own zip code destination number: Smokey Bear Headquarters, Washington, D.C. 20252.

Children felt they now had a very important job as Junior Forest Ranger. This promotion became so involved that groups with Scout leaders and clubs began popping up around the country, promising to help Smokey in his mission to prevent forest fires.

The real Smokey bear died in 1976. He was buried near the place of his discovery at the Smokey Bear Historical State Park, New Mexico.

Smokey may be gone, but his message lives on. REMEMBER, ONLY *YOU* CAN PREVENT FOREST FIRES!

Please help me PREVENT FOREST FIRES!

Smokey

LEFT: *Illustration 248.* Smokey's home at the National Zoo in Washington became a favorite spot for thousands of youngsters. *Used by permission of the U.S.D.A. Forest Service, Smokey Bear Program.*

ABOVE: *Illustration 249.* One of Smokey Bear's familiar posters. *Used by permission of the U.S.D.A. Forest Service, Smokey Bear Program.*

TOP LEFT: *Illustration 250.* Ideal Smokey. c.1953. 26in (66cm); brown plush body; vinyl head, hands and feet; glass eyes; unjointed body; swivel head; kapok stuffing. Silver buckle reads "Smokey." Incised on back of head "C 1953//Smokey says//Prevent Forest Fires//Ideal Toy Company." Printed white label reads: "Smokey//Official License authorized by the U.S. Department of Agriculture//18 U.S.C. 711//Prevent Forest Fires//Made by Ideal Toy Corp." Condition: Good. Missing his Smokey Ranger badge and shovel. Comments: Ideal's first Smokey edition. *Courtesy Helen Sieverling.*

TOP RIGHT: *Illustration 251.* Ideal Smokey. c.1954. 20in (50.8cm); rust plush; vinyl head; glasene brown eyes; unjointed body and head; kapok stuffing. Condition: Fair. Missing hat and shovel. Comments: Silver badge reads "Junior//Forest Ranger//Prevent Fires." *Courtesy Helen Sieverling.*

BOTTOM LEFT: *Illustration 252.* Collection of Smokey memorabilia. *Courtesy Bob Baldwin.*

BOTTOM RIGHT: *Illustration 253.* "Smokey." Knickerbocker. c.1968. 36in (91.4cm); dark brown plush; brown realistic eyes; unjointed body; soft stuffing; denim pants; monogrammed belt; yellow plastic Smokey hat; ranger badge; coonskin tail attached to belt; sewn-on-tag reads: "The Official Smokey Bear, Help Prevent Forest Fires, CAL T-5, All new cotton and Foam, Knickerbocker Toy Co., Inc. Middlesex, N.J. 08856, USA." Condition: Mint. Comments: Rare size. Knickerbocker was the company licensed to produce a 3ft (91.4cm) Smokey Bear. They continued to be manufactured up until 1977. A 3ft (91.4cm) Smokey Bear was presented to President Johnson's granddaughter in 1968. *Courtesy Broder Collection.*

English Bear Companies

Many of the Teddy Bears sold in England during the early 1900s were imported from Steiff.

The increased popularity of bears induced the English toy makers to create their own version of the Teddy Bear. The toy manufacturers, up until this time, concentrated mainly on doll making, but they had all the basic requirements for Teddy Bear making right at their finger tips. Even the mohair plush for making the bearskins and already supplying Steiff, was made in Yorkshire, principally at Dewsbury and Huddersfield, north of London.

History of English Bears

William J. Terry of Kingsland, London, and William Henry Jones are remembered as two of the largest soft toy manufacturers of those early days. Another company called "The Bear Pit," of St. Peters Road, London, is noted for its specialization in Teddy Bears.

J. K. Farnell and Company designed Teddy Bears made out of natural skin and fur.

In 1909, a realistic cut-out printed cotton flannelette bear made by Samuel Finsberg and Company could be assembled at home. This inexpensive kit bear met with a good deal of success. In 1908, Samuel Dean, founder of the Dean's Rag Book Company, Ltd., published a half crown book called *The Teddy Bear*. He also designed (1912) a cut-out Mama Bear, Teddy and Susie in their popular "Knock-about" Toy Sheets.

Window displays throughout London influenced by the Teddy Bear craze showed artistic displays of bears. Morrell's of Oxford Street featured a 1909 Christmas display "old mistress Teddy that lived in a shoe." A crimson shoe with a sledge and ladder showed a large Teddy and twelve baby bears performing all sorts of feats. It sold for 21 Shillings.

Teddy Bears were offered in six sizes with growlers by the Star Manufacturing Company in 1916. A 36in (91.4cm) promotional bear was made by Ralf Dunn and Company of the Barbican for a newly introduced line of Teddy Bear biscuits made by Peak Freans in 1909. They also advertised them with paintings of the bears on the company vans.

Identification of the early English bears is difficult because so many were unmarked.

The Teddy Bear's construction was very similar to that of Steiff and Ideal. They were jointed at the head and body. The early bears were filled with excelsior, but kapok was introduced and by the 1920s was used quite widely. Although, in many cases, to obtain good head shaping, the head would still be stuffed with excelsior.

The average English bear is slightly plumper than others of this era. In some cases the arms were shorter and the feet more rounded and smaller. The animal had a flatter appearance with a short nose and wide head.

The majority of the early 1900s bears had the type of growler designed to sound when the bear was tipped backwards. This was eventually replaced with a less expensive press-type squeaker.

Plastic noses were also used in later years.

The eyes on the early bears were made of glass and imported from Germany, but England soon started manufacturing a less expensive, slightly flatter eye with the color painted on the back. Birmingham was the principle center for this trade. *(Illustration 255.)*

Felt pads were used at first, but later on a material resembling oilcloth (called Rexine) was introduced and is found in a large percentage of English bears. *(Illustration 254.)* Leather, and later velveteen, were also used on the paw pads of these bears.

The Teddy Bear obtained popularity in England as it did in America. Women could even be seen proudly out for walks carrying a Teddy Bear. Photographers included them in their portrait photos. They became household decorations. It wasn't surprising to see a car or motorcycle driving down the road with a Teddy Bear hood ornament.

The Teddy Bear is still extremely popular in England today.

English toymakers produce a variety of bears and soft toys. Many of these companies are noted for a particular style or innovative creation.

English Bears

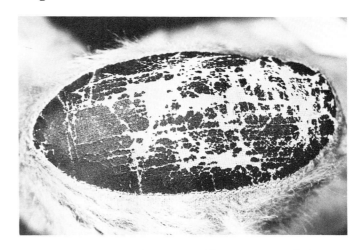

TOP: *Illustration 254.* The material used for the pads on many of the English bears is called "rexine." It resembles a painted oilcloth. Felt, velveteen and leather were also used.

BOTTOM: *Illustration 255.* Glass eyes with the color painted on the back were less expensive to make and replaced the German blown glass eyes on many English Teddy Bears.

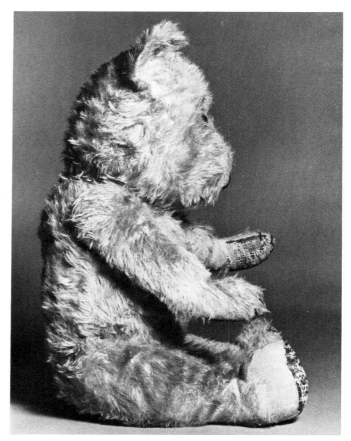

ABOVE: *Illustration 256.* Manufacturer unknown. c.1930. (Left) 24in (61cm), (Right) 17in (43.2cm); gold mohair; glass eyes; jointed arms and legs; swivel heads; heads stuffed with excelsior; bodies stuffed with kapok; rexine paw pads. Condition: Good. Comments: One of the more common designs of an English bear. *Author's collection.*

ABOVE: *Illustration 257.* Side view of English bear shows distinguishing features. Large head; short nose; large ears; plump body; short arms.

LEFT: *Illustration 258.* Manufacturer unknown. c.1930. 20in (50.8cm); gold mohair; glass eyes; jointed arms and legs; swivel head; rexine paw pads; head stuffed with excelsior; body stuffed with kapok. Condition: Fair. Comments: Typical English design. Wide head; plump body. *Author's collection.*

Note: The characteristics of English bears are a large wide head; short nose; fairly large ears; plump body and short arms.

OPPOSITE PAGE TOP LEFT: *Illustration 259.* Manufacturer unknown. c.1940. 15in (38.1cm); gold mohair; glass eyes; jointed arms and legs; swivel head; kapok stuffing; velveteen pads. Condition: Good. Comments: Winnie-the-Pooh type face. *Author's collection.*

TOP RIGHT: *Illustration 260.* Manufacturer unknown. c.1950. 16in (40.6cm); gold mohair; glass eyes; jointed arms and legs; swivel head; body stuffed with kapok; head stuffed with excelsior; worn rexine pads; "plastic nose." Condition: Good. *Author's collection.*

BOTTOM LEFT: *Illustration 261.* Panda. Manufacturer unknown. c.1940. 18in (45.7cm); black and white mohair; glass eyes; jointed arms and legs; swivel head; excelsior stuffing; rexine paw pads. Condition: Good. *Author's collection.*

BOTTOM RIGHT: *Illustration 262.* Manufacturer unknown. c.1950. 12in (30.5cm); silky gold mohair; glass eyes; jointed arms and legs; swivel head; body stuffed with kapok; head stuffed with excelsior; worn rexine pads. Condition: Good. *Author's collection.*

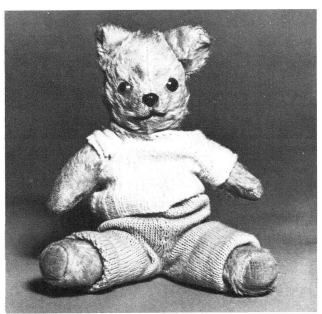

TOP LEFT: *Illustration 263.* Manufacturer unknown. c.1920. 33in (83.8cm); gold mohair; glass eyes; jointed arms and legs; swivel head; excelsior stuffing; leather pads. Condition: Excellent. Comments: Wide head; short nose; short arms. Typical English style. *Author's collection.*

TOP RIGHT: *Illustration 264.* Made in Eire (Ireland). c.1950. 16in (40.6cm); gold mohair; glass eyes; jointed arms and legs; swivel head; kapok stuffing; red felt pads. Condition: Mint. Comments: Tag on foot reads "made in Eire." *Courtesy Volpp Collection.*

BOTTOM LEFT: *Illustration 265.* Pedigree Soft Toys Ltd. c.1950. 11in (27.9cm); gold mohair; glass eyes; jointed arms and legs; swivel head; kapok stuffing; plastic nose. Condition: Fair. Comments: This company was founded before 1938 as Lines Bros. factories, Merton, London. The "Pedigree" trademark was registered in 1942. In 1968, Rovex Industries Ltd., another Lines Bros. company took over Pedigree and moved the business to Canterbury. As well as soft toys, the company produced many varieties of dolls. After the collapse of the Lines Bros. Group (1972), Rovex and Pedigree were taken over by Dunbee Combex Marx Company. When this company collapsed in 1980, Pedigree Soft Toys was bought out by Tamwade Ltd. *Author's collection.*

BOTTOM RIGHT: *Illustration 266.* Ealon Toys. c.1940. 12in (30.5cm); gold mohair; glass eyes; jointed arms and legs; swivel head; kapok stuffing. Condition: Good. Comments: Ealon Toys was the trademark of the East London (Federation) Toy Factory founded c.1915. They manufactured dolls as well as soft toys. *Courtesy Volpp Collection.*

J. K. Farnell

The history of J. K. Farnell's toys adds one more mystery of Teddy's roots. A 1954 statement by H. E. Bryant, then Director of Dean's Rag Book Company, Ltd., and Chairman of the British Toy Manufacturing Association, claimed that an unnamed Englishman invented the idea of the Teddy Bear.

Bryant wrote that since 1897 the firm of J. K. Farnell produced toys "from rabbit skins and took the form of ...monkeys, rabbits, etc." These toys were, according to Bryant, distributed "the world over."

According to the toy maker, Margarete Steiff "immediately saw the possibilities...(and) Farnell's took every advantage of this development and by their own new methods invaded the original home of toy makers by exporting quantities to Germany."

Joseph Susskind is said to have been the distributor in that country.

This interesting, though unsubstantiated twist in Teddy's history is simply more proof in the number of companies and people who wish to be credited with the creation of this special toy.

The famous English toy firm of J. K. Farnell claims existence since 1840. A large Farnell ad of 1965 announced the company to be "Makers of High Quality Soft Toys for over 125 Years."

By 1870, it appears the toy firm was founded by Agnes Farnell. Her father and brother, J. K. Farnell took an active part in business operations.

After World War I the private company built a factory called the Alpha Works and extra staff was hired. One of Farnell's most popular characters were "Alpha Bears," with most of the creative work done by J. K. Farnell's sister Agnes and a brilliant animal designer named Sybil Kemp.

Dogs were popular off-shoots of the Teddy Bear craze and the firm tried out various models of Terriers, Spaniels and Scotties.

A disastrous fire severely damaged the old company in 1934. Miss Agnes Farnell died soon afterwards and one director (J. C. Janisch) left to join the newly formed Merrythought, Ltd. in Shropshire.

Then in 1938, Farnell took over two companies: Trojan Toys, which manufactured wood toys and Dunham White and Company Ltd., which specialized in metal toys.

J. K. Farnell continued to produce more dolls than animals. Alpha Cherub and Joy Day are two that are officially registered. Farnell also produced soft toys throughout World War II. Eventually, their lease expired at Acton in 1964 and the business moved to Hasting. In 1968, the out-of-business J. K. Farnell Company was sold to a finance company.

J. K. Farnell bears are known for their high quality. Although machine seamed, they achieved an individuality from hand embroidery on the faces, noses and paws.

It is interesting to note that the prototype of Winnie-the-Pooh was thought to be a Farnell bear purchased at Harrods (London).

J. K. Farnell

ABOVE: *Illustration 267.* A white label was attached to the foot of the early J.K. Farnell Teddy Bears. Woven in blue silk were the words "A Farnell Alpha Toy. Made in England." Taken from the bear in *Illustration 269.* Later the words "This is a Farnell Quality Soft Toy. Made in Hastings, England" was printed in red and blue on a white label.

RIGHT: *Illustration 268.* J.K. Farnell. c.1936. 27in (68.6cm); long silky gold mohair; glass eyes; jointed arms and legs; swivel head; body stuffed with kapok; head with excelsior; rexine pads. Condition: Excellent. Comments: White label woven in blue silk thread attached to foot reads: "A Farnell Alpha Toy. Made in England." Note the resemblance in photos to Christopher Robin's actual Teddy Bear, Pooh. *Courtesy The Ted Tear Collection. Photograph Gale Darter.*

Chad Valley

A leading toy maker in England was Chad Valley. The company was founded in 1823 by Anthony Bunn-Johnson. He started as proprietor of a small printing and bookbinding company in Linchfield Street, Birmingham. Johnson's two sons, Joseph and Alfred, opened a printing concern called Johnson Brother Ltd. in 1860. It was situated in George Street Parade.

The Johnsons main business was stationary and peripheral paper supplies. Their business did so well they moved (1897) to a larger factory located near a stream named "Chad" in the village of Harborne near Birmingham.

The importing of German goods was banned during World War I, which gave the Johnson family the opportunity to further expand their company. The old Harborne Institute (and later a building at Welling [Salop]) was taken over for the production of dolls and soft toys.

In 1919, the company located on the stream "Chad," took the trade name Chad Valley. Chad Valley manufactured board games and jigsaw puzzles.

The merging of the three companies took place in 1920, under the one title of the Chad Valley Company. It specialized in making Teddy Bears, Mascots, grotesque animals, and popular commercially known subjects (such as Dame Quack who carried an umbrella under her wing, Bobby Penguin wearing a policeman's helmet and The Padre). These characters were made of soft velveteen with felt hats.

Early versions of their toys appeared to be of poor quality, but they soon improved and in the 1920s the company could justifiably advertise their toys as the most lifelike ever produced, completely made of hygienic British materials.

In the 1920s, Chad Valley purchased one company after another. Issa Works, manufacturing soft toys, and Warrillows and H. S. Hooper were acquired during this time.

The combined companies had more resources now. They created the famous bull terrier pup Bonzo, originally drawn by G. Studdy for the *Daily Sketch* newspaper. As part of their Bonzo promotion at the British Industries Fair (1920), Chad Valley entertained King George V and Queen Mary with a dwarf dressed in a Bonzo suit.

Chad Valley manufactured Teddy Bears in thirteen sizes and six qualities of fur, with cry boxes. The largest size of bears had "Patent Chad Valley growlers." One of their special traits (although quite rare) was brightly colored mohair bears.

Fortunately for the collector, Chad Valley was one of the few companies that labeled their toys. Before the 1930s, they appear to have labeled their Teddy Bears on the foot with the words "Hygienic toys, made in England by The Chad Valley Co., Ltd." printed or embroidered in black or red. Also a metal button with the words "Chad Valley English Hygienic Toys" covered over with clear plastic was implemented. In addition, small narrow labels have also been found stitched into the side seam of Chad Valley bears.

In 1938, Chad Valley was appointed "Toymakers to Her Majesty the Queen" and it seems that then a square label was stitched to the foot of the bear with the words printed "The Chad Valley Co., Ltd., by appointment Toy Makers to H. M. Queen Elizabeth, The Queen Mother." What appears to be a picture of the royal family crest is part of this label.

When World War II was declared the majority of factories changed over to government contract jobs. Yet, some production for boxed games still occurred for the armed forces and the home market.

When the war ended the company continued to prosper, buying other well-established factories.

In 1950 the Chad Valley Company dissolved the family business and was declared a public company. By 1960 three other companies had been acquired and, with increased export trade, now employed 1000 people in seven factories.

Palitoy (a subsidiary of the American firm General Mills, U. K. Limited) purchased the Chad Valley Company in September of 1978.

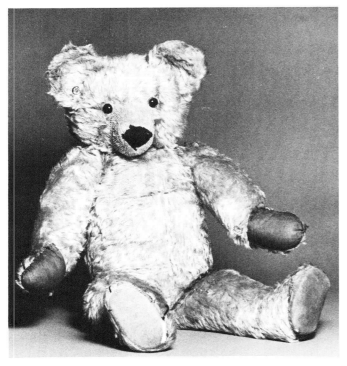

Chad Valley

TOP RIGHT: *Illustration 272.* The Chad Valley trademark. A clear celluloid covers a metal button with the words "CHAD VALLEY BRITISH HYGIENIC TOYS." This button is affixed to the early bear's ear.

MIDDLE LEFT: *Illustration 273.* A label was attached to the foot of the bear. The early versions were woven with silk thread with the words "HYGIENIC TOYS MADE IN ENGLAND BY CHAD VALLEY CO. LTD." Later versions were printed in black or red.

MIDDLE RIGHT: *Illustration 274.* The woven label was changed to a larger, printed one with the words "THE CHAD VALLEY CO. LTD. BY APPOINTMENT TOY MAKERS TO H.M. QUEEN ELIZABETH THE QUEEN MOTHER" and included a picture of the royal family crest.

LEFT: *Illustration 275.* Chad Valley. c.1930. 24in (61cm); long beige shaggy mohair; glass eyes; jointed arms and legs; swivel head; kapok stuffing. Condition: Good. Comments: Wide head. Note: Wide stitched nose characteristic of Chad Valley. *Author's collection.*

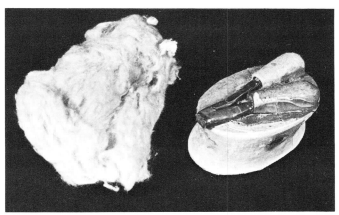

ABOVE LEFT: *Illustration 276.* Chad Valley. c.1930. 24in (61cm); long beige shaggy mohair; glass eyes; jointed arms and legs; swivel head; kapok stuffing. Condition: Good. Comments: Wide head. Note: Wide stitched nose characteristic of Chad Valley. *Author's collection.*

TOP RIGHT: *Illustration 277.* Kapok stuffing and squeeze-type cry box. A large spring is held together by two pieces of oval cardboard, encased with an oilcloth material. Sound is produced by squeezing the air through the large cardboard dowel. Stuffing and cry box were taken from Chad Valley bear shown in *Illustration 275.*

BOTTOM RIGHT: *Illustration 278.* (Left) Chad Valley. c.1950. 18in (45.7cm); light gold mohair; glass eyes; jointed arms and legs; swivel head; kapok stuffing; rexine pads. Condition: Excellent. Comments: Label on foot reads "The Chad Valley Co. Ltd., By Appointment Toy Makers to H.M. Queen Elizabeth The Queen Mother." (Center) Chad Valley "Sooty." c.1950. 9in (22.9cm); gold mohair; black ears; orange plastic eyes; rexine pads. Condition: Excellent. Comments: White label stitched into back seam, printed in blue letters: "Hygenic Toys Made in England by The Chad Valley Co. Ltd." Because Sooty represents a character his nose isn't the recognizable Chad Valley design. (Right) Chad Valley. c.1935. 22in (55.9cm); turquoise blue mohair; glass eyes; jointed arms and legs; swivel head; body stuffed with kapok; head stuffed with excelsior; turquoise blue felt pads. Condition: Excellent, replaced eyes. Comments: Fine example of early Chad Valley Bear in a rare beautiful color. White cloth label with red woven silk reads "Hygenic Toys, Made in England by Chad Valley Co. Ltd." Original metal button covered with clear plastic affixed to ear reads "Chad Valley, British Hygenic Toys." Example of button shown in *Illustration 272. Courtesy Darter Collection. Photograph Gale Darter.*

TOP LEFT: *Illustration 279.* Chad Valley Bear. c.1950. 12in (30.5cm); gold mohair; glass eyes; jointed arms and legs; swivel head; kapok stuffing. Condition: Excellent. Comments: Label on foot reads "THE CHAD VALLEY CO. LTD. BY APPOINTMENT TOY MAKERS TO H.M. QUEEN ELIZABETH THE QUEEN MOTHER." It also pictures the family crest. Chad Valley Doll. c.1930. 10in (25.4cm). *Author's collection.*

TOP RIGHT: *Illustration 280.* Kapok stuffing and tilt-type cry box. Cardboard encases a metal weight and bellows. Sound is produced when bear is tilted back and forth, forcing air through the holes on the metal top. This was another type of cry box used by Chad Valley and is taken from the bear shown in *Illustration 279.*

BOTTOM LEFT: *Illustration 281.* Chad Valley. c.1940. 21in (53.3cm); gold mohair; glass eyes; jointed arms and legs; swivel head; kapok stuffing. Condition: Good. Comments: Unusual head shape. Label on foot reads: "CHAD VALLEY 'MAGNA SERIES' HARBORNE ENGLAND." *Courtesy Volpp Collection.*

BOTTOM RIGHT: *Illustration 282.* Chad Valley. c.1950. 28in (71.1cm); light beige mohair; glass eyes; jointed arms and legs; swivel head; kapok stuffing; rexine pads. Condition: Excellent. Comments: Label attached to side seam of bear's body reads: "HYGIENIC TOYS MADE IN ENGLAND BY THE CHAD VALLEY CO. LTD." Note: Wide stitched nose. *Author's collection.*

TOP LEFT: *Illustration 283.* Chad Valley. c.1940. 30in (76.2cm); gold mohair; glass eyes; jointed arms and legs; swivel head; kapok stuffing. Condition: Mint. Comments: Fine example of Chad Valley, especially showing the large wide stitched nose design. *Courtesy Sally Bowen. Photograph by Warren Bowen.*

MIDDLE LEFT: *Illustration 284.* Chad Valley (Musical). c.1950. 16in (40.6cm); gold mohair; glass eyes; jointed arms and legs; swivel head; kapok stuffed body; excelsior stuffed head; rexine pads. Condition: Good. Comments: Key located on back of bear plays music box "Teddy Bear's Picnic" when wound. *Author's collection.*

ABOVE: *Illustration 285.* Chad Valley Bears. c.1940-1950. A rare 36in (91.4cm) Chad Valley Bear is surrounded by smaller Chad Valley Bears. Comments: Note the similar nose shape. *Author's collection.*

Sooty

When Harry Corbet purchased a little handmade puppet-bear from an elderly lady in a novelty shop on the North Pier at Blackpool in 1948, his only intention was to amuse his three-year-old son, David. Because the bruin's nose resembled a smudge of soot, they named the bear "Sooty." Corbet and Sooty began performing magic acts to amuse families and children.

Four years later, when Corbet and Sooty made their first television appearance, they were an instant success. They quickly gained popularity and were given their own show, which became a family favorite for many years. Sooty's reputation as a star was increased when he also became a comic strip. Little replica Sooty puppets were designed and then manufactured by Chad Valley.

BOTTOM LEFT: *Illustration 286.* Chad Valley Sooty Puppet. c.1950. 10in (25.4cm); gold mohair; black ears; plastic eyes; rexine pads. Condition: Good. Comments: Famous Teddy Bear puppet brought to life by Harry Corbet. Egg Cups. c.1960. 2½in (6.4cm); colored picture of Sooty with his name on the front of the cups; markings on base read "Keele st. Pty. Co. Ltd. Reg. by Sooty Concessions Ltd. No. 743610." *Author's collection.*

Fleet Street, London, in 1903 was the center of the newspaper industry. It was here Samuel Dean founded the Dean's Rag Book Company, Ltd. Dean's Rag Book Company, Ltd., is a subsidary of Dean and Son Ltd. Dean's Childsplay Toys, Ltd., became a subsidary of Dean's Rag Book Company, Ltd. in 1960.

Dean's famous trademark (registered c.1910) shows two dogs fiercely tugging on one of the company's books. This picture demonstrated the durability of their cloth books which were also washable and hygenically safe. The appropos logo was designed by Stanley Berkley. Dean's humourous slogan was "These rag books are for children who wear their food and eat their clothes."

Although known for their children's books, it is thought that Dean's first produced soft toys. One of their most popular lines were printed toys that came in sheets. Printed mechanically from hand-engraved rollers, the kits were designed for home-assembly.

In 1912, the "Rag Knock-about Toy Sheets" series produced glove puppets, toy animals and dolls. These were made in a soft wooly cloth material. This series proved so successful it continued to be manufactured after World War I when the Three Bears were introduced.

The company moved their factory to London's well-known area The Elephant and Castle. Here a brightly lit sign displayed the trademark of the two fighting dogs advertising the factory's new location.

Dean's manufactured Teddy Bears in many shapes and forms. One feature of their toys were "evripose" joints. The unique construction allowed the bears to be posed in any position.

In 1920 bears on wheels were produced. Dean's advertisement stated "It follows like a well trained pet —all you have to do is pull the string." Other animals on wheels were also made.

Perceiving the popularity of characters in children's literature, Dean's produced many of these memorable creatures including Bobby Whitetail and Peter Rabbit (from the Beatrix Potter books) and the grotesque figure of "Gilbert the Filbert" the Nursery Knut.

Other popular animals were "Dismal Desmond," a pitiful looking Dalmatian dog issued in 1923. He was supplemented ten years later by a happier looking "Cheerful Desmond." The poor little dog called "Tatters the Hospital Pup" with bandaged upraised paw came on the scene in 1928.

In 1930 an historic event occurred for Dean's. They were contracted by Walt Disney to be the sole manufacturer of the first Mickey Mouse. The honor of the contract was not evident in the beginning. It is thought Walt Disney came to England to find a manufacturer since Mickey Mouse had not been too well received by manufacturers in America (Dean's manufacturer's trademark number for Mickey Mouse is #750611).

With new laws requiring more information on the labeling of toys, Dean's deleted the picture of the famous two dogs.

When Samuel Dean died the business was taken over by his son and daughter who then owned controlling interest. After World War II, Teddy Bears, Golliwogs, animals and soft cuddly toys of many types became the firm's main products.

In 1956 the factory moved to the beautiful country town of Rye in Sussex. Then in 1974 they moved to their present home in Pontnewynydd, the industrial town of Pontypool, Gwent, in South Wales.

Three directors, Ian Scott, Michael Crane and Ron Green now own controlling interest in the company.

It was at their new location that my husband and I enjoyed a wonderful tour with Ian Scott during our 1984 visit to my homeland. Ian's convivial personality is projected to visitors and employees alike. He proudly showed us the care and craftsmanship that went into manufacturing their beautiful soft toys which have brought Dean's so much recognition.

Ian enthusiastically showed us the prototype of the Schoonmaker Bear which was in production at the time of our visit. He pointed out how Dean's had reproduced its likeness in every detail.

In 1972, Dean's Rag Book Company, Ltd., merged with Dean's Childsplay Toy divisions. Already manufacturing quality plush toys in 1960, they also purchased Gwent Toys of South Wales which produced a lower-end price range plush line. This enabled Dean's to have a broader priced market and enlarge its domestic line.

The Rockwell series of three bears, introduced in 1981, was the turning point for Dean's movement into the collector's market.

The beautiful "Schoonmaker Bear" designed as an exact replica of Patricia Schoonmaker's (historian and author of *A Collector's History of the Teddy Bear*) original bear was another of Dean's additions to the world of collectibles. The second series of the Schoonmaker Bears was a clown.

At this writing, Dean's plans to open an American branch of its company. Dean's America will be completely separate from its English parent company.

Dean's Childsplay Toys

Illustration 287. 1920 Catalog of Dean's Rag Productions showing the Dean's famous trademark of two dogs fiercely tugging on one of the Dean's Rag Books demonstrating their durability.

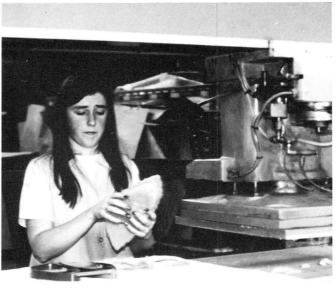

TOP LEFT: *Illustration 288.* Page from the 1920 Dean's catalog advertising jointed Teddy Bears with hygienic stuffing.

TOP RIGHT: *Illustration 289.* Page from the 1920 Dean's catalog showing their "Knockabout Toys."

BOTTOM LEFT: *Illustration 290.* Inside the Dean's factory.

BOTTOM RIGHT: *Illustration 291.* A machine stamps out the patterns for some of the designs of Teddy Bears.

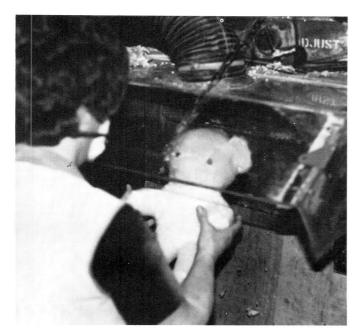

TOP LEFT: *Illustration 292.* Teddy Bears account for a large percentage of Dean's business. Here a stuffing machine is blowing in just the right amount of filling in one of Dean's unjointed Teddy Bears.

TOP RIGHT: *Illustration 293.* Dean's famous Rag Books are still manufactured and remain a popular item in their line.

BOTTOM LEFT: *Illustration 294.* Careful inspection is made of every item before it is packed and ready for shipping.

BOTTOM RIGHT: *Illustration 295.* Ian Scott proudly displays the Dean's reproduction of the "Schoonmaker Bear." The original is on the right.

TOP LEFT: *Illustration 296.* Label identifying Dean's Rag Book soft toys. A silver metal button with the incised words "Dean's Rag Book Co. Ltd" was affixed to the early soft toys. With the success of Steiff using a button for their trademark it would appear many companies adopted similar methods of identification.

MIDDLE LEFT: *Illustration 297.* Dean's. c.1920. 14in (35.6cm); gold mohair; glass eyes; jointed arms and legs; swivel head; kapok stuffing; squeeze type voice box. Condition: Fair. Comments: Original label on foot reads "Made in England by Dean's Rag Book Co. Ltd. London." *Author's collection.*

BOTTOM LEFT: *Illustration 298.* Dean's Dismal Desmond. c.1923. 14in (35.6cm); white soft flannel material with black spots and features; kapok stuffing. Markings: "Made in England by Dean's Rag Book Company. Hygienic stuffing. Dismal Desmond." Condition: Fair. *Author's collection.*

TOP RIGHT: *Illustration 299.* Dean's "Tatters the Hospital Pup." c.1928. 9½in (24.2cm); gold soft flannel material with black spots and features; upraised bandaged paw; kapok stuffing. Markings read "Made in England by Dean's Rag Book Co. Ltd. Hygienic Stuffing. Regd. Design No. 751488 'Tatters' The Hospital Pup." *Author's collection.* Dean's Golliwog. c.1940. 19in (48.3cm); black felt face; applied red mouth; celluloid eyes; black wool hair; yellow felt shirt and green jacket with orange trousers; black and white felt shoes; black felt hands. All clothes are made as part of the body and cannot be removed. Label on right foot reads "Made in England by Dean's Rag Book Co. Ltd. London." *Author's collection.*

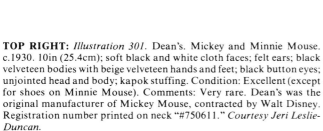

TOP RIGHT: *Illustration 301.* Dean's. Mickey and Minnie Mouse. c.1930. 10in (25.4cm); soft black and white cloth faces; felt ears; black velveteen bodies with beige velveteen hands and feet; black button eyes; unjointed head and body; kapok stuffing. Condition: Excellent (except for shoes on Minnie Mouse). Comments: Very rare. Dean's was the original manufacturer of Mickey Mouse, contracted by Walt Disney. Registration number printed on neck "#750611." *Courtesy Jeri Leslie-Duncan.*

ABOVE: *Illustration 300.* Dean's. c.1915. 15in (38.1cm) honey colored mohair; glass eyes; jointed arms and legs; swivel head; excelsior stuffing. Condition: Good. Comments: Label on foot reads "Made in England by Dean's Rag Book Co. Ltd. London." *Courtesy Pam Hebbs.*

MIDDLE RIGHT: *Illustration 302.* Dean's. c.1940. 22in (55.9cm); gold mohair; glass eyes; jointed arms and legs; swivel head; kapok stuffing; velvet pads. Condition: Good. Comments: Original label on foot reads "Dean's Rag Toy." *Courtesy Sally Bowen. Photograph Warren Bowen.*

BOTTOM RIGHT: *Illustration 303.* Dean's (Polar Bears). c.1930. (Left) 8in (20.3cm), (Center) 17in (43.2cm), (Right) 20in (50.8cm); white mohair; glass eyes; unjointed head and body; leather noses on the 17in (43.2cm) and 20in (50.8cm) bears; kapok stuffing. Condition: Good. *Courtesy Sally Bowen. Photograph Warren Bowen.*

Chiltern

H. G. Stone (a partner in J. K. Farnell Company) and Leon Rees (a director of Ellison, Rees and Company in London) founded the H. G. Stone Company, Ltd. in 1920.

The Bavarian born Rees then acquired the Chiltern Teddy Bear Factory at Chesham and opened a factory (with Stone as his partner) in the north of London where they manufactured Chiltern plush animals.

Two well-known examples of these early Chiltern toys are a baby bruin and an Angel Face Chimpanzee, both made in 1922.

Registration of the brand name Chiltern for plush and velvet toys came about 1924.

When H. G. Stone died in 1935, his son continued the business at 35 Wilson Street in London.

Chiltern's Hugmee Bears" were introduced in 1947.

Twenty years later (1967) the company was bought by Chad Valley.

Chiltern

TOP LEFT: *Illustration 304.* Chiltern Teddy Bears are identified by a label attached to the side seam in the body of the bear. Label reads "CHILTERN HYGIENIC TOYS MADE IN ENGLAND."

TOP RIGHT: *Illustration 305.* Chiltern. c.1950. Both 36in (91.4cm); honey colored mohair; glass eyes; jointed arms and legs; swivel head; kapok stuffed body; excelsior stuffed head; plastic nose; velvet pads. Condition: Mint. Comments: Rare size. Typically English style of wide head and plump body. The plastic nose and velvet pads are features used by Chiltern. *Author's collection.*

BOTTOM LEFT: *Illustration 306.* Side view of one of the bears shown in *Illustration 305.*

BOTTOM MIDDLE: *Illustration 307.* Chiltern. c.1940. (Left) 10in (25.4cm), (Right) 17in (43.2cm); beige mohair; glass eyes; jointed arms and legs; swivel head; kapok stuffed body; excelsior stuffed head; plastic nose on 10in (25.4cm) bear; resewn nose on 17in (43.2cm) bear. Condition: Good. *Author's collection.*

BOTTOM RIGHT: *Illustration 308.* Chiltern. c.1946. 10in (25.4cm); beige mohair; glass eyes; jointed arms and legs; swivel head; kapok stuffed body; excelsior stuffed head; plastic nose. Condition: Good. Comments: Label attached to side seam of body reads "CHILTERN HYGIENIC TOYS MADE IN ENGLAND." *Courtesy Susan Allen.*

Merrythought

Although Merrythought entered into the toy world in 1930, its origin came from the roots of milling fine mohair fabrics.

The old company began in 1919 when W. G. Holmes joined forces with G. H. Laxton to open a small spinning mill to convert raw mohair to yarn. With the invention of synthetic fibers, during the 1920s, a number of mohair mills suffered business losses.

One of Holmes and Laxton and Company's customers was a plush weaving factory (Dyson Hall and Company). Holmes and Laxton bought them out and needed a way to put their mohair yarn and cloth to work.

The sales director of the newly combined companies knew both C. J. Rendel (of Chad Valley) and A. C. Janisch (of J. K. Farnell). Rendle, dissatisfied with his position as toy production chief, and Janisch, unhappy as sales director, hired on at Holmes and Laxton — and Merrythought Toys were born.

Holmes and Laxton and Company had operations along the river Severn, on the Welsh border in the agricultural county of Shropshire. Today that valley is called "The Cradle of the Industrial Revolution." The town where Merrythought is located is called Iron Bridge, named after its landmark, a majestic iron forged bridge, the first of its kind in the world.

I was fortunate enough to visit this area and Merrythought in particular in 1984. The Merrythought factory is one of the foundry buildings of the Coalbrookdale Company, which built the famous iron bridge in 1779.

The name Merrythought came from an archaic English word meaning forked bone. Hence the trademark of the wishbone, combined with the word Merrythought.

Along with Rendle came a number of unhappy Chad Valley workers, including Florence Atwood. Florence was a deaf-mute who learned her designing craft at The Deaf and Dumb School in Manchester, which Rendle's daughter also attended.

Florence had also gained experience at Chad Valley working with the designer Norah Wellings, who in turn left the company to form her own soft toy business.

The first Merrythought line was entirely produced by Florence in 1931. Some of these toys are still in production. She served as chief designer for the company until she succumbed to cancer in 1949.

In addition to her own creations, Florence Atwood translated well-known drawings into toys including MGM's Jerry Mouse. MGM was particularly pleased with the added publicity Merrythought's toys gave them.

The Merrythought facilities I visited were purchased from the Coalbrookdale company in 1956. Of course, they've undergone refurbishing and new buildings have been added, but the main portion of the factory is still the original brick structure built by the iron foundry in 1898.

Merrythought prides itself on keeping employees happy. I experienced a friendly atmosphere as I visited with the women going about their craft. Their policies are so strong that eight of the early 1930s employees are still with them. In addition, their methods have changed very

little since the "old days." All Merrythought animals are produced by hand, although they have made some cost-cutting concessions, such as automatic cutters.

One of those original eight employees is Mrs. Fanny Elizabeth Davis (still lively at 80) who began in the accounting department. Now, as a director of the firm, she remembers the Merrythought effort during World War II when they manufactured a variety of soft cloth products for the army, including chevrons, gas mask bags and covers for hot water bottles. After the war, toy production went back to full throttle. A flood in 1946 took away much of Merrythought's pre-war toy samples and many of their supplies.

The business continued as a family concern with the son Trayton Holmes entering the company in 1949. Later, in 1972, he was followed by Oliver Holmes (his son and grandson of W. G. Holmes) who now serves as managing director.

It was under Trayton Holmes that Dean and Son Ltd. began to represent Merrythought as a marketing arm, and with the increase in orders an automatic stuffing machine (imported from the United States) took over much, but not all, of the filling of the soft animals.

In 1958, the company took their toys to the giant toy fair in Nürnberg, Germany, one of Europe's most important trade shows.

The Holmes family still resides in the sheep raising, wool making rural area of Shropshire. Trayton Holmes, in fact, runs a sheep ranch near the village of Clun and has the utmost integrity to continue producing toys of high quality fabric.

The family based operation uses two types of plush in producing Merrythought animals: an imported woven plush and a British domestic knitted plush.

Since high quality is difficult to maintain on a large scale, and Merrythought insists on retaining a great deal of handiwork in its product, eighty percent of its production is sold in better stores in England. Only twenty percent is exported to other countries.

Oliver Holmes, who personally toured Wally and me through the factory, says his firm is "a traditional private British company...If one of our animals makes one smile, then it is a successful toy."

In the United States, Merrythought is represented by Tide-Rider, Inc. of Baldwin, New York.

Quality made soft toys of felt and fur fabric have been produced by Merrythought over the years. Some of their main productions are Teddy Bears, Golliwogs and whimsical animals.

One of their most famous character bears is "Cheeky." Made for the 1955 British Toy Fair, he had a bell in his ear and a velvet muzzle. His individualistic expression prompted a very important person to comment "Isn't he Cheeky?"...and the name stuck. He's been Cheeky ever since.

One particular bear made by the company represented a character appearing in the "Robin" comic books' first edition in 1953. It became the mascot of the famous

Donald Campbell, an Englishman who held the world record for driving a jet propelled Bluebird Hydroplane. "Mr Whoppit," as he was christened by Donald, sat in the cockpit of every daring record breaking attempt made by his owner.

Merrythought's 1984 beautiful mohair bear is a limited edition of 2500 bears. It is styled from their first 1930s bear.

Initially the company identified their bears with a metal plastic-covered ear button depicting their trademark, and additionally a stitched label to the foot of the bear.

It is thought (due to some controversy with Steiff's existing button in the ear) that Merrythought changed to using a label by itself. The first labels were machine embroidered with the words "Merrythought Hygienic Toys, made in England." It was changed (c. 1950) to a printed label which reads: "Merrythought, Ironbridge, Shrops, made in England." Another identifying feature is the design of the paw stitching.

The first Merrythought catalog (1931) showed approximately 150 styles of animals. Today, that catalog reveals about 200 different and even more "appealing" styles.

Merrythought

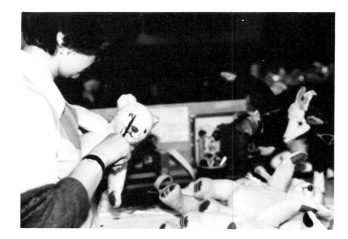

TOP LEFT: *Illustration 309.* The world's first iron bridge is located close to the Merrythought factory in Ironbridge, Shropshire. The bridge was built in 1779 by Abraham Darby III. He was the first iron worker to smelt with coke at his foundry in Coalbrookdale, Shropshire, England.

MIDDLE LEFT: *Illustration 310.* The word Merrythought is an archaic English word meaning forked bone. Here Oliver Holmes, managing director of Merrythought, stands in front of a large sign showing their trademark.

BOTTOM LEFT: *Illustration 311.* The Merrythought label is attached to each animal before assembly.

TOP RIGHT: *Illustration 312.* The finishing touches are carefully applied to each animal before inspection.

BOTTOM RIGHT: *Illustration 313.* Signed, sealed and approved, the Teddy Bear is package ready for the shipping department.

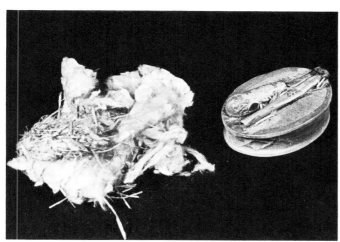

TOP LEFT: *Illustration 314.* Clear celluloid covers a metal button showing the Merrythought trademark: a wishbone with the words "Regd. trademark HYGIENIC MERRYTHOUGHT TOYS, MADE IN ENGLAND" is affixed to left ear of the bear. Taken from the c.1930 Merrythought Bear in *Illustration 318.*

MIDDLE: *Illustration 315.* The early labels were woven with silk thread with the words "Merrythought Hygienic Toys Made in England."

TOP RIGHT: *Illustration 316.* Printed labels replaced the woven type and the words are changed to read "Merrythought Ironbridge Shrops. Made in England."

BOTTOM LEFT: *Illustration 317.* Kapok and excelsior stuffing; squeeze type voice box. A large spring is held together by two pieces of oval cardboard, encased by an oilcloth material. Sound is produced by squeezing the air through the large cardboard dowel. Marked: "Germany." Taken from the c.1930 Merrythought Bear in *Illustration 318.*

BOTTOM RIGHT: *Illustration 318.* Merrythought. c.1930. 18in (45.7cm); light beige curly mohair; glass eyes; jointed arms and legs; swivel head; body stuffed with kapok; head stuffed with excelsior. Condition: Good. Comments: Clear celluloid covered metal button in left ear reads "Regd. Trademark Hygienic Merrythought Toys Made in England." Note wide head; large ears and wide stitched nose are characteristic of early Merrythought Teddy Bears. Also notice the similarities to the Chad Valley bears. Original woven Merrythought label on foot. *Author's collection.*

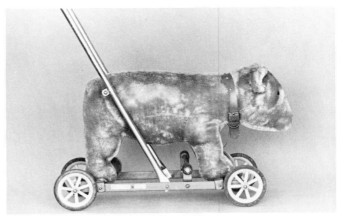

TOP LEFT: *Illustration 319.* Merrythought. (Left) c.1940. 21in (53.3cm), (Center) c.1930. 15in (38.1cm), (Right) c.1940. 20in (50.8cm). The two larger bears are gold and the one in the center is beige mohair. Glass eyes; jointed arms and legs; swivel head; kapok stuffing; metal buttons in left ear; original woven Merrythought labels on foot. Condition: Excellent. Comments: Note the different shape of the heads. *Author's collection.*

TOP RIGHT: *Illustration 320.* Merrythought. c.1950. 22in (55.9cm) long; 14in (35.6cm) high; gold mohair; glass eyes; unjointed head and body; metal frame; plastic wheels with rubber tires. Label on frame reads "Merrythought Toys" with the wishbone trademark. *Author's collection.*

BOTTOM LEFT: *Illustration 321.* Merrythought (pajama case). c.1930. 15in (38.1cm); white mohair; pale blue glass eyes; excelsior stuffing. Condition: Excellent. Comments: Zipper in center of body opens to store pajamas. Note stitching on paws characteristic of Merrythought. *Courtesy Sally Bowen. Photograph Warren Bowen.*

BOTTOM RIGHT: *Illustration 322.* (Left) Merrythought "Cheeky." c.1957. 10in (25.4cm); bronze and gold mohair; long gold mohair topknot; velveteen snout and feet; foot pads are velour; paw pads are brown felt; glass eyes; jointed arms and legs; swivel head; excelsior stuffing. Condition: Excellent. (Right) Merrythought "Punkinhead." c.1952. 10in (25.4cm); brown and gold mohair; glass eyes; jointed arms and legs; swivel head; excelsior stuffing. Condition: Mint. Comments: Rare. *Courtesy Beverly Port.*

The House of Nisbet

In the heart of the beautiful English countryside lies the House of Nisbet. Established at Dunster Park, the old Victorian estate in the nearby West Country Village of Winscombe is situated on the borders of Somerset.

The Nisbet story began in 1953 when families and friends of British people around the world celebrated the Coronation of Her Majesty, Queen Elizabeth II.

An enterprising woman, Peggy Nisbet, created a portrait doll who was the exact replica of H. M. Queen Elizabeth II in her coronation robes. On the basis of this commemorative piece, Peggy Nisbet obtained permission to carry on her work from The Lord Chamberlain.

With the assistance of her Aunt Kate, her sitting room was transformed into a workroom and her dining room became the office. The first portrait replica doll of the Queen evolved with much hard work and exhausting research.

Peggy Nisbet's small idea grew into a larger venture. Other historical characters followed in quick succession. A two-story building in Weston-super-Mare became available with much more space for expansion. The Nisbet enterprise grew rapidly.

Then, in 1970, disaster struck when a fire destroyed the entire premises. Everything was lost. Mrs. Nisbet's home once again was the headquarters where loyal supporters were soon back at work making dolls.

At the same time, work commenced on a new building. The company, under the leadership of Mrs. Nisbet and her daughter, Alison, continued to prosper during the invervening years.

In approximately 1977, Jack Wilson (Alison's husband) entered the company as Chairman. He changed the name to The House of Nisbet, Ltd. It was Jack who approached Peter Bull with the concept of Nisbet creating an original Peter Bull Bear. Fifteen months later after their original meeting in Bull's Chelsea flat, "Bully Bear" was handborn in the Nisbet workrooms by Alison Nisbet Wilson. Bully was fashioned after Peter's wonderful old bear Delicatessen/Aloysius (see chapter on Peter Bull). Young Bully and Bully Minor were designed to complete the family.

In 1983, Nisbet entered the publishing business, reprinting Peter Bull's *The Teddy Bear Book*, which had been out of print for several years.

Peter was so enthusiastic about this reissue, he authored a new last chapter and agreed to sign every one of the 10,000 numbered limited edition books.

Early in 1983, Peter shared some extraordinary artwork of bears with Jack Wilson. He also revealed a mass of draft manuscripts which he envisioned publishing.

Peter told Jack of a talented artist named Pauline McMillian who painted stones, postcards and gift items for his Astrological Emporium and how, under his guidance and inspiration, she had begun creating these wonderful drawings of bears. Jack was impressed. Not only could he appreciate the potential of Bull's book, but he could also visualize the actual Zodiac Teddy Bears.

So, with Peter's enthusiasm, Pauline's enormous imaginative talent, and the teamwork of The House of Nisbet, The Zodiac Bears and book came into being.

The Zodiac Bears are made of the highest quality plush, are 14in (35.6cm) tall, fully jointed and display boxed. The first 1000 of each bear, plus the first 1000 books are signed and numbered. (For more information on the Zodiac Bears and Peter Bull please refer to Chapter 19, A Tribute to Peter Bull).

House of Nisbet

Illustration 323. The home of the House of Nisbet is an old Victorian estate. It is located in the beautiful English countryside of Dunster Park, Winscombe, on the borders of Somerset, in England.

Little Folk

Little Folk has a most enchanting and fascinating location for a Teddy Bear Factory. Maggie Breedon and Graham McBride live and manufacture their wonderful creations in a 700 year old mill, known as The Mill House, located in Tiverton, Devon.

The upper part of the mill is used for production purposes and for years it was quite dark. Only electricity lit this area which had no windows. In 1983, remodeling took place and a new roof with sky lights was added.

The first animals made by the talented couple were rabbits and foxes. These wonderful toys were completely dressed in all their finery, with their heads, hands and feet made of fur.

In 1980, Charles and Gail Garrett (now the United States representative) suggested Breedon (a former bookeeper) and McBride (an automobile designer) try their hand at a Teddy Bear. The couple studied a wild animal book and created the Little Folk Bear which is now the most popular animal in their line.

The Canterbury Bear Company

John and Maude Blackburn who have been married for 27 years live in Westbere, a suburb of Canterbury, County of Kent, England. From their home one can see the famous Canterbury Cathedral. John began as a designer and painter, working in a wide spectrum of media.

Commissioned by a client to design a traditional jointed bear as a gift for his client, John created the original design for the basis of the famed Canterbury Bear. Using an incredible series of unique, high quality and original designs, the Blackburns opened the Canterbury Bear Center which continued to grow by leaps and bounds.

The Blackburns have three children and most of the family is involved in the bear business. Maude acts as Financial Manager and oversees about 25 women in a management merchandizing firm. Their second child, Kerstin is the manager of the company while their son Mark, markets the bears.

Little Folk

The Canterbury Bear Company

ABOVE LEFT: *Illustration 326.* Little Folk's 1983 traditional Teddy Bear. Comes in two sizes: 12in (30.5cm); 22in (55.9cm). Made in "London gold" mohair; features reminiscent of the original Teddy Bears — slight hump; hand-embroidered nose and mouth. Characteristic of other Little Folk creations shown as these bears will stand on their feet or heads without support. The importers for Little Folk line in America are Oxford Properties of Huntington Beach, California. *Courtesy Little Folk.*

ABOVE RIGHT: *Illustration 327.* A group of current Canterbury Bears. The Oxford Bear, which is seated in the center, is 14in (35.6cm). He is fully jointed and made of beautiful white mohair; the smaller bears are 8in (20.3cm) and are made in mohair and synthetic fabrics. *Courtesy Lillian Rohaly.*

Chapter Five

Unidentified Bears

As much as we try to discover the history behind Teddy Bears, the heritage of many is difficult to document. Insufficient background information, the vast number of Teddy Bear manufacturing companies, lack of labeling and specific markings, and the inability of original owners to provide thorough "genealogies," create a great deal of frustration to collectors. Bears without roots are as important and loved just as much as their pedigreed brothers.

This chapter is filled with photos of bears in this limbo state. My hope is that you readers may be able to share some important data with us all. So, if you own or know a similar bear, or have some knowledge to offer regarding these unidentified bears, please write to me in care of Hobby House Press, Inc., 900 Frederick Street, Cumberland, Maryland 21502.

Illustration 329. Manufacturer unknown. c.1930. 18in (45.7cm); light gold mohair with pale blue mohair formed trousers; glass eyes; unjointed body; swivel head; excelsior stuffing; rexine pads. Condition: Good. Comments: Rexine pads are an indication the bear could have been made in England. *Author's collection.*

Illustration 328. Manufacturer unknown. c.1920. 17in (43.2cm) long, 12in (30.5cm) high; short beige mohair; glass eyes; unjointed head and body; excelsior stuffing; wooden wheels. Condition: Excellent. Comments: Probably German; possibly Hermann. *Author's collection.*

ABOVE LEFT: *Illustration 330.* Manufacturer unknown. c.1915. 21in (53.3cm); gold mohair; replaced shoe button eyes; jointed arms and legs; swivel head; excelsior stuffing. Condition: Excellent. Comments: Very flat feet. Cardboard underlines felt on feet. *Author's collection.*

LEFT: *Illustration 331.* Manufacturer unknown. c.1925. 15in (38.1cm); bright gold mohair; glass eyes; jointed arms and legs; swivel head; excelsior stuffing. Condition: Good (repaired pads). China cup. c.1910. 3in (7.6cm); mark on base "Made in Bavaria." Condition: Fair. Comments: Colorful picture of The Three Bears. *Author's collection.*

ABOVE RIGHT: *Illustration 332.* Manufacturer unknown. c.1910. 24in (61cm); short beige mohair; large shoe button eyes; jointed arms and legs; swivel head; excelsior stuffing. Condition: Mint. Comments: Unusual wide body shape. *Author's collection.*

ABOVE: *Illustration 333.* Manufacturer unknown. c.1930. 28in (71.1cm); white mohair; glass eyes; jointed arms and legs; swivel head; body stuffed with kapok; head stuffed with excelsior. Condition: Good. Comments: Replaced pads. Possibly manufactured by J. K. Farnell. *Author's collection.*

ABOVE LEFT: *Illustration 334.* Manufacturer unknown. c.1915. 12in (30.5cm); light beige mohair; glass eyes; jointed arms and legs; swivel head; excelsior stuffing. Condition: Excellent. Comments: Exceptionally wide large head. *Courtesy Colleen Tipton.*

LEFT: *Illustration 335.* Manufacturer unknown. c.1915. 13in (33cm); honey colored mohair; glass eyes; jointed arms and legs; swivel head; excelsior stuffing. Condition: Mint. Comments: Cardboard underlining felt on feet enables bear to stand. *Author's collection.*

ABOVE RIGHT: *Illustration 336.* Manufacturer unknown. c.1910. 29in (73.7cm); gold mohair; replaced glass eyes; jointed arms and legs; swivel head; excelsior stuffing. Condition: Good. *Author's collection.*

ABOVE: *Illustration 337.* Manufacturer unknown. c.1908. 33in (83.8cm); honey colored mohair; glass replaced button eyes; jointed arms and legs; swivel head; excelsior stuffing. Condition: Good (replaced pads). Comments: Rare size. Smaller bear is a Steiff. c.1907. 17in (43.2cm). *Author's collection.*

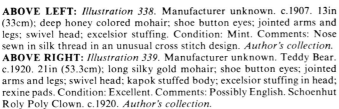

ABOVE LEFT: *Illustration 338.* Manufacturer unknown. c.1907. 13in (33cm); deep honey colored mohair; shoe button eyes; jointed arms and legs; swivel head; excelsior stuffing. Condition: Mint. Comments: Nose sewn in silk thread in an unusual cross stitch design. *Author's collection.*

ABOVE RIGHT: *Illustration 339.* Manufacturer unknown. Teddy Bear. c.1920. 21in (53.3cm); long silky gold mohair; shoe button eyes; jointed arms and legs; swivel head; kapok stuffed body; excelsior stuffing in head; rexine pads. Condition: Excellent. Comments: Possibly English. Schoenhut Roly Poly Clown. c.1920. *Author's collection.*

ABOVE: *Illustration 340.* Manufacturer unknown Bear Bell Toy. c.1910. 10in (25.4cm) long, 4in (10.2cm) high; dark brown burlap; glass eyes; unjointed papier mâché body; metal wheels on feet. Comments: Probably German. When toy is pulled, wheels rotate and bell rings. *Author's collection.*

RIGHT: *Illustration 341.* Manufacturer unknown. c.1930. 17in (43.2cm); worn gold mohair; painted glass eyes; jointed arms and legs; swivel head; kapok stuffing. Condition: Fair (replaced pads). China Mug. c.1930. 3in (7.6cm). Condition: Good. Comments: Picture of large gold Teddy Bear playing English football. Many pieces of china in this series; each bear is shown playing a different sport. *Author's collection.*

ABOVE: *Illustration 342.* Manufacturer unknown. Teddy Bear. c.1910. 18in (45.7cm); gold mohair; large button eyes; jointed arms and legs; swivel head; excelsior stuffing. Condition: Mint. Comments: Paw stitching resembles the Merrythought design (see *Illustration 320*). *Author's collection.* Miniature car. American National Packard Roadster. c.1930. 29in (73.7cm) long x 14in (35.6cm) high; completely original. Painted in red with black fenders. Emblem attached to the radiator shell "The American National Co., Packard, Toledo, Ohio. Made in U.S.A." This name also appears on the instrument panel with decals duplicating the gauges. This extremely rare car is a perfect size for this 18in (45.7cm) Teddy Bear to ride. *Courtesy Carl Burnett.*

Illustration 344. Manufacturer unknown. c.1930. 17in (43.2cm); gold curly cotton plush; metal painted eyes; jointed arms and legs; swivel head; excelsior stuffing. Condition: Good. Comments: Unusually large head and .fat cheeks. Stuffed extremely firmly. *Courtesy Volpp Collection.*

Illustration 343. Manufacturer unknown. c.1910. 15in (38.1cm); dark honey colored mohair; shoe button eyes; jointed arms and legs; swivel head; excelsior stuffing. Condition: Good. Comments: Both bears have extremely hard stuffed bodies with cardboard lining under their felt feet. *Author's collection.*

ABOVE LEFT: *Illustration 345.* Manufacturer unknown. c.1910. 16in (40.6cm); gold mohair; shoe button eyes; jointed arms and legs; swivel head; excelsior stuffing. Condition: Good. *Author's collection.*

ABOVE RIGHT: *Illustration 346.* Manufacturer unknown. c.1915. 12in (30.5cm); light gold mohair; glass eyes; jointed arms and legs; swivel head; excelsior stuffing. Condition: Mint. Comments: Unusual cone shaped head and pointed nose. Flat feet lined with cardboard under felt pads. *Author's collection.*

ABOVE: *Illustration 347.* Manufacturer unknown. c.1920. 20in (50.8cm); honey colored mohair; glass eyes; jointed arms and legs; swivel head; kapok stuffing. Condition: Fair. *Author's collection.*

RIGHT: *Illustration 348.* Manufacturer unknown. c.1920. 18in (45.7cm); worn honey colored mohair; shoe button eyes; jointed arms and legs; swivel head; excelsior stuffing. Condition: Fair. *Author's collection.*

Illustration 349. Manufacturer unknown. c.1910. 15in (38.1cm); light beige mohair; shoe button eyes; jointed arms and legs; swivel head; excelsior stuffing. Condition: Excellent. Comments: Ears placed low on head. *Author's collection.*

Illustration 350. Manufacturer unknown. c.1915. 8in (20.3cm); dark honey colored mohair; googlie painted tin eyes; jointed arms and legs; swivel head; excelsior stuffing. Condition: Excellent. Comments: Unusual eyes. *Author's collection.*

Illustration 351. Manufacturer unknown. c.1910. 13in (33cm); pale apricot mohair; shoe button eyes; jointed arms and legs; swivel head; excelsior stuffing; 'rust velveteen nose;'' velveteen pads. Condition: Good. Comments: Unusually shaped nose. Twin bears belonged to two sisters. Advertising Box. c.1930. 8½in (21.6cm) x 7½in (19.1cm); cardboard box advertising chocolate covered Teddy Bears. Box contained 24 bars. Manufactured by James O. Welch Co., Cambridge, Massachusetts. *Author's collection.*

Illustration 352. Manufacturer unknown. c.1910. 13in (33cm); light beige mohair; shoe button eyes; jointed arms and legs; swivel head; excelsior stuffing. Condition: Mint. Comments: Exceptionally large ears. *Author's collection.*

163

Illustration 353. Manufacturer unknown. c.1930. 16in (40.6cm); white mohair; glass eyes; jointed arms and legs; swivel head; excelsior stuffing. Condition: Excellent. *Author's collection.*

Illustration 354. Muff. Manufacturer unknown. c.1940. 12in (30.5cm); white mohair; velvet muzzle; glass eyes; stationary head. Condition: Excellent. *Author's collection.*

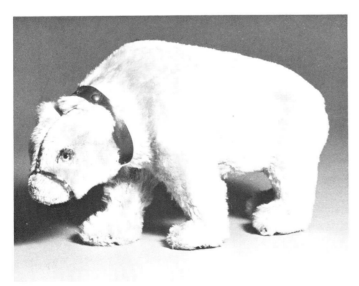

Illustration 355. Manufacturer unknown. c.1920. 12in (30.5cm); light beige mohair; glass eyes; papier mâché unjointed head and body. Condition: Mint. *Courtesy Colleen Tipton.*

Illustration 356. Manufacturer unknown. c.1910. 9in (22.9cm) tall x 9in (22.9cm) long; honey colored mohair; glass eyes; papier mâché unjointed head and body. Condition: Excellent. *Author's collection.*

RIGHT: *Illustration 357.* Manufacturer unknown. c.1930. 26in (66cm); long rust mohair with short mohair muzzle; glass eyes; jointed arms and legs; swivel head; excelsior stuffing. Condition: Excellent. *Courtesy Flore Emory.*

BELOW: *Illustration 358.* Manufacturer unknown. c.1920. 25in (63.5cm); honey colored mohair; large shoe button eyes; jointed arms and legs; swivel head; excelsior stuffing. Condition: Excellent. *Courtesy Flore Emory.*

BELOW RIGHT: *Illustration 359.* Manufacturer unknown. c.1920. 14in (35.6cm); pink and blue mohair; glass eyes; jointed arms and legs; swivel head; excelsior stuffing. Condition: Excellent. Comments: Clown type bear; original ruffle around neck. Probably American. *Courtesy Volpp Collection.*

ABOVE LEFT: *Illustration 360.* Manufacturer unknown. Bottle Holder. c.1950(?) 11in (27.9cm); white cotton plush; glass eyes; unjointed head and arms. Condition: Good. Comments: Zipper opens to reveal compartment to store bottle. *Author's collection.*

ABOVE RIGHT: *Illustration 361.* Manufacturer unknown. c.1910. 16in (40.6cm); dark honey colored mohair; shoe button eyes; jointed arms and legs; swivel head; excelsior stuffing. Condition: Excellent. *Author's collection.*

BELOW LEFT: *Illustration 362.* Manufacturer unknown. c.1915. 6in (15.2cm); honey colored mohair; shoe button eyes; jointed arms and legs; swivel head; excelsior stuffing. Condition: Good. Comments: Rather large head for body. *Author's collection.*

ABOVE: *Illustration 363.* Manufacturer unknown. c.1920. 3in (7.6cm); light brown mohair; glass eyes; unjointed papier mâché head and body. Condition: Excellent. *Author's collection.*

ABOVE: *Illustration 364.* Manufacturer unknown. c.1920. 3½in (8.9cm); gold mohair; glass eyes; jointed arms and legs; swivel head; excelsior stuffing. Condition: Excellent. Comments: Rather grotesque looking large head. *Author's collection.*

ABOVE RIGHT: *Illustration 365.* Manufacturer unknown. c.1930. 4in (10.2cm); gold velveteen; black glass eyes; jointed arms and legs; stationary head; kapok stuffing. Condition: Good. *Author's collection.*

BELOW RIGHT: *Illustration 366.* Manufacturer unknown. c.1910. 2in (5.1cm); all bisque; painted features; jointed arms and legs; stationary head. Condition: Excellent. *Author's collection.*

Chapter Six

Special Bears: Mechanical, Battery-Operated, Musical, Rare and Unusual

Mechanical Bears

Over the past 80 years, many Teddy Bear manufacturers have contributed to the world of mechanical bears in one way or another. Walking, climbing, tumbling, drinking — almost every human activity possible, has been recreated in bears. Their charm and humor never cease to intrigue children and collectors alike.

Some of the most intricately made and exquisitely costumed bears were created in the late 1800s and early 1900s. These magnificent works of art were primarily designed for adult amusement and were too delicate to be played with by mischievous little children. Many of these early examples of automatons were covered with real fur, with fierce expressions looking startlingly realistic.

To add to the entertaining quality of these mechanical wonders, musical movements were also encased in a box at the base of many. Production of these magnificent toys took place mainly in Germany and France, where papier-mâché forms were used for lightness and also to house the mechanical apparatus.

One noted French company is that of Roullet and DeCamp (founded in 1865, Paris, France). Roullet and DeCamp are particularly noted for award-winning walking and mechanical dolls. The firm also manufactured key-wound bears covered with real fur in the early 1900s. The identifying features on these bears is the large key with the initials R. D.

Using a method similarly found in fine old clocks, mechanical bears work on the principle of the spring as the driving power. In most cases, music was produced by winding a key. A true automaton (after its initial winding) works totally on its own, with outside help.

In walking, growling bears, for instance, a key-wound mechanism activates a cam. This cam then pushes a lever which squeezes the bellows causing the bear to growl. In this type of toy, the turning cam operates leg movement so the bear walks five steps, growls, walks another five steps, growls again and so on until the winding has run down.

In the case of trapeze bears, the inner spring is wound by twisting the arm round and round.

Nodding bears use levers and weights to make their heads move up and down.

A particularly intricate automated bear was the drinking bear which incorporates a rubber tube extending up one arm, continuing across the back and then down the other arm to a pewter bottle. When liquid is poured into the bottle, the bear seems to drink it down by lifting the cup. Gravity keeps the liquid flowing back into the bottle.

Due to the time and materials involved creating these museum quality pieces, the cost became prohibitive. New methods and less expensive materials were invented.

Manufacturers economized with recycled materials, that could easily be stamped out or cut. Fewer parts were used with simplified assembling methods, such as tabs and holes that could be joined either by hand or easily soldered.

New types of ingenious mechanisms accomplished more complex results with minimum means.

Despite their rather frail appearance, these mechanical toys were more durable than they looked and many have survived to take honored positions in wonderful collections today.

ABOVE LEFT: *Illustration 368.* Unknown French Manufacturer. c.1890. 14½in (36.9cm) high, 13½in (34.3cm) long, 7in (19.1cm) wide. When porcelain handle is turned, Punch and Judy turn their bisque heads as the white "real fur" covered bear cranks the Hurdy Gurdy which in turn activates the black wool covered poodle causing him to twirl around to the sound of the music. The framework is made of papier mâché and cardboard. *Courtesy Volpp Collection.*

ABOVE RIGHT: *Illustration 369.* Manufacturer unknown. c.1900. 20in (50.8cm); dark brown "real fur" covers papier mâché body; carved wooden hands, feet, nose and mouth; felt tongue; glass eyes; bear permanently stands on velvet covered wooden base; key wind chain driven mechanism; on and off lever. Condition: Mint. Comments: Rare. Action: Head turns towards cigarette to inhale; smoke travels through rubber tube concealed in arm holding cigarette which is attached to the inside of the nose causing smoke to be exhaled through the nostrils as head turns to the front. The resemblance to a real bear was very typical of the bears that were manufactured before the Teddy Bear. Possibly manufactured by Roullet and DeCamp of Paris. *Author's collection.*

RIGHT: *Illustration 370.* Manufacturer unknown. c.1900. 14in (35.6cm); dark brown "real fur" covers papier mâché body; carved wooden feet, paws, mouth; felt tongue; glass eyes; wire muzzle; key wind chain driven mechanism; on and off lever. Condition: Mint. Comments: Rare. Action: Head moves from side to side as mouth opens and closes; one hand beats the drum and the other clangs the cymbals. The same manufacturer made several versions of this bear playing different instruments. Note: the fierce realistic looking expression, characteristic of the early bears made before the Teddy Bear. Possibly manufactured by Roullet and DeCamp of Paris. *Author's collection.*

OPPOSITE PAGE: *Illustration 367.* Moses Kohnstam "Moko." German. c.1928. 12in (30.5cm); clown has papier mâché head; metal body; clockwork mechanism concealed in tin hurdy gurdy. 5in (12.7cm); gold mohair Teddy Bear. Action: Key wind clockwork mechanism causes clown to crank musical hurdy gurdy as Teddy Bear revolves to the sound of the music. Condition: Excellent. Comments: Rare. *Courtesy Volpp Collection.*

ABOVE LEFT: *Illustration 371.* Drinking Bear. Roullet and DeCamp (R.D.). French. c.1900. 15in (38.1cm); dark brown and white rabbit fur; glass eyes; unjointed. Condition: Mint. Comments: Rare. Key wind mechanism. Action: Water is poured into cup; as arm raises to drink the water flows down rubber tube concealed in arm; tube continues across the back, down to the other arm, refilling the pewter bottle. *Courtesy Helen Sieverling.*

ABOVE RIGHT: *Illustration 372.* Mechanical Polar Bear. c.1890. 18in (45.7cm); papier mâché body covered with real white fur; brown glass eyes; key-wound clockwork mechanism encased in body; white papier mâché iceberg. Condition: Excellent. Comments: Rare. Action: The bear's mouth opens and shuts resembling a breathing movement as he nods his head. *Courtesy Helen Sieverling.*

BELOW LEFT: *Illustration 373.* Nodding-breathing bear. c.1910. 22in (55.9cm) long; brown fur covers papier mâché body; brown glass eyes; key-wound clockwork mechanism encased in body. Condition: Excellent. Comments: Rare. Action: When wound with key the bear's head will continuously nod while opening and closing his mouth as if breathing for 6 to 8 hours. However, this action may be halted by lightly touching the bear's head. *Courtesy Helen Sieverling.*

BELOW RIGHT: *Illustration 374.* Bell-ringing mechanical bear. c.1900. 15in (38.1cm); real brown fur covers papier mâché body; carved wooden paws and feet; key-wound clockwork mechanism encased in body; carved bone teeth; brown glass eyes. Condition: Good. Comments: Rare. Action: When wound with the key, the bear turns his head from side to side as he raises his right arm and strikes the brass bell. Possibly manufactured by Roullet and DeCamp of Paris. *Courtesy Helen Sieverling.*

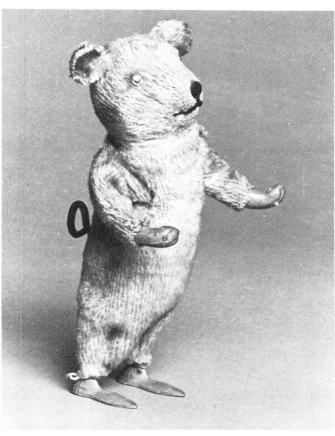

ABOVE LEFT: *Illustration 375.* Drinking Bear. c.1900. 14in (35.6cm); papier mâché body covered with white fur; key-wind mechanism encased in body; carved wooden paws and feet; pewter cup and bottle. Condition: Excellent. Comments: Rare. Action: When activated bear raises bottle and pours liquid into the cup, he then raises to drink. The liquid flows back through the rubber tube in the arm attached to cup, continues through the body, and re-enters the bottle through the other arm, ready to start the drinking action once again. *Courtesy Helen Sieverling.*

ABOVE MIDDLE: *Illustration 376.* Bike riding bear. c.1948. 5in (12.7cm) high; gold mohair covers metal (tab jointed construction) jointed body. The three wheel bike has key-wind mechanism. Condition: Excellent. Comments: Printed on the three-wheeler are the words "U.S. Zone, Germany." Action: When activated, the bike goes around in circles. *Courtesy Helen Sieverling.*

ABOVE RIGHT: *Illustration 377.* Climbing Bear. F.M. System. French. c.1910. Bear is 8in (20.3cm); bear has metal frame assembled with tabs and covered with white wool material. Key wound mechanism. Condition: Mint. Comments: Inexpensive construction. Action: Bear climbs to top of ladder by means of metal paws gripping each rung of the ladder. Markings on base of ladder read "F.M. System B^te S.G.D.G. France Et. Etranger." *Author's collection.*

LEFT: *Illustration 378.* Manufacturer unknown. c.1930. 7in (17.8cm); gold wool material covers metal frame; glass eyes; green painted metal feet and paws; plastic nose; key wound mechanism. Condition: Excellent. Comments: Inexpensive construction of metal frame assembled with tabs. Action: Bear dances and rocks from side to side. *Author's collection.*

RIGHT: *Illustration 379.* Manufacturer unknown. "Musical." c.1900. 11in (27.9cm); brown burlap covers unjointed body; shoe button eyes; black leather muzzle with chain attached to wooden staff; musical movement encased in wooden box. Condition: Excellent. Comments: Rare. Sound is produced by cranking small wooden handle on left side of box. *Courtesy Celia Sawyer. Photography by Ronald L. Sawyer.*

Japanese Battery-Operated Bears

During the 1950s and 1960s, the Japanese became the leaders in the automated tin toy industry. Up until this time, they had manufactured cheap copies of foreign designs. With World War II behind them the technically oriented culture began to rebuild their industrial strength. The next 20 years came to be known as the "Golden Age of the Battery-Operated Toy" for the Japanese.

Because of the continuing popularity of the Teddy Bear and the way they simulate human activities in every conceivable way, they were a natural subject in many variations of the battery-operated toys. The first wind-up clockwork and friction drive mechanical bears (severely limited in running time) were soon replaced by the most ingenious automatons, with small continuously running electric motors. A battery-driven motor was the source of power for the numerous actions of the unequalled toys.

Approximately 95 percent of the battery-operated toys sold in America and Europe came from Japan. With their labor costs far lower than their German and American competitors, and their innovative creations, the Japanese invaded the toy industry causing many foreign toy companies to go out of business.

War-time machinery tin now was recycled to supply the growing Japanese toy industry.

In the late 1940s, the first versions used only one D-cell battery. The toy was made from celluloid and tin. Due to its highly flammable nature, celluloid was outlawed and replaced by plastic.

Unlike other collectibles the individual manufacturer's themselves do not have too much bearing on the value or rarity of the battery-operated toys.

Some of the most well-known are Cragstan, ElectroToy, Alps, Linemar and Marx. Many manufacturers are identified only by initials or single letters. T-N is the trademark used by Normura Toy, Ltd., founded in 1923, and the Masutoku Toy Factory, founded in 1924 (later the Masudaya Toy Company), used the letter M. T. (Modern Toy) as their trademark.

Value and collectible desirability of these original toys is based on many criteria. The main ones are condition, the amount of separate actions, and the bear's original box.

Unfortunately, over the years, from mistreatment and lack of care, batteries corroded in the toys. Bears that used water for their activities not only rusted beyond repair, but the rubber hoses and bellows hardened and cracked. One of the worst causes of damages to the toy was the attempts made to interfere and stop the bear during its cycle. The delicate, intricate gears, mechanism and tiny wires were camouflaged with plush and tin. They would easily break or come loose with over-play. So, finding a mechanical bear in mint condition is indeed rare.

The original box not only increases the bear's value by approximately 10 percent, but important information printed on the box describes the bear's abilities and appearance. This enables you to discern if your bear is complete and has all his parts and facilities.

The more movable actions, the more valuable the bear. Some rare toys have over three actions.

These fascinating creatures that come alive and personify carpenters, blacksmiths, musicians and clowns, with just a small battery, are fast becoming high on the list of popular collector's items today.

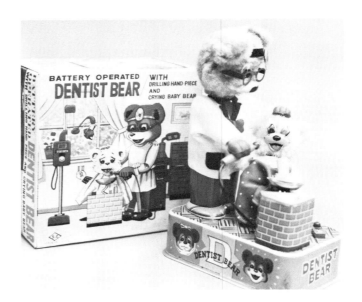

Illustration 380. (Left) A. 1. "Blacksmith Bear." c.1950. 9in (22.9cm); battery-operated; black plush bear on tin base holds a horseshoe over a forge; he then moves it across to his anvil where he strikes it with his mallet. The anvil, forge and bears eyes light up while in motion. Condition: Mint in box. (Right) T.N. "Bear the Shoemaker." c.1950. 9in (22.9cm); battery-operated; black plush bear on tin base hammers on a boot as he shakes his head and smokes a pipe. Condition: Mint. *Courtesy Sandy Madden.*

Illustration 381. S & E Co., "Dentist Bear." c.1950. 9½" (24.2cm) tall; 6¾in (17.2cm) long; battery-operated; seven actions; dentist, light brown plush; patient, white plush; tin base. Dentist's head moves as he drills on the little bear. When he stops he pushes his young patient's head forward to expectorate (drill lights up). Condition: Mint in box. Comments. Rare. *Courtesy Sandy Madden.*

Illustration 382. San Co., "Shooting Bear." c.1950. 9½in (24.2cm); battery-operated; remote controlled; five actions; gray plush and tin bear. His eyes light up, he walks forward, lifts his gun, closes one eye and takes aim; then he shoots and smoke appears from end of barrel. Condition: Mint. Comments: Very rare. *Courtesy Sandy Madden.*

Illustration 383. Y. Co., "Teddy the Artist." c.1950. 8½in (21.6cm); battery-operated; three actions; cinnamon plush bear on tin base. He moves his head and closes his eyes; as he draws any one of the nine different interchangeable picture templets (templets are included). Condition: Mint. Comments: Rare. *Courtesy Sandy Madden.*

Illustration 384. Kramer "Accordion Bear." c.1950. 10in (25.4cm); battery-operated; remote controlled; black plush and tin bear; eyes light up as he sways back and forth playing his accordion. The remote control is contained in the microphone. Condition: Mint in box. Comments: Very rare. *Courtesy Sandy Madden.*

Illustration 385. M-T Co., "Bear — The Cashier." c.1950. 7½in (19.1cm); battery-operated; brown plush bear on tin base; five actions. The bear continuously moves the items on the conveyer belt while ringing them up on the cash register. Condition: Mint. Comments: Rare. *Courtesy Sandy Madden.*

Illustration 386. Alps Co., "The Busy Housekeeper." c.1950. 8½in (21.6cm); battery-operated; four actions; brown plush bear moves back and forth turning her head while vacuuming. Condition: Mint. Comments: Several versions in this series including upright and canister vacuums. *Courtesy Sandy Madden.*

Illustration 387. S & E Co., "Popcorn Vendor." c.1960. 8in (20.3cm) high; 7in (17.8cm) long; battery-operated; six actions; black plush bear pedals his tin cart as he sways from side to side. The umbrella spins as the popcorn pops. Condition: Mint. Comments: Rare. *Courtesy Sandy Madden.*

Illustration 388. (Left) Alps Co., "Barney Bear Drummer." c.1950. 11in (27.9cm); battery-operated; five actions; remote controlled; dark brown plush bear's eyes light up while beating his drum as he walks and turns. Condition: Mint. (Center) "Bruno the Accordion Bear." c.1950. 11in (27.9cm); battery-operated; remote controlled; beige plush bear's eyes light up as he dances sideways and plays his accordion. Condition: Mint. (Right) "Musical Marching Bear." c.1950. 11in (27.9cm); battery-operated; remote controlled; brown plush bear toots his tin horn as he beats his drum. Condition: Mint. *Courtesy Sandy Madden.*

Illustration 389. Unknown manufacturer. "Musical." c.,1920. 19in (48.3cm); bright gold mohair; glass eyes; jointed arms and legs; swivel head; excelsior stuffing; squeeze type bellows encased in body. Condition: Mint. Comments: Rare. Very long narrow snout giving an almost fox-like appearance. Bellows produce music when left side of bear is squeezed. Music Box. Swiss. c.1925. 2½in (6.4cm) diameter; wooden box with colored lithograph picture, porcelain crank turns to produce music. *Author's collection.*

Illustration 390. Unknown manufacturer "Musical." c.1930. 12in (30.5cm); long pale beige silky mohair; glass eyes; jointed arms and legs; swivel heads; excelsior stuffing; squeeze type bellows concealed in bodies. Condition: Good. Comments: Rare. Bellows produces music when tummy is squeezed. Clothes not original. (A 1928 issue of *Toy World* reported Helvetic exclusively manufacturing Teddy Bears with squeeze-operated music boxes encased within the bodies.) *Courtesy Volpp Collection.*

ABOVE LEFT: *Illustration 391.* Gebrüder Süssenguth (German) "Peter." c.1925. 14in (35.6cm); gray mohair varigated with black; glass googlie eyes; jointed arms and legs; swivel head; carved teeth and tongue; excelsior stuffing. Condition: Mint. Comments: Rare. When head is turned, eyes and tongue move from side to side. This bear also was made in brown and gold (gold being the rarest color). A large percentage came with wooden eyes. The original tag reads "Peter, Ges. Gesch. (legally protected) Nr. 895257." He came in a box with a label illustrating the bear with the words "Neuheit (novelty) Bar Wei Lebend (Bear most nature-like finish)." The factory Gebrüder Süssenguth was in Neustadt near Coburg, Thuringia, Germany. A stock of these bears were discovered in an old closed-down toy shop in Germany, in 1976. It is thought because of their fierce life-like expressions they terrified young children and never sold. *Author's collection.*

BOTTOM LEFT: *Illustration 392.* Gebrüder Süssenguth (German). "Peter." c.1925. 14in (35.6cm); brown mohair varigated with light beige; glass googlie eyes; jointed arms and legs; swivel head; carved teeth and tongue; excelsior stuffing. Condition: Mint. Comments: Rare. When head is turned, eyes and tongue move from side to side. This same bear also came with wooden eyes, the glass are the rarest, however. The original tag reads "Peter, Ges. Gesch." (legally protected) Nr. 895257. Both bears have their original boxes which are the same as the box in *Illustration 391. Courtesy Beverly Port.*

ABOVE RIGHT: *Illustration 393.* Manufacturer unknown. c.1930. 15in (38.1cm); honey colored light mohair; glass eyes; jointed arms and legs; swivel head; kapok stuffing in body; head stuffed with excelsior; rexine pads. Condition: Good. Comments: Rare. Lever at back of head opens and closes mouth when moved up and down. *Courtesy Volpp Collection.*

BOTTOM RIGHT: *Illustration 394.* Manufacturer unknown. "Laughing Bear." c.1915. 17in (43.2cm); beige mohair; glass eyes; jointed arms and legs; swivel head; excelsior stuffing. Condition: Excellent. Comments: Rare. (A similar version to the Roosevelt Laughing Bear in *Illustration 212.*) Action: When stomach is squeezed the wooden mouth opens and closes revealing pointed teeth. Note the unusually large ears and feet. *Courtesy Celia Sawyer.*

Illustrations 395, 396 & 397: Louis S. Schiffer. "Two Face Bear." 1914. 17in (43.2cm); gold mohair; jointed arms and legs; swivel head; excelsior stuffing. Teddy Bear has shoe button eyes. Bisque doll's face is German with glass eyes. Condition: Mint. Comments: Extremely rare. Head swivels to change faces. Patent date June 9, 1914. *Courtesy Beverly Port.*

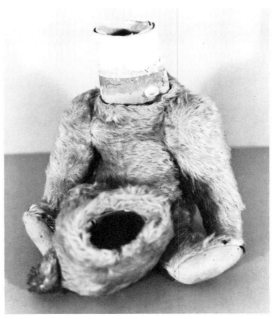

ABOVE LEFT: *Illustration 398.* Manufacturer unknown. "Sleeping Bear." c.1926. 14in (35.6cm); deep rust cotton plush; wooden eyes with metal rims; jointed arms and legs; swivel head; excelsior stuffing. Condition: Good. Comments: Eyes will close when bear is laid on his back. *Courtesy Volpp Collection.*

TOP RIGHT & MIDDLE: *Illustrations 399 & 400.* Manufacturer unknown. Candy Container. c.1907. 14in (35.6cm); grey mohair; shoe button eyes; jointed arms and legs; swivel removable head; excelsior stuffing. Condition: Excellent. Comments: Rare. Removing the cardboard lined head reveals the cardboard tube that contains the candy. *Courtesy Kathy George.*

LEFT: *Illustration 401.* Unknown manufacturer. Bear in Cage. c.1910. Wooden cage 7in (17.8cm) high x 8in (20.3cm) long; bear on all fours. Short gold bristle type mohair; unjointed head and body; glass eyes. Condition: Excellent. Comments: Rare. Action: When door is opened bear springs out and squeeks. *Courtesy Celia Sawyer.*

Chapter Seven

The Beauty Of Tomorrow's Antique Bears

An important impact on the popularity and growth of the Teddy Bear market are the talented efforts of a new breed of handmade bear artists.

Early antique bears are increasingly difficult to find. And when discovered, these older bears are often extremely expensive. With a deep affection and love for these little furry fellows, more and more collectors choose to seek out the excellent workmanship, individuality and quality of today's handmade bears.

Of course, there are plenty of people for whom making Teddy Bears remains a delightful hobby. In fact, most of the bear artists I know began their careers just as a pleasurable pastime. Even Margarete Steiff never intended to market her soft animals for profit. She, and her modern day emulators, created these toys as gifts for the children in their life. Now, this joyous avocation has turned into a business for many.

For some, bear making has remained a self-contained small cottage industry. For others it has grown into a large, money-making business with assistants, marketing representatives and wide recognition.

Southern California is known for its excellent climate, Disneyland, freeways, Hollywood and pretty women. Among Teddy Bear aficiandos, this part of the country is quickly gaining recognition for producing some of the best in a new form of folk art — Teddy Bears.

Many people make Teddy Bears, but most of the primary bear artists live in Southern California. I feel fortunate to live nearby and know most of these talented people who are creating tomorrow's antique bears. It is interesting to realize that this new world of Teddy Bear artists evolved here in America.

Pat Carriker (Pat C. Bears)

Pat Carriker is a prime example of maintaining bear making as a small cottage industry. Her bear world is small in two ways.

First, most of her creations measure no more than 2¼in (5.7cm). Secondly, Pat's love for her home, family and pleasurable hobby keeps this creative artist from going "big time." She's never exhibited at a show, nor advertised. In fact, you almost have to be a detective to find where she lives.

When I first approached Pat to be part of this section on bear artists she claimed "there's nothing really special about me." I think she's wrong. Only a unique artist like Pat has both the patience and talent to produce such wonderful "little people."

This is her story.

"Even as a little girl in Sacramento, California, I loved to sew tiny doll clothes. When I left school, however, I decided to work in a local bank with people I knew.

"Later, when I married, I spent many a happy hour making clothes for my little girl and her dolls. Delicate, intricate work still holds special rewards for me.

"As time went on, I began making Christmas ornaments and miniature stuffed dolls including a Santa and Mrs. Claus.

"The ornaments brought many requests from friends. One of those requests was for a Teddy Bear ornament.

"Up until this time, the only contact I'd had with a Teddy Bear was watching my younger brother play with his. He and that bear were so inseparable that the poor, furry toy finally disintegrated. It came to the point my mother couldn't stand to see her son carrying around this awful piece of fur anymore, so she conveniently pretended it was lost and replaced it with a brand new bear.

"It turned out my Teddy Bear ornament worked out very well. I went on to designing other bears in small sizes.

"Now, with eighteen bears in my line, people seem to love The Teddy Bear Family the most. This tiny foursome consists of a distinguished-looking Papa Bear (5in [12.7cm]), a prim and proper Mama Bear (4½ [11.5cm]), a mischievous Little Boy Bear (3½in [8.9cm]) and a tiny Baby Bear (2½in [6.4cm]). All are jointed except for their heads.

"Since it's difficult to find the right material for the little guys, I had to dye the fabric myself. This way I get just the shaded color I want. Keeping this craft a hobby allows me to keep on enjoying the creation of new bears."

Illustration 402. Pat Carriker, surrounded by materials, ribbons, and her own collection of Teddy Bears and dolls.

Illustration 403. Finished products of beautiful little Teddies, patiently waiting to see who their new parents will be.

Illustration 404. All five of these Pat C. Bears are 2¼in (5.8cm) tall and are made in caramel cotton velour. The arms and legs are jointed and the head is stationary. Tiny black beads are used for eyes; faces are hand-embroidered.

ABOVE: *Illustration 405.* Pat C. Bears "Little Family." (Left) "Mama Bear." 4½in (11.5cm); caramel cotton velour; jointed arms and legs; stationary head; eyes are black beads; hand-embroidered face; dressed in gray dress with white lace trim; straw hat with red flowers on brim. (Center) "Baby Bear." 2½in (6.4cm); caramel cotton velour; jointed arms and legs; stationary head; eyes are black beads; hand-embroidered face; dressed in cream lace dress and hat with pale pink rosette. (Right) "Papa Bear." 5in (12.7cm); caramel cotton velour; jointed arms and legs; stationary head; eyes are black beads; hand-embroidered face; dressed in white shirt and bow tie; red velvet vest and black jacket. (Standing) "Little Boy." 3½in (8.9cm); caramel cotton velour; jointed arms and legs; stationary head; eyes are black beads; hand-embroidered face; dressed in red sweater with white collar and black tie; beige cap.

BELOW: *Illustration 406.* Pat C. Bears. "Mama Bear." 4½in (11.5cm); light beige cotton velour; jointed arms and legs; stationary head; eyes are black beads; hand-embroidered face; cream lace dress. "Baby Bear." 2½in (6.4cm); light beige velour; jointed arms and legs; stationary head; eyes are black beads; hand-embroidered face; dressed in beige lace dress and bonnet.

Flore Emory (Flore Bears)

If you were to imagine a home where bears live, it would be Flore and Neil Emory's old-fashioned country farmhouse, nestled in the woods of rural Fallbrook in California's San Diego County.

The first time I drove down the country lane leading to their charming, rustic, rambling home, I knew I was in fairyland. The abundantly blooming wild flowers could not hide the little bunnies as they hopped in and out of hollow logs along the way. And then, in the clearing, surrounded by giant old oak trees, was the dream home the Emory's constructed themselves. The used lumber, the finely handcrafted window panes, the natural combination of the land and homesite all gave the feeling that the place had been there forever and ever.

I felt like Goldilocks when Flore opened the door to greet me. The entire interior decor of her home creates an ambiance of days gone by. The country antiques, handmade quilts and primitive furniture all add to the idea that time has stood still here since the early 1900s.

BELOW *Illustration 407.* Flore Emory's rustic country home is just the sort of place bears would live.

Three fireplaces take the place of central heating. My favorite is a huge hearth reminiscent of one used by pioneer women long before we discovered convenience foods and microwave ovens. It is here, in front of a cozy fire, that Flore spends many an evening putting the finishing touches on her recreated antique bears.

In Flore's home, there are bears everywhere. They line the stairs and play in the loft overlooking the dining room. They're propped up in wagons and sit snuggly in corners. They greet you in bathrooms and bedrooms, on the front porch and in trees — there is no doubt this is their home.

Flore's workroom is a friendly, slightly haphazard nook behind her bedroom. It is here her bears are born.

As she tells it:

"I have thirteen grandchildren. Finding gifts for them all is no easy task. I've always enjoyed making gifts for my family and friends, so I started making Teddy Bears for the children.

"They loved them!

BELOW: *Illustration 408.* Flore's "Old Woman in a Shoe." 26in (66cm) high; 24in (61cm) long. A wire frame covered with papier mâché forms the shoe. Two kittens play on top of the shake roof. The shoe has a battery that lights up the interior. Peeking through the upstairs bedroom window you can see Mama Bear showing Papa how to change Baby Bear's diaper. Bears (2½in [6.4cm]) to 7in [17.8cm]) play around the garden while the old woman happily watches from her rocking chair.

Illustration 410. Flore's Bumble Bear. 14in (35.6cm); beige acrylic fur; body is brown, black and gold striped; shoe button type eyes; jointed arms and legs; swivel head; yellow felt wings; hand-embroidered face.

Illustration 409. Flore's Mailbear and Mailbearess. 14in (35.6cm); beige acrylic fur; shoe button type eyes; jointed arms and legs; swivel head; hand-embroidered face. Clothes made from an original mailman's outfit and designed to represent their uniforms as closely as possible.

"Pretty soon the grown-ups expressed an interest in the bears as well. So I sewed some bears for them too.

"One day, my daughter-in-law showed me a handsome old Teddy she inherited from her grandfather. I decided to try to see if that early look could be captured in my bears.

"Now people tell me that my bears look just like the original old ones. Duplicating this authentic style, the early Steiff design with the hump and long arms, still allows my bears to become individuals. The Jester, Uncle Sam, Pilgrims and a Rough Rider have all come from the basic bear design.

"I'm never happier than when I'm making bears. I just love it!

"At first, my bears were unmarked, so you may own one without even knowing it.

"By 1979, I was amazed to find orders coming in from all over America. The popularity of my jointed bears was heartwarming; but creating new challenges still brings me great satisfaction. Now Flore Bears range from 3in (7.6cm) to 41in (101.6cm)...there are bears on wheels... fireman bears...policeman bears...even convict bears.

"Sometimes in the middle of the night a new idea will strike me. My husband's finally become used to my midnight brainstorms when I wake up and write down the concept on a pad next to our bed. Staying up 'til 3 o'clock in the morning working on a new project is not unusual either.

"Neil makes the wheels for the roller bears, so he's in on the act too.

"Until I met Linda, personally appearing with my work at shows was not something I did. Linda talked me into exhibiting at her first Teddy Bear Show. She felt it would be good for me to enjoy the feelings and responses of those who purchase bears. I must admit it was a thrill to experience the joy and satisfaction one of my bears gives another person.

"Bears always make me so happy. It's just a pleasure to share that happiness with others."

ABOVE: *Illustration 411.* (Left) Flore's Convict. 15in (38.1cm); brown acrylic fur; natural brown eyes; jointed arms and legs; swivel head; hand-embroidered face. Outfit is white and black stripe mattress ticking; black felt boots; metal chain and wooden ball. (Right) Policeman. 15in (38.1cm); beige acrylic fur; natural brown eyes; jointed arms and legs; swivel head; hand-embroidered face. Outfit is heavyweight navy blue wool suit; navy blue felt hat; wooden Billie Club.

RIGHT: *Illustration 412.* Flore's Possums. "Mama." 10in (25.4cm); short white acrylic fur; white felt tail and ears; shoe button type eyes; jointed arms and legs; swivel head; shaved nose; hand-embroidered face; wearing antique lace hat. "Papa." 12in (30.5cm); short white acrylic fur; white felt tail and ears; shoe button type eyes; jointed arms and legs; swivel head; shaved nose; hand-embroidered face; dressed in black tuxedo, white shirt and black bow tie. "Baby." 7in (17.8cm); short white acrylic fur; white felt tail and ears; shoe button type eyes; jointed arms and legs; swivel head; shaved nose; hand-embroidered face; antique ribbon bow.

Colleen Tipton (Collee Bears)

I'm proud to say this talented bear maker is my step-daughter. Colleen never had her father's interest in collecting. Before I began my love affair with the Teddy Bear, dolls were my primary hobby. Colleen shared very little enthusiasm for my collection.

I'd been collecting bears for several years when Colleen suddenly showed an interest in them. I started giving her Teddy Bears for special occasions.

The first bear Colleen ever made was a Christmas present for me. It brought tears to my eyes. Of course, now she'd like me to get rid of him because he's not very good compared to the sought-after Collee Bears that have become a profitable business for her. But I could never part with him.

"Linda calls me 'a bit of tomboy!' It's true in a way. My father gave me 'Joker,' a black and white pony when I was twelve and from that time on, all I wanted to do was ride horses.

"I've always been good with my hands. In fact I was a dental assistant for seven years. Needlework was always a craft I enjoyed.

"When Linda introduced me to Teddy Bears, I took to them right away. When she suggested I try to make my own bear, I went for it.

"The first attempt at making a bear is not easy. We all still laugh at my first bear's difficulty in sitting up. But, after awhile I managed to get it all together.

"All of my bears are jointed and they measure from 10in (25.4cm) to 30in (76.2cm). One of my most popular creations is a climbing bear. He's pretty little (just 3in [7.6cm]) and attached to two sticks. My husband makes all the movable parts. When you move the sticks up and down the little bear does tricks. My son Loren gets a big kick out of that one.

"I guess my simple, no frills attitude still shows in my line of bears. I like to dress them in Levi's®, or down home outfits. My bears are sturdy creatures who'd rather shoot slingshots and go fishing than go to fancy dress balls. So far I've named them all after members of the family.

"Making a bear today is not much different than it was so many years ago. In fact, the way we do it by hand is much the same as it was originally and the way it is still done in even the big factories."

Fabrics

"Many types of fabrics are suitable for making Teddy Bears. It all depends on the kind of look you want to achieve. The mohair originally used for early bears is beautiful, but very expensive and hard to locate. A large percentage of Teddy Bear makers, including myself, get good results from acrylic fur, which comes in an array of colors and is available in short or long pile. It is washable and feels very good. Some acrylics do have a tendency to stretch. This may be a real problem when finally stuffing the bear. Be careful that it doesn't distort the shape of the head. Be sure to watch out for this situation.

"A variety of other fabrics are used in modern day Teddy Bear making: *Dralon* (an acrylic staple and tow made in a wide range of deniers primarily for knitting, produced by Bayer, G.G., West Germany). *Jersey* (originally made of wool but now also made of worsted, cotton, silk, man-made fibers or a combination of fibers; its principal distinction is that it has no distinct rib. It was first manufactured on the island of Jersey, off the English coast). *Polyester Fiber* (a crease-resistant, quick drying and shape retaining fabric in which the fiber-forming substance is any long-chain, synthetic polymer composed of at least 85% of an ester). *Polyurethane Fiber* (a synthetic fiber produced in Germany during World War II with high strength and low moisture absorption). *Rayon* (a generic term for man-made fibers composed of regenerated cellulose derived from trees, cotton and woody plants; it was originally called 'artifical silk,' 'wood silk,' and 'glos'); and *Velour* (a French word meaning velvet derived from the Latin *vellosus,* meaning hairy).

Illustration 414. Collee Climbing Bear. 8in (20.3cm): brown polyester velour; eyes are black beds; jointed arms and legs; swivel head; hand-embroidered face; ruffle collar. Bear does stunts on 16in (40.6cm) wooden stick. The original concept by William Tipton.

Illustration 413. Collee Bear. 20in (50.8cm); gold acrylic fur; natural brown eyes; jointed arms and legs; swivel head; shaved nose; hand-embroidered face. Comments: Colleen's original design won first place in the Handmade Bear Competition at Bob and Rebecca Collin's 1st Great Western Teddy Bear Show and Gathering, San Jose, California, 1983.

ABOVE LEFT: *Illustration 415.* Collee Junior. 12in (30.5cm); short beige acrylic fur; shoe button-type eyes; jointed arms and legs; swivel head; hand-embroidered face; old Levi® overalls with fishing fly and bandanna in pocket; carries twig fishing pole. 1984 limited edition of 125. Numbered on paw.

BELOW LEFT: *Illustration 416.* Collee Wabbits. 14in (35.6cm); white acrylic fur; natural brown eyes; jointed arms; stationary legs; swivel head; hand-embroidered face. Boys shoes and trousers are form fitting and cannot be removed. Girls pinafore is removable.

ABOVE RIGHT: *Illustration 417.* Collee Frenzel. 16in (40.6cm); cream colored acrylic fur; natural brown eyes; jointed arms and legs; swivel head; reddish-brown hand-embroidered face and claws; olive green lederhosen; holding edelweiss in paw. 1985 limited edition of 85.

RIGHT: *Illustration 418.* Collee Robin Hood. 14in (35.6cm); gray acrylic fur; shoe button type eyes; jointed arms and legs; swivel head; hand-embroidered face; brown velveteen hat, belt and boots; green velour vest; carrying a wooden bow across chest; holds wooden arrow in paw. 1985 limited edition of 100.

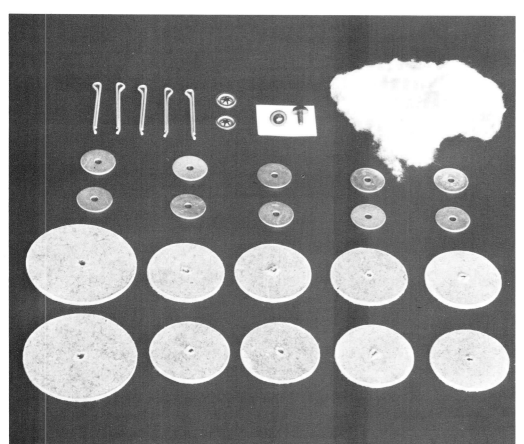

Colleen Tipton's Bear Making Method

LEFT: *Illustration 419.* Bear making supplies (from top left hand corner): 5 metal cotter pins; 1 pair washers for eyes; 1 pair acrylic safety eyes; sample of polyester fiber fill used for stuffing; 10 metal washers to reinforce cotter pins; 8 small wooden disks used for limb joints; 2 large wooden disks for head joint.

BELOW LEFT: *Illustration 420.* Tools: long nose pliers; sharp scissors; long needle used for sewing eyes (if using shoe button eyes); embroidery needle; wooden dowels for stuffing.

BELOW: *Illustration 421.* Patterns: If you're only making a couple of bears, a paper pattern is sufficient. But, if you intend to use the same pattern over and over again, it's a good idea to trace it out and cut onto a more permanent material like plywood or thick cardboard. You will find this more durable and easier to work with. Be sure to mark and trace each piece of the pattern and remember to point an arrow in the direction the pattern is to be placed on the fabric.

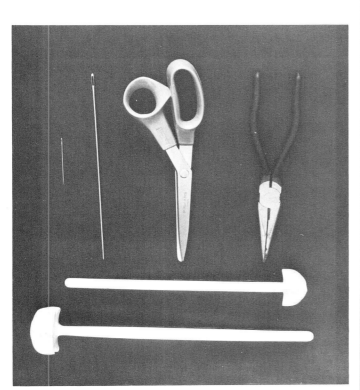

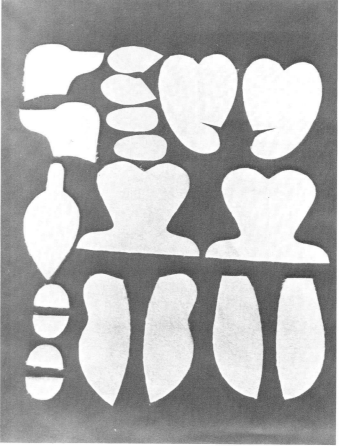

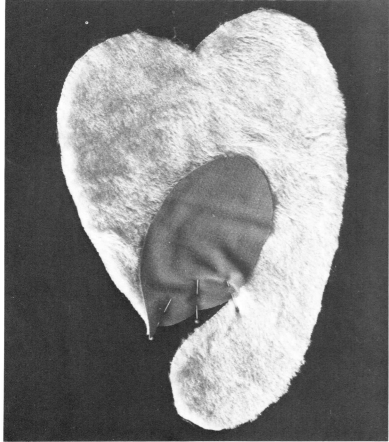

ABOVE: *Illustration 422*. Step 1. My working area is the den where there's plenty of room and I can keep an eye on my son Loren playing in the yard. First, with a felt marking pen (on the wrong side of the fabric) I trace around the entire pattern of the bear. Each limb is then carefully pinned together.

LEFT: *Illustration 423*. Step 2. (With right sides of the fabric together) I sew the paw pads to the two inner arm pieces.

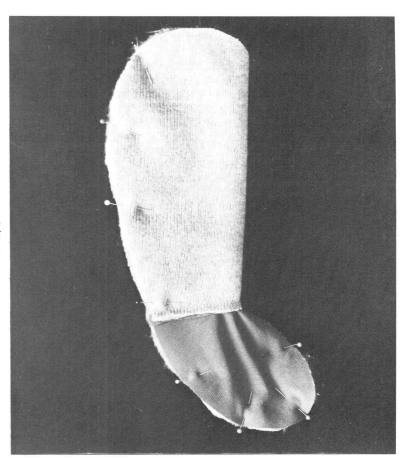

Illustration 424. Step 3. Then (with the right sides of the fabric together) I seam around the paw pads and bottom of the arm. Leave an opening at the top for stuffing and joints.

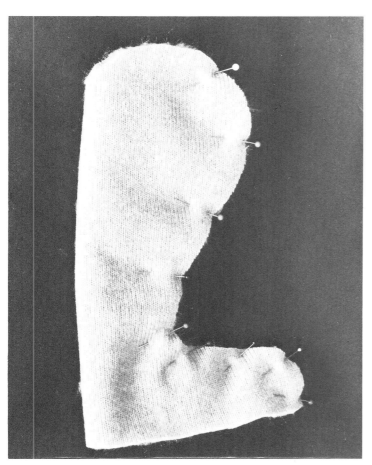

Illustration 425. Step 4. (With right sides together) seam around the legs. Leave the top open for stuffing and the bottom open for pad application.

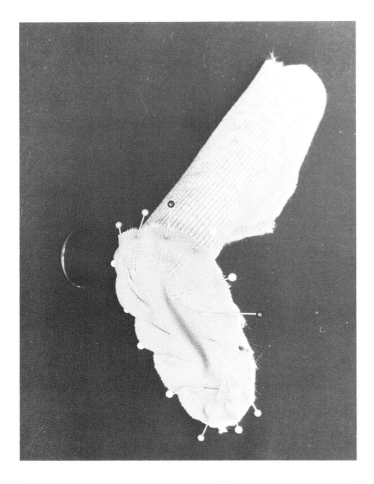

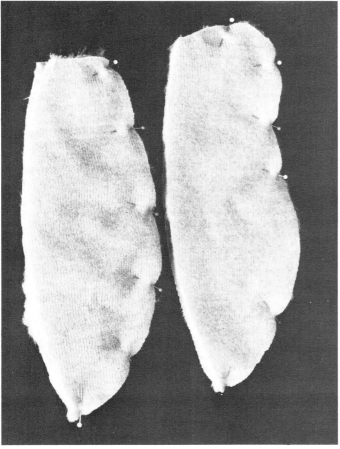

ABOVE LEFT: *Illustration 426.* Step 5. (With right sides together) carefully pin the foot pads to the bottom opening on each leg. Seam them into place.

LEFT: *Illustration 427.* Step 6. (With right sides of fabric together) sew center seams of the body front pieces and center seams of the body back pieces.

ABOVE RIGHT: *Illustration 428.* Step 7. Leave a 6in (15.2cm) opening at the body back seam.

ABOVE: *Illustration 429.* Step 8. (With right sides of fabric together) sew the two head side pieces at the chin seam.

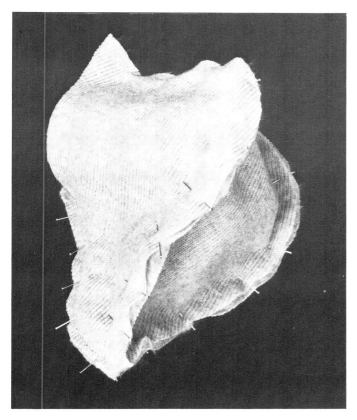

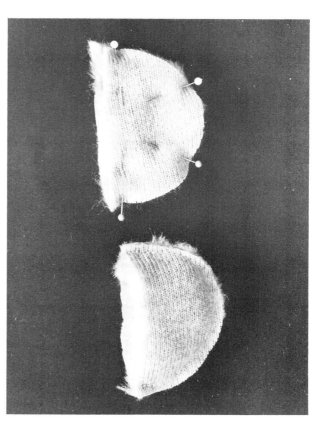

Illustration 430. Step 9. (With right sides together) pin and seam the head center in place.

Illustration 431. Step 10. (With right sides together) pin and sew each of the two ears together.

Illustration 432. I enjoy working with an old 1940 Singer Sewing machine my dad gave me one Christmas. I find it withstands the heavier work with the fur fabric more than my newer model.

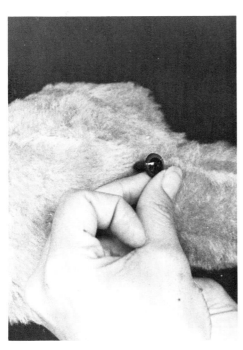

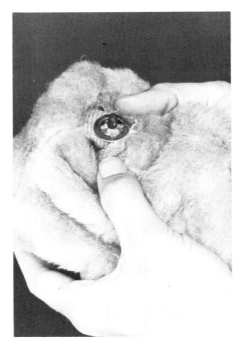

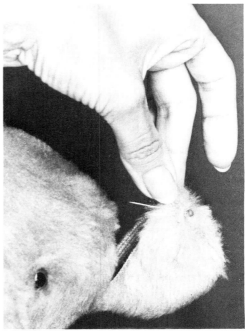

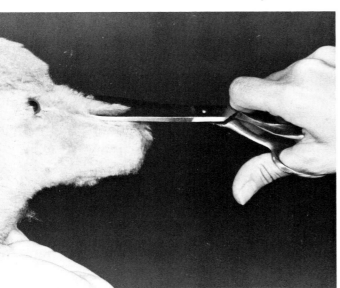

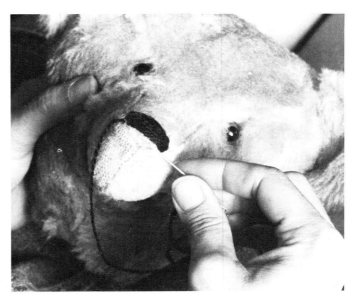

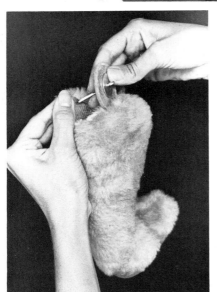

TOP LEFT: *Illustration 433*. Step 11. To be sure of the exact placement of the eyes, I stuff the head first, check the position and punch a hole through the material.

TOP MIDDLE: *Illustration 434*. Step 12. Then I unstuff the head, insert the eyes inside the fabric and (on the wrong side of the fabric) push the safety washer onto each post. Stuffing the bears firmly is really important. Not only do I get a more tailored look, but since the stuffing will soften up as time goes on, it must be packed as tightly as possible in the beginning. Stuff each limb.

MIDDLE LEFT: *Illustration 435*. Step 13. To give my bear an early and slightly worn look, I trim some of the fur around his snout.

TOP RIGHT: *Illustration 436*. Step 14. Position each ear with the ends slightly curved forward. Hand sew them in place.

ABOVE: *Illustration 437*. Step 15. The type of nose and mouth embroidered on your bear gives him his own personality. I also embroider the claws onto the pads and feet.

LEFT: *Illustration 438*. Step 16. The metal cotter pin is pushed through the metal washer and wooden disk. (On the wrong side of the fabric) I make a small hole for the cotter pin. This method is used for each limb and the head.

Divided cabinets enable you to make separate scenes and yet the overall picture can look very interesting and decorative without looking too cluttered. *Author's collection.*

A rocking chair set in a corner gives Grandpa the ideal place to tell stories of the early 1900s to his grandchildren. *Author's collection.*

OPPOSITE PAGE: An old oak school desk makes these two 25in (63.5cm) Steiff Teddy Bears look very studious. It's also fun to hunt for related Teddy Bear accessories to make your set-ups look more realistic. *Author's collection.*

OPPOSITE PAGE: Antique glass candy containers filled with colorful candy are made more tempting by the hungry looks of the Teddy Bears. *Author's collection.*

Two small Steiff bears are waiting to be bathed in an early 1900s hand-painted washstand by the beautiful Jumeau doll (26in [66cm]). All the time, the J.D. Kestner googlie (16in [40.6cm]) and Steiff bear play on the floor together. *Author's collection.*

A fireplace is the ideal spot to display your Teddy Bears. Perhaps there are a few too many bears in this particular fireplace, but because the local Teddy Bear Collectors Club was visiting, it was a special occasion. *Author's collection.*

OPPOSITE PAGE: Collecting miniatures to add to your displays can also provide much enjoyment. The colorful blue enamel ware and miniature kitchen items enliven this scene. *Courtesy Sally Cain.*

OPPOSITE PAGE: These mischievous Flore bears look very realistic getting into things they shouldn't. Flore's husband, Neil, made the cabinet from old lumber. A stained old wooden box conceals the mechanism that makes the ladder go back and forth, giving the impression the Teddy Bear at the bottom is trying to shake the little bear off the top of the ladder. The action enhances this already lifelike scene. *Author's collection.*

An antique high chair creates a domestic scene for these three early 1900s bears. The type of clothes chosen for each bear distinguishes which part they portray. *Author's collection.*

ABOVE: Pat C. Bears tiny 2¼in (5.8cm) creations also make ideal Christmas tree ornaments.

OPPOSITE PAGE: A wall hanging corner cabinet doesn't take up too much space, but it is the ideal place for small toys and bears. *Author's collection.*

Although Colleen Tipton diversifies her line of Teddy Bears with different outfits and facial expressions, she still retains the shape and characteristics of the early Steiff Teddy Bears that she herself collects.

Joanne Purpus is surrounded by her tailored-looking bears with sweet faces. Her famous Roller Bear is copyrighted.

BELOW: Linda Spiegel is encircled by many of her wonderful creations. Linda is renowned for the wide variety of Teddy Bears in her line.

Pat Rypinski (left) and Lynn West (right) proudly display some of their wonderful creations.

Flore Emory is never happier than when she makes Teddy Bears in her fantasyland-type home in the country setting of Fallbrook, California. Here a family of Flore Bears watch her put the finishing touches to the clothes of a newly born bear.

Bears and Bibs. "Teddy, King of the Toys." 24in (61cm): beige acrylic fur; natural brown eyes; jointed arms and "bent" jointed legs; hand-embroidered face; suede paws. Regally dressed in a red velvet robe with white polyester satin lining edged in gold; jeweled crown and holding a gold-leafed scepter with crystal top.

BELOW: Cheryl Lindsay constantly stays busy working in her studio. Shelves are conveniently stocked with dainty laces, ribbons and silks waiting to enhance the beautiful clothes which add the finishing touches to the successful "Elegant Fantasies" bears. "The White Rabbit" (her first rabbit creation) keeps an eye on the situation.

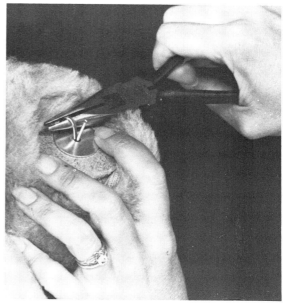

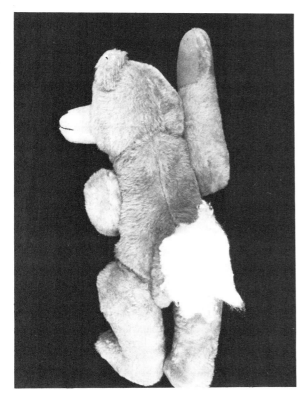

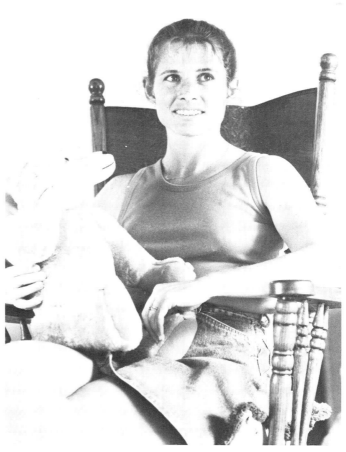

ABOVE LEFT: *Illustration 439.* Step 17. Neat hand stitching encloses the stuffing and joints of each limb and head.

ABOVE RIGHT: *Illustration 440.* Step 18. Attach the bear's arms, legs and head onto its body. Working from inside the body, turn the cotter pins that have been punched through the body and secured through another wooden disk and metal washer.

LEFT: *Illustration 441.* Step 19. All parts are firmly attached to the body. Tightly stuff the filling through the opening in back. Neatly hand sew the opening closed.

RIGHT: *Illustration 442.* The newly born Collee Bear gives Colleen a look of gratitude.

Joanne Purpus (Joanne Purpus Ltd.)

The first bear Joanne Purpus ever made was created for a nostalgic 1930s art exhibit at the Palos Verdes Art Museum near Los Angeles, California. Joanne, a teacher of every form of needlework and a custom clothes designer, was contemplating an original entry for the show when she came upon some old photos. A child herself during the 1930s, Joanne's eye was caught by a picture of her twin sister and herself holding their favorite Teddy Bears. The photo inspired her to create a 1930 Teddy Bear for her entry. It was such a tremendous success that she immediately sold all of the Teddy Bears in her exhibit — and was deluged with orders for more.

That was in 1981. Now, Joanne is renowned for her handmade Bears with "sweet faces." Her famous Roller Bear is copyrighted and was exhibited at the National History Museum (Los Angeles) American show in 1982.

Today, Joanne enjoys sharing her talents, teaching Teddy Bear making classes and presenting slide shows about "The Life of a Teddy Bear Maker."

The Life Of A Teddy Bear Maker

"In the olden days, before bear makers had their patterns and many companies had their kits, you were really on your own when it came to making Teddy Bears. Sometimes the bear came together easily; but often that step between the concept and the creation of that darling little creature meant months and months of hard work and trial and error — not to mention yards of wasted fabric. My own design took six months to perfect.

"After the pattern was finalized, came the problem of finding decent material. A bear out of an old bedsheet just doesn't give the same feeling as one covered with plush or high quality wool.

"Supplies abound now, but they didn't use to. Now it's fairly easy to find fine plushes, good quality glass eyes, felt, leather, ultra suede for paw pads and even antique shoe buttons for eyes.

"Heavy woolens are really hard to find here on the west coast. I buy woolens in short lengths from a special place and order custom colors. But this limits the size of series. It's difficult to dye yards and yards of wool in a dye pot. And even though the short pieces are dyed in the same vat with the same dye, they all come out just a tiny bit different. But that's good. Because dyed wools all have such gorgeous character.

"I used to try trotting to all the Good Will stores looking for heavy woolen coats, but that didn't work out too well even though I do try to use camel hair and good coat woolens from time to time.

"Stuffing is important too. And expensive. For wool, velvet and felt Bears, the stuffing must be the same quality doll makers use in stocking dolls. With fake fur or plush Bears, you can get by with a cheaper stuffing because under all that fur it doesn't show.

"Once all the materials are gathered, you're in for some very hard work.

"Oh, four to six of the little guys is not bad. But then you start to think big. You continue sewing the same little body; the same struggle with the paw pads; you stuff, stuff, stuff and crimp those stubborn cotter pins...then you embroider those adorable faces.

"I think this is where a lot of bear makers who use assistants go wrong. The faces on *your* bears should all look alike. They should be sweet, not sappy. When other people help it's difficult to maintain continuity with your particular design.

"And once you have your adorable little bear, which you've created with skill and caring, it's to market, to market.

"Remember, nobody cares as much about your bear as you do. So, if you're not into hiring little bear sewers, you must set aside so much time, so many days per week to sew, embroider, package, market and ship out. If you do it all yourself, there will be no huge orders coming in. The only thing to do is work at your own pace and keep a good eye on quality control.

"The next step is to figure out who is buying your little wonders? If you have a big business, you'll need a rep to push your work at gift shows, take them to shops and hustle them for you. If you don't have a rep, you have to do it yourself. You'll worry about advertising, taking the bears hither and yon, placing them in the right spot, keeping them out of shops that are too close together. After awhile, you run out of friends, neighbors and relatives to sell to; so you must think ahead.

"If you think that bear makers make big money, think again. Making bears is very time consuming and the amount of money invested for quantity supply orders can be tremendous. Shopkeepers will probably buy your bear for half of what they can sell it for themselves.

"So — with all the hassles — why do we do it? Simply because bear makers are creative and want to see their very own thing come to life. Many of us truly enjoy sewing eight hours a day. A bear maker's success really all depends on how ambitious they are.

"When you purchase a handmade bear, you are investing in a work of art. Always look at the bear's face. Would you like to have that face looking at you for a long time? If so, good. Buy it. Take it home. And love it. And remember, the creator of that wonderful creature loves it too!"

Illustration 443. Joanne Purpus carefully chooses quality woolen fabrics to give her fine looking bears the look of distinction.

Illustration 444. Joanne Purpus' famous roller bear. 14in (35.6cm) long; 14in (35.6cm) tall; finest English wool material; shoe button eyes; wooden frame and wheels.

Linda Spiegel (Bearly There Company)

Linda Spiegel made her first Bear in 1973 as a door prize for a local doll club. Her success has been overwhelming and truly shows how a small creative endeavor can grow to a full-scale business.

In affirmation of Linda's acclaim as a Bear artist, the Effanbee Doll Company selected her to create a Bear for the Cristina Doll modeled after the well-known print "Cristina and her Bear" by Jan Hagara. The original Bear is an old 12in (30.5cm) Teddy from artist Hagara's personal collection. Linda Spiegel's miniature version of the Bear measures just 5¼in (13.1cm).

"I started making handmade Bears when my friend Joan suggested I come over and try out a pattern for a Bear she had. In fact, we both made Bears. I enjoyed the experience so much, I began trying to make my own designs. I'd joined some doll clubs and these first bears were frequently door prizes at meetings.

"Friends became interested in my bears, so in 1980, I quit my job at Woolco as a 'hamburger queen' and opened up the Bearly There Company in my garage. For a year and a half, the garage took care of my needs. But everything seemed to grow and grow. It was time for a very big step. Thinking, 'oh, if it doesn't work out we can always go back to the garage,' we plunged into a very scarey step and moved to a warehouse.

"Now that warehouse has a showroom and eight full time employees. In addition there are eleven ladies who

Illustration 446. Ready for assembly, the individual pieces are returned to the factory.

Illustration 445. The bears are hand cut following lines drawn from a wooden pattern. The cut pieces are then taken to the homes of eleven cottage industry workers who carefully sew them together.

Illustration 447. Linda herself still embroiders the faces on her bears. She believes their cute facial features are a primary factor in the success of Bearly There Bears.

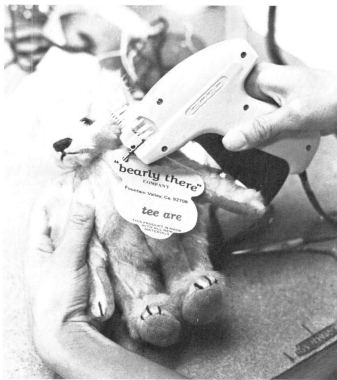

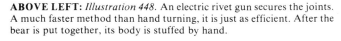

ABOVE LEFT: *Illustration 448.* An electric rivet gun secures the joints. A much faster method than hand turning, it is just as efficient. After the bear is put together, its body is stuffed by hand.

LEFT: *Illustration 449.* The company tag is fastened to the bears.

ABOVE RIGHT: *Illustration 450.* Effanbee Doll Company's "Cristina," was created by Jan Hagara. The doll holds a tiny Teddy Bear which Linda recreated from an old Teddy Bear from Jan's private collection.

RIGHT: *Illustration 451.* Silly Old Bear. 8½in (21.6cm); antique-gold velvet upholstery material; black wooden bead eyes; jointed arms and legs; swivel head; hand-embroidered nose and facial features. Copied from E.H. Shepard's illustration of Winnie the Pooh.

sew for us in their homes on a contract labor basis. Five sales reps market our product all over the country. It's hard to imagine that a business that started on $150 in 1980 grew to a steady six-figures firm in just three years.

"Bearly There Company took its name from a battered old Bear owned by a friend of mine. That tattered old Bear inspired a whole new career for me.

"Designing copies of very old bears is my favorite activity. Frequently it takes about four tries before the pattern is as close as possible to the original. Father Christmas, copied from a turn-of-the-century Christmas ornament is special to me. He's so ugly, he's cute. Plus, he's the only pattern I've cut out and had it fit on the first attempt!

"Now my business is still on the move. Not only has The Bearly There Company achieved national distribution, but we've also been approached by a Japanese cosmetic company to create a bear for promotional purposes.

"Signing the exclusive contract with Effanbee to manufacture the miniature bear for Cristina was a major honor. The bear will be produced for just two years (1984-85) with consecutive numbering. If you're a collector, here's a tip. The first 1,000 bears bore a cloth label with *Christina* spelled incorrectly. Corrected labels *(Cristina)* appear on bears numbered 1,001 and up."

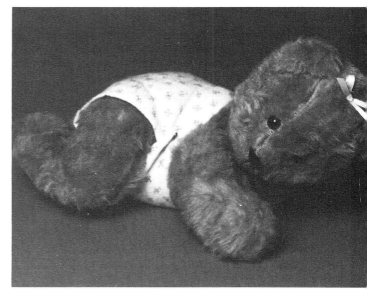

Illustration 452. Cubbie. 7in (17.8cm) tall; 11in (27.9cm) long; camel acrylic fur; jointed arms and legs; swivel head; natural brown eyes; hand-embroidered nose and facial features; modern design of a baby bear crawling on all fours, wearing a diaper and bow in hair.

Lynn West (Creator of Lasting Endearments)

Lasting Endearments, conceived by Lynn West and now owned by Alan and Pat Rypinski, create a fairy tale fantasy world from a lifelike family of Bears. Lynn West, originator of the Grizzlynn Bear Clan tells her story about a small hobby that grew into a dynamic, prospering business.

"I've lived in a fantasy world ever since I was a little girl. I used to pretend I was Cinderella and one day I'd become a princess. My adult life does seem like a modern day fairy tale come true.

"I've always loved art. When I was seven years old my parents enrolled me in drawing and painting classes. My first paying job in any artistic field was sewing and designing childrens clothes for a shop in Laguna Beach, California.

"Not too long after I was married, my husband, Bert, was in a bad accident. As a result of Bert's injuries he couldn't continue in his regular line of work. So we decided, along with my mother and sister, to go into business together. We worked out of our home, making and selling the Christmas ornaments and soft-sculpture dolls which I'd originally made to share with friends and for the sheer enjoyment of creating beautiful objects of art.

"My mother was my driving force, showing up every morning to get me going and encouraging me — all for no pay for four years! I was also inspired by my friend Kitty Coleman. She'd load up my car with laces, ribbons and silk — imploring me to go home and make beautiful things. So, with her encouragement, that's exactly what I did.

"Kitty worked with renowned decorating genious Jack Eshbauch of Newport Beach, California. When jack saw my ornaments and asked me to do some work for him, I couldn't believe I was that good!

"In 1975 Jack decided to sell his business. By now I'd gained a lot of self-confidence in my abilities. A number of Jack's former employees (Kitty and the women who made the ornaments for Jack's store) and I opened our own shop, called St. Nicholas.

"Seasonal items and dolls were my primary focus at that time. But, I'd always appreciated antique dolls and toys. I began studying their early methods of construction, concentrating mainly on toys covered with material. Not having the proper equipment for metal frames, I investigated various materials which would be firm enough to cover with fur. After numerous experiments, including *papier-mâché,* I finally came up with the idea to try styrofoam. Professor Grizzlyn was my first attempt. The results were much better than anticipated. He was a realistic looking bear with his tongue showing in his open mouth.

"Everyone loved him. He made people smile and feel happy and that was my main intention.

"In January 1982, I received a phone call from my old employer, Jack Eshbauch. That call changed my life.

"He'd arranged a meeting for me to show my work to Pat and Alan Rypinski. Pat was a representative for an exclusive, well-known gift boutique. When we met, her arms were full of bears from an earlier buying engagement. Then she saw Professor Grizzlyn and dropped everything. He completely won her over.

"Alan, a prominent manufacturer, intensely inspected my samples and interrogated me with endless questions. I didn't know Alan was considering buying my entire company. But, that's just what he did.

"Now, for almost two years, I've worked for the Rypinskis. It's just like a dream come true. I design for them. I travel to gift shows throughout the country. I'm treated like a true princess.

"Lasting Endearments has grown into a tremendous business with nationwide accounts including Nieman-Marcus. Yet, even with our success, Pat and Alan still insist on retaining the highest standards in quality control. Each bear is a handmade work of art, sewn and inspected by the finest of craftspeople.

"Lasting Endearment Bears are a treasure to add to any collection. In addition to ensuring excellence in the unique quality of our line, our objective is to make our bears come alive with their own distinct personalities. To this aim, Pat is now working on a series of fairy tale bear stories, including a captivating saga of each member of the Grizzlynn Bear Clan."

BELOW: Illustration 453. A three piece mold produces the form for the Grizzlyn Bear Clan.

BOTTOM LEFT: *Illustration 454.* The fur pattern is meticulously cut to exactly fit the mold, then securely glued to the mold piece-by-piece. A sleeve of fur for covering the arms is sewn. A wooden dowel is tightly secured and glued into position, attaching the arm to the body.

BOTTOM RIGHT: *Illustration 455.* The eyes are glued into place. Fine quality leather is used for the eyelids, nose and mouth. The eyelashes are carefully measured and applied separately. High gloss paint is used to give the eyes realism.

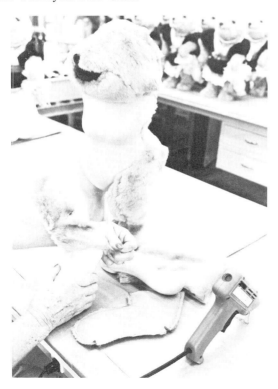

Illustration 456. Lynn's mother has worked with her daughter from the very beginning. Here she puts the finishing touches on Nellie's elegant clothes, which are all hand-made on the premises.

Dorothy Kunkle (Bears and Bibs)

Dorothy Kunkle and I first met in 1983 at the Teddy Bear Collectors Club Love Boat Affair in Long Beach, California. Both bears and club members enjoyed the afternoon touring the ship and sipping afternoon tea. The afternoon concluded with an exciting Teddy Bear making competition.

"Even though I'd only been making bears a few months, I'd entered John Bearmore and Clara Boa in the contest. They managed to win the Presidents Choice and the award for Best Dressed!

"The success of these elegant bears encouraged me to make Mr. Oly M. Pic. From the very beginning, I felt he was destined for greatness. He was patriotic and All-American, right down to his music box which plays "The Star Spangled Banner."

"I'm also a member of the Teddy Bear Club in Glendale, California. One of our special dinner guests was Hans-Otto Steiff. Imagine my delight when my fellow club members selected Mr. Oly M. Pic to present to our honored guest as a gift!

"A short time ago I purchased 'Bearcat,' a beautiful, bright shiny new pedal car made by the Bartholomew Company. I had the brainstorm to design a Teddy Bear with 'bent legs' so he was just right for any sitting position. Not only does he look perfect, proudly sitting at the wheel of the pedal car, but he's able to ride scooters and trikes too!

"I was so excited with my new idea, that my husband Elton and I applied for a patent for the design.

"What I enjoy most about bear making are the endless possibilities that exist. It has been a very challenging part of my life but my belief in being busy is the secret of happiness and health."

Illustration 457. Dorothy Kunkle proudly presents Hans Otto Steiff and Mrs. Steiff a gift of one of her handmade bears, "Mr. Oly M. Pic." The event took place when the Steiffs were guests of honor at Dorothy's bear club in Glendale, California, in 1983. *Photography by Warren Bowen.*

Illustration 458. The "bent leg" bear is a 1983 creation of Bears and Bibs. This innovative design makes it easy for the bear to ride scooters or cars. He also sits perfectly in a chair or on benches. *Photography by Warren Bowen.*

Illustration 459. Dot Kunkle has only been making Teddy Bears since 1983, but she finds creating new ideas makes her happy and keeps her collectors interested.

Cheryl Lindsay: *Elegant Fantasies*

Cheryl Lindsay, who never owned a bear as a child, possesses a teaching credential in college-level needlecraft and clothing construction. The talented teacher discovered bear making while recuperating from surgery in 1981. Cheryl sewed her first bear (from a Mary Hardy pattern in *Family Circle*) completely by hand. A reunion with a long time friend eventually propelled Cheryl into professional bear making.

"My teaching career entailed a great deal of travel. Even though I found the work plentiful and rewarding, the never ending travel tired me. So, I enrolled in a two year program in Northern California and graduated as a registered nurse.

"Toward the end of my nursing studies, my mother mailed an article to me. It was about my friend and teacher Joanne Purpus and her Teddy Bear making class. I couldn't wait to see her again. When I did, she asked me to assist in her growing Teddy Bear business. And I accepted.

"We worked so well together and had so much fun! We formed the Lindsay-Purpus Partnership and our bears gained national recognition.

"As frequently happens, our intense working relationship eventually made us both recognize the need for a change, to do our own thing.

"So, in 1983, I set out on a new path. With my roots in embroidery and needlecraft, it was only right to dress my bears in elegant, intricately designed and detailed clothing.

I named my new company 'Elegant Fantasies.'

"My head was full of so many outfits to create. I put together a line of storybook bears, sewing costumes for all the little characters.

"Elegant Fantasies" creations are fully jointed with my own hardwood, hand-cut joints. The bears are machine sewn, hand stuffed and assembled. The faces are always hand embroidered with either glass or shoe button eyes; on several of the larger bears I actually use 1920s antique shoe buttons. Most of my dressed bears are constructed from English Coat Woolens, with paw pads of ultra suede.

"The business has been growing by leaps and bounds since beginning with one store in 1982 (Earth Bound, in Long Beach, California) which is still one of my best customers. In 1983, at the Los Angeles Gift Show, three new editions sold out in three days to storeowners from all over the country. We've now gone international with a store in Vancouver, Canada.

"Besides myself, Elegant Fantasies has one other full-time employee and at any one time can employ 5-6 part time seamstresses. Two of my sisters often work with me. One (Linda) is the designer of our new bunny line.

"Although the business gets bigger each year, our main goal is quality. I am frequently called a perfectionist and I take it as a compliment. I feel that Elegant Fantasies' animals and their clothing reflects my attention to detail and craftsmanship. I prefer to do all sewing by hand, but because of the need for durability and the lack of available time, I've had to give in and use a sewing machine, especially for the actual bears. I still do a great deal of hand sewing finish work on each costume.

"Currently, we are putting together a line of storybook bears: "Mother Goosebeary," "Little Bear Peep," and "Beary had a Little Lamb" are only a few. Our bears will serve as the illustrations for two forthcoming books.

"Elegant Fantasies are either limited or numbered editions complete with a hand numbered tag. Several of the editions, including the storybook series, come with parchment certificates of authenticity, numbered, signed and dated for collectors' records. Because of the quality of the materials and the long hours involved, Elegant Fantasies gears its products specifically to the collector.

"When I'm making bears they seem to run every part of my life. I've spent 16-18 hours a day in my studio when orders are at their peek.

"One of the reasons the world of bear making is so exciting is the ongoing challenge to keep on your toes. It's the new additions to your line that keep customers coming back to buy yet another bear to add to their collection."

Illustration 460. Cheryl stands at the doors of her studio which have the name of her company beautifully hand painted in a style representing her elegant bears.

Illustration 461. Elegant Fantasies. "Bearlin the Magician." 14in (35.6cm); gray wool; shoe button eyes; jointed arms and legs; swivel head; hand-embroidered face; ultra suede pads. His magical outfit is made of black satin with silver and crystal stars and beads. He was featured on a 1983 Exclamations Valentine and birthday card.

Illustration 462. Elegant Fantasies. "Little Bear Peep." 14in (35.6cm); camel colored wool; shoe button eyes; jointed arms and legs; swivel head; hand-embroidered face; ultra suede pads; pink cotton dress with separate hand-smocked pinafore; custom made cane staff.

Illustration 463. Elegant Fantasies. "Alice in Bearland" and the "White Rabbit." 14in (35.6cm); bear is white wool; shoe button eyes; jointed arms and legs; swivel head; hand-embroidered face; ultra suede pads; blue dress with white polka dots; separate white pinafore. Rabbit is also white wool; shoe button eyes; jointed arms and legs; swivel head; hand-embroidered face; ultrasuede pads; white satin lining in ears; blue vest with white polka dots; decorative watch; blue satin bow tie.

Illustration 464. Elegant Fantasies. "Mother Goosebeary." 14in (35.6cm); cream sheerling; glass eyes; jointed arms and legs; swivel head; hand-embroidered face; ultra suede pads; green patterned dress; shawl and black felt hat; glasses. "Goose." 18in (45.7cm); ecru painters cloth; taxidermy glass eyes. Mother Goosebeary is a limited edition of 25. She sold out in three days at the 1983 Beckman Gift Show in Los Angeles, California.

Wendy Brent

Wendy Brent moved from her California home to live in an area untouched by the progress of high tech skyscrapers and freeways. She now lives in northern Idaho in a rustic log cabin surrounded by majestic pines. She looks out her window onto the beautiful Lake Pend Orielle, the deepest lake in the United States.

Wendy's love of nature and natural lifestyle is exemplified on her kitchen shelves, lined with herb teas, handmade pottery and books about organic medicine and natural cooking.

It is only fitting that Wendy chose to use materials from her rural environment when she entered the wonderful world of toy making.

"When I was eleven years old, I was offered $150 for one of my paintings. So you could say I have had a paintbrush in my hand most of my life. I've always focused on art since I was a child.

"After leaving high school, I attended the Hollywood Art Center. Studying the fine arts of painting, drawing and sculpture. I also concentrated on fashion design.

"My first attempts at three-dimensional sculpture were a disaster. At that time I was living in the mountains, unable to buy supplies and materials. I formed my first doll by using an apple for a head. To my despair, the head shrank, the apple expanded and the back of the head exploded!

"After gradually experimenting with wild flowers and weeds mixed with various chemicals, I discovered a hard, durable ingredient that was impervious to deterioration. I became fascinated by the utilitarian aspects of sculpture.

"The Pioneer doll was one of my first creations and to my amazement sold quickly. I was so proud when the third purchaser was the daughter of one of the curators of the Smithsonian Institution. My doll was exhibited there!

Illustration 465. (Left) Wendy Brent's rose petal rabbit. 1984. 20in (50.8cm); fragrantly scented crushed rose petal composition head, hands and feet; large blown glass German eyes; hand-painted facial features; felt body; stuffed with polyester fiber. Exquisite hand-made silk and satin clothes. (Right) Wendy Brent's rose petal bear. 1983. 25in (63.5cm); fragrantly scented crushed rose petal composition head; large blown glass German eyes; hand painted facial features; beige acrylic fur; polyester filled body; ball-jointed neck; all wooden jointed arms and legs; leather paws. Swiss music box encased in body.

"I began to find my interests working towards the finer, more aesthetic aspects of art.

"I worked with porcelain for awhile and designed a "Fairie Princess" and "Spirit of the Dawn." They were so delicate compared to my previous work. Each doll had its own character since I used no mold, but my original sculpturing from the rose petal composition offered me more inspiration.

"I've experienced some of the greatest rewards from my fragrantly scented jester animal creations. Their clothes present as much a challenge to me as the sculpting of the animal itself.

"The Teddy Bears I designed in 1983 have proved to be the most loved of all my creations. Their skin tones are beautiful colors. Their large blown glass German eyes and hand-painted facial features reveal definite characters. Their firmly stuffed bodies have wooden ball joints. Real leather forms paws and feet, and a music box is encased in all their bodies.

Each art piece takes me about sixty hours from beginning to end. I have perfected my rose petal basic ingredients that I originally put together in 1976 to an even more permanent consistency. No additives are used. I let the natural color of the flower dictate the interesting hues that result.

"Each sculptured piece is entirely handmade, signed, dated and numbered. They carry a certificate of authenticity, including a detachable section to be returned to me so I may keep a file of owners of my work. The American Ambassador to Malaysia was presented with my Puss in Boots as a gift.

"As my business increased I found less time to be able to exhibit at shows, so in 1980 I made the decision to have my creations sold commercially.

"Since then I've also hired three representatives and five cottage industry workers who sew the clothes to my design.

"I set such a high standard for my work I interviewed many girls before I found suitable seamstresses. All the girls have a degree in home economics, and one has even worked for a museum restoring antique clothes.

"The latest phase of my doll creations is a real llama fur Teddy Bear. Living in the land of pine trees, I had the idea to stuff him with cedar sawdust. This stuffing protects the fur from moths. You will still be able to recognize his family heritage by his distinctive rose petal nose.

"I'm never happier than when I'm hunting the woods for natural dyes and creating new ideas. So I will work hard to try to continue to bring about objects of art to be treasured and loved."

Charleen Kinser (Forever Toys)

Charleen Kinser, a native of Long Beach, California, lives and makes her toys in a New England atmosphere in Central Pennsylvania. The countryside sings of real America. The changing seasons, the hardwood forests, the flowing creeks and rivers running down to the richer dairy farmlands and orchards prove to be a fitting background for Charleen to create her toy characters.

The source of the quality of Forever Toys grows from her studies at Los Angeles' Chouinard Art Institute and a careful attention to character developemnt initially learned at U.P.A., the innovative animation studio.

She also produced TV commercials, designed exhibits and packaging before working for a large toy company in Chicago. There she designed a toy which at first delighted her. The finished products lost their fun and vitality in mass production. Says Charleen:

"Our business is a cottage industry. It will always be a cottage industry because emotion cannot be mass produced.

"I made my first bear in 1976. I still follow the same recipe. It consists of *Character*, a *Demand for Respect* and a *Warm Personality*.

"When I design a new toy, first I think of its place in my family of characters, because each toy has a personality. I think specific shapes and textures — and gestures — that describe a character in a toy are more exciting than nondescript ones. It's more exciting to be able to touch bear-like foot pads or the complexities of a nose that's different from our own.

"I use the best materials I can find and make many prototypes leading to one finished toy. If it's perfect, I then explain it to the people who sew, stitch, assemble and finish. This may be the most important step, because to me, a seam is never just a seam, a shape never just a shape — it's the creation of a character.

"Our toys are handmade from primarily those basic, familiar materials that can be easily mended with needle

Illustration 466. Forever Toys. Thaddeus P.J. Bear. 26in (66cm); soft acrylic fur; glass eyes; polyester stuffing; jointed underbody; cowhide nose and paw pads.

. . .Strange, being a bear

220

and thread, or sandpaper for the wood pieces. I chose leather for some of our pieces not only for its resemblance to skin — believeable in a toad or gnome or troll — but because it will last to play out all the dramas through a childhood or two. Leather wears the years well even with stains and scuffs. If a seam tears, it can be sewn the same as fabric. If it gets really grubby, it can be cleaned with saddle soap. The surface will just look lovelier with the years.

"When our children were young I made stuffed toys for them — toys that had some of our playing built in, just as most mothers who sew do. We made our toys now with that same intent — with enough little details to make unique characters that will fit in with other families' play. I like to give a child or even an adult nice things to touch — different things — soft long fur or coarse frizzy stuff. Forever Designs can be carried around or swung by the legs or propped up in some human-like gesture by a bowl of cereal or ride around in wagons.

"At Charleen Kinser Designs I'm proud to say no one just 'does a job.' Everyone cares to know exactly what the purpose of his/her job is, and everyone makes suggestions when they have them. We have about 8 reps now and 27 people work with us. Our animals are sold all over the United States and parts of Canada.

"Special events involving our bears are common. Mostly kidnappings and thefts. One theft in Vail, Colorado, inspired a car chase through the town and a posse of townspeople. We recovered the bear: A TR's Bear, five feet tall!"

Gnome Tom Griswold

he wind kicks around in the dry leaves atop the trees as the moonlight throws its eerie light on woods where the creatures live together in a silent clamorous world. Comfort fills your soul as this new friend leads you along the moonlit path, promising to show you the secrets of the forest. No

Tom twirls, stomps,

Illustration 467. Forever Toys. Gnome Tom Griswold. 22in (55.9cm); deerskin head, hands, feet; poly/cotton body; acrylic hair; glass eyes; polyester stuffing movable head and legs.

Beverly Port

Beverly Port has loved Teddy Bears since she was a child. She started collecting Teddy Bears long before they were regarded as valuable collectibles. With a background in art at Olympic College, Washington, Beverly excelled first in designing original dolls. Soon afterwards, she discovered the rewards of Teddy Bear making.

Today, Beverly is a renowned Teddy Bear and doll artist. She travels throughout America lecturing at Teddy Bear conventions, sharing her extensive knowledge and magnificent collection of slides of Teddy Bears throughout the ages.

Illustration 468. Beverly Port. "Clown Bear." 18in (45.7cm); blue and gold acrylic plush; hand carved and painted porcelain face; antique glass eyes; jointed arms and legs; swivel head; antique lace ruffles and braided ribbon. Handle at back of body activates music box when turned.

Illustration 469. Beverly Port. "Snowflake." 6½in (16.5cm); white mohair and wool; hand-painted bisque face; glass eyes; jointed arms and legs; swivel head.

221

Judy Lewis (Judy Lewis Collectibles)

Illustration 470. Judy Lewis, the daughter of a U.S. Army Cavalry Officer, discovered arts and crafts offered her both entertainment and companionship as she traveled with her family to isolated areas throughout this country, Panama and Japan.

But not until she married and had two sons did she discover a hidden talent. Her first bear making attempt was a class project — a family of three felt bears. Judy had so much fun, she's never stopped creating bears and now counts more than 1400 members in her bear family.

Although her early bears were wool, Judy Lewis now also incorporates fur, velvet and textured upholstery fabrics into her designs.

Bear making is a full-time occupation for Judy. The entire family pitches in with shows, or just plain stuffing.

She produces between 300-500 bears a year. Most of them are owned by serious collectors, including, it is said, Stephanie Powers and Jonathan Winters. Larry Linville of M.A.S.H. fame purchased several of her creations.

Illustration 471. Judy Lewis' "Little Family." Made entirely of felt and exquisitely attired in handmade clothes. The original concept was from Mary Hardy who taught the first Teddy Bear making class Judy attended.

Sue Kruse (Bears by Sue Kruse)

Illustration 472. Sue Kruse is another popular southern California bear artist who found herself in the bear business before she knew what happened. One day she saw an advertisement in a catalog for a book on Teddy Bear making. She thought it would be fun to make one for her new baby. Very soon, her friends and family inundated her with orders and her new career was on its way. Recently, Sue has branched out into creating Teddy Bear stationary, note pads, small clay bears, and bears cast in metal. Here she is seen surrounded by some of her wonderful creations.

Chapter Eight

The Art Of Displaying Bears

Bears are toys. They're meant to be played with. As a grown-up, this means that I'd rather not just buy a bear and pack it alongside others in a glassed-in, sterile shelf. I like to have fun with my bears. And displaying bears, dressing bears and creating an atmosphere from bears will be fun for you, too!

Although some people do have an exceptional flair and eye for showing off their bears in the best light, you don't have to be an expert to display bears. Just use your imagination. And remember, since bears don't break, you can experiment all you want.

Bears are not masculine or feminine. Even though they were invented as a boys' toy, the environment and clothing dictates their gender. They can decorate a boy's or girl's room they can plop their chubby little bodies in a toy wagon to greet guests at a party; they can eye a cookie jar full of delicious goodies: peek around a corner to hide out in a tree near your front door.

One home I know practically changes it whole decor based on the season and Teddy Bears. In summer, they feature a gay May Pole with a fabulous collection of creatures encircling it, dressed in filmy, colorful summer party clothes, complete with hats and baskets of flowers.

At Halloween, the furry creatures become trick or treaters, dressed in costumes that range from Darth Vader to the more traditional ghosts and goblins.

Christmas time is a natural season for displaying your bears. My friend, bear artist, Flore Emory, dresses one of her big handmade bears like Santa Claus, seated at an antique desk, making out his Christmas list. The long scroll in front of him contains the names of Flore's thirteen grandchildren.

Some bear lovers go all out when it comes to displaying their prize possessions. For instance, a couple of bear collectors I know keep their most precious bear in a tiny brass bed with lace coverlets in their own bedroom. On their bureau, where some folks might keep wedding photographs, is an entire wedding procession made up of bears. The bride, the groom, the wedding party — even the ring bearer — are all present.

On the other hand, there are those who prefer to keep their bears bare. Use your own discretion. If you own an antique bear that is in mint condition, display them in their natural "birthday suit."

And speaking of elderly bears, remember their poor, failing eyes. A seventy year old bear would certainly

Illustration 473. By just the right placement of one Teddy Bear, this wonderful kitchen scene of rare early 1900s miniatures is brought to life. *Courtesy Sally Cain.*

appreciate a pair of spectacles to give him an extra touch of character.

With the right props and clothes, bears reveal your personal preferences and tastes. If your home is country style, your bears can wear jeans and perch on top of a rustic wooden box. If you lean toward the more formal or French surroundings, bears can be dressed elegantly in lace, dinner attire and tuxedoes while relaxing in a hand carved chair.

Let me offer one little piece of advice I've picked up from experience. When you go shopping for bear clothes, take your Teddy Bear along. If you don't, you may discover his plump little body just won't squeeze into the doll clothes you've purchased.

Even though some bear aficionados spend many pleasant hours searching for authentic props such as miniature wagons, ladders and exquisite toy furniture, it is not always necessary to spend a lot of money to display your bears. Be ingenious! You undoubtedly have all you need right in your own home.

Stand an inquisitive bear near a picture frame positioned as if he's looking at it. Lean a Teddy Bear against a stack of books with one of them opened and he'll appear to be reading. You may even want a couple of bears in the bathroom near the soap dish. One may hold a washcloth, threatening to scrub the other.

To get more ideas for displaying and dressing your bears, join a Teddy Bear Club. These clubs will frequently hold theme parties. Even if you only have one bear, you'll have the opportunity to dress him many ways. A favorite theme is nursery rhymes and storybook characters. Who knows? Maybe your special bear could dress as Little Bo Peep, Little Miss Muffet, Little Jack Horner, the Queen of Hearts, the Pied Piper, the Old Woman in the Shoe or Peter Pan. The possibilities are endless!

Teddy Bear clubs are just one good way to get display ideas or to share your concepts with fellow bear lovers.

The photographs here will give the sample of ways to display Teddy Bears. But remember, each person has his/her own style, own creativity and own bears. The best ideas will always be your own.

ABOVE: *Illustration 474.* Grouping the tiny 3½in (8.9cm) Teddy Bears together (Steiff c.1910-1950) can make them look even more impressive. The rare German googlie-eyed dolls (Kestner #221; 16in [40.6cm]; 11in [27.9cm]) are standing looking surprised at the many Teddies in the sleigh. (French, c.1900). *Author's collection.*

Illustration 475. Two rare cinnamon Steiff bears (c.1904, 16in [40.6cm]) are given more character by just adding a small toy to the scene. *Courtesy Sally Cain.*

Illustration 476. The beautiful French doll (F. Gaultier, 24in [61cm]) is easily made to look like she is playing with Ten Pin Cats (Steiff, c.1913, 8in [20.3cm]) while the Teddy Bear watches curiously (Steiff, c.1905 16in [40.6cm]). *Author's collection.*

Illustration 477. The Steiff camel (c.1905, 9in [22.9cm]) looks more appealing when accompanied by the beautiful French doll (Jumeau; 15in [38.1cm]) and the Steiff Teddy Bear (c.1904; 18in [45.7cm]). *Author's collection.*

Illustration 478. A small table and miniature china make the setting for a tea party for the beautiful early 1900s bears (c.1907), elegantly dressed in antique silks and laces. *Courtesy Sally Cain.*

225

Chapter Nine

Teddy Roosevelt

The evolution of our little friend the Teddy Bear is only one of the many events in Theodore Roosevelt's life we must honor him for. He was one of the greatest statesmen in the country and the youngest President of the United States.

Born October 27, 1858, in a house at 28 East 20th Street in New York City, Roosevelt came from Dutch, Scotch and Irish ancestry. The son of Theodore Roosevelt Sr. and Martha Bulloch, the young Theodore was strongly influenced by his father who died in 1878.

Martha, his mother, was a sweet, gracious beautiful southern woman beloved by everyone.

From boyhood, Teddy Roosevelt was deeply involved in the study of natural history. Suffering an acute and often agonizing asthma, he was unable to attend boarding school (as was fashionable for children of his social stature) and had to be educated by tutors. He entertained himself by reading travel and adventure books. Even at a young age, he showed a terrific power of concentration which served him well in later life.

At the age of ten he wrote his first book *Natural History of Insects.* He wrote 34 more books throughout his life, including *The Naval History of the War of 1812* and *The Winning of The West* which are considered classics.

Teddy Roosevelt adored children and was a good father. No interest of the children was too small that the busy President did not find time to share it.

His children are said to have rollerskated in the White House and legend has it their pony once was a passenger in the elevator there.

Playing with his children was an important and necessary part of Roosevelt's day. The favorite amusement is said to be the game of *Bear.* Acting the part of the ferocious animal himself, the President was chased across the floor by the young hunters who armed with umbrellas, walking canes or any other objects which were close at hand, hunted down their prey. When the hunt was complete and the "bear" had been killed or captured, the roles were reversed and the President became the hunter while the children scrambled to safety behind the large furniture which decorated the White House.

Although he was remembered as a great hunter, Roosevelt loved animals and nature. His passion for hunting bears in particular wasn't solely to kill them but to observe their natural habits.

Roosevelt's book, *Outdoor Pastimes of an American Hunter* (1905) tells how he frequently watched the bears while he himself was unnoticed. The grizzlies became his favorites.

Because of his eventful and adventuresome life, his role as a dominant figure in American history, and his distinctive facial features and robust smile, Teddy Roosevelt was often characterized in one form or another.

Clifford Berryman's famous "Drawing the Line in Mississippi" cartoon was only one of the artists numerous outlandish cartoons covering President Roosevelt's career.

Roosevelt collectibles ranges from buttons, post cards, books, tins and advertising to figurines and dolls.

A major Roosevelt antique collectible is Schoenhut's "Teddy's Adventures in Africa." Based on Roosevelt's legendary African Safaris, the toy company marketed the 53 piece, wooden jointed set of characters in 1909.

The star of the collection is the remarkably designed Roosevelt doll. Wearing a khaki hunting outfit, the doll looks very much like its human inspiration. Other finely carved members of the hunting expedition include appropriately attired natives, a photographer, gun bearer and animals from Schoenhut's popular Humpty Dumpty Circus.

In the fall of 1984, my husband and I had the good fortune to visit Teddy Roosevelt's birthplace in New York City. It is a large home, furnished in the solid, but rather gloomy style which was generally accepted in those days.

The narrow five-story home retains approximately 40 percent of its original furnishings.

Climbing the steep steps to the entrance of the old city home, a wonderful feeling enveloped me as I reflected on following the same paths that little "Teedie" (his family nick-name) did so long ago.

At the top of the stairs a guide, bearing an uncanny resemblance to Roosevelt, greeted us at the door. His appearance undoubtedly contributed to his selection for the position. He personally delighted in recounting events in the Roosevelt boy's life.

Teedie's actual crib and rush-seated chair are still in the nursery. Our guide explained how the little boy's growth was measured in ratio to the height of the chair. (At full growth, Roosevelt only reached 5 feet 8 inches.)

Beyond the nursery lies a gymnasium which Theodore Sr. built for his asthmatic son.

Our guide astonished us with the late 19th century cures forced on little Teedie for his condition. The sickly child drank black coffee and smoked cigars in an effort to induce vomiting. The asthma attack tended to cease after this torturous treatment.

Moving into the magnificent library, highlighted by mementos of the wealthy family's journey to Egypt, and the formal dining room, we discovered that the high horsehair covered chair seats scratched little Teedie's legs, causing him a great deal of discomfort.

A Teddy Roosevelt museum of rare items covers a large portion of the Roosevelt birthplace. Dominating the exhibit is an impressive bronze statue of Roosevelt astride his horse. The statue's domain is filled with stuffed trophies from the President's hunting expeditions.

After a serious illness, President Teddy Roosevelt died peacefully in his sleep at his home in Sagamore Hill, Oyster Bay, Long Island, on January 6, 1919, at the age of 60.

The Teddy Roosevelt Association has been formed in honor of this national hero. A non-profit organization chartered by Congress in 1920, they invite you to join to help perpetuate the memory and ideas of Teddy Roosevelt. They are a historical association and public service group, with members throughout the United States. They publish and disseminate the Teddy Roosevelt Association Journal. Published four times a year, the Journal is available by writing to: Teddy Roosevelt Association, Box 720, Oyster Bay, Long Island, New York 11771.

Illustration 479. Theodore Roosevelt (or "Teedie" as his family called him) about the age of four. *Courtesy Harvard College Library.*

BELOW: *Illustration 480.* President Roosevelt with his family at Sagamore Hill, 1903.

PRESIDENT ROOSEVELT AND FAMILY

THE PRESIDENT'S DREAM.

Illustration 481. With the popularity of Teddy Bears and the derivation of their name from President Roosevelt's nickname "Teddy," many of Clifford Berryman's cartoons depicted bears. *Courtesy Harvard Library.*

BELOW: *Illustration 482.* Oxford University June 1910. The students play a prank on President Roosevelt by placing a Teddy Bear in his path. *Courtesy Harvard Library.*

BEASTLY PRIDE.

ABOVE LEFT: *Illustration 483.* This picture drawn by the famous political cartoonist Clifford Berryman shows the popularity of the Teddy Bear and his relationship with President Roosevelt. c.1905. *Courtesy Harvard Library.*

ABOVE: *Illustration 484.* Theodore Roosevelt (Teddy Bear) campaign pin. c.1904. Teddy Bear. 3in (7.6cm); white plush; black button eyes; unjointed head and body; white cardboard pads. Comments: Rare. With Theodore Roosevelt's association with the Teddy Bear, political campaign items would use the Teddy Bear. This bear originally was mounted to a stick pin. The ribbon and Roosevelt button have been assembled for display purposes. *Author's collection.*

LEFT: *Illustration 485.* 1904 Teddy Roosevelt campaign button. 1¾in (4.5cm) in diameter. Original pin. *Author's collection.*

LEFT: *Illustration 486.* 1904 Teddy Roosevelt campaign button. 1¾in (4.5cm) diameter; manufactured by Torsch and Franz Badge Company of Baltimore, Maryland. Extremely rare; only four specimens are known to exist. Taken from the Clifford Berryman cartoon, the button depicts Teddy and his running mate trailed by a Teddy Bear. This cartoon button was never made in large quantities or widely distributed as were so many T.R. button designs. It could have been a salesman's sample for which orders were never received, as was the case with many rare political buttons. In 1904, political campaign buttons were relatively new, and manufacturers outdid themselves producing buttons of great beauty. It was possible this plain black and white button was overlooked amongst all the other colorful designs available. It appears this is the only known Roosevelt campaign button picturing the Teddy Bear. *Courtesy Fred H. Jorgensen.*

RIGHT: *Illustration 487.* Embossed brass clothing button. 3/4in (2cm) diameter; shows Roosevelt riding on his horse; gun in hand; the words "The Rough Riders Brigade" are around the top edge and "Roosevelt 1904" on the bottom. *Author's collection.*

Illustration 488. "Teddy and the Bear." Iron Mechanical Bank. 1910. 10in (25.4cm) long; 8in (20.3cm) high; when coin is inserted into bank the bear springs out of the tree stump. *Courtesy Volpp Collection.*

Illustration 489. Schoenhut. "Teddy Roosevelt doll." c.1909. 8in (20.3cm); carved jointed wooden body. Khaki hunting outfit. Condition: Excellent. Comments: Rare. Part of Schoenhut 53-piece set "Teddy's Adventures in Africa." *Courtesy Helen Sieverling.*

Illustration 490. The Cracker Jack Bears climb the tree to escape from President Roosevelt. The Cracker Jack Series. Copyright 1907. B. E Moreland. Rueckheim Bros. Eckstein, Chicago, U.S.A. *Author's collection.*

1858	Born October 27 at 28 East 20th Street, New York City.
1880	Graduated from Harvard; married Alice Hathaway Lee on October 27.
1882-84	Member, New York State Assembly.
1882	Published *Naval War of 1812,* first of many books on history, nature, travel and public affairs.
1884	Death of Alice Lee Roosevelt on February 14.
1884-86	Rancher in Dakota Territory.
1886	Unsuccessful candidate for Mayor of New York City; married Edith Kermit Carrow on December 2.
1889-95	Appointed U.S. Civil Service Commissioner.
1895-97	Commissioner, New York City Police Board.
1897-98	Assistant Secretary of the Navy.
1898	Organized Rough Riders.
1898-1901	Governor of New York State.
1901	Vice President of the United States; becomes President September 14, upon the death of McKinley; began policy of "trust busting" in 1901.
1902	Began vigorous conservation program.
1904	Elected President of the U.S.A. on November 8.
1905	Brought Russia and Japan to peace table at Portsmouth, New Hampshire.
1906	Pure Food and Drug Act passed for consumer protection.
1909-10	Hunted big game in Africa.
1910	Received Nobel Peace Prize in Oslo, Norway.
1909-14	Contributing editor of *The Outlook* magazine.
1912	Unsuccessful Progressive (Bull Moose) Party candidate for President.
1914	Expolored "River of Doubt" in jungles of Brazil.
1914-17	Prominent advocate of American preparedness and intervention in World War I.
1919	Died at home, Sagamore Hill, Oyster Bay, Long Island, on January 6.

Chapter Ten

Billy Possum

The Teddy Bear had a younger cousin. His name was Billy Possum and he appeared on the toy scene in approximately 1909. Billy never became the darling of the toy world, even though the industry made every effort to artificially foist his merits on the public and to create a popular successor to the Teddy Bear. No matter how hard toy makers tried, poor Billy simply could not compete with Teddy.

Billy Possum, like his cousins, was conceived after a political incident. When William H. Taft dined at a banquet in his honor held in Atlanta, Georgia, the then President-elect ordered "'possum and 'taters" as his main course.

So taken was Taft with the possum delicacy he made the statement: "for Possum first, last and all the time."

The press capitalized on this speech and announced it was the death of the Teddy Bear (alluding to Theodore Roosevelt) and the beginning of a life-long reign for Possums (meaning William Taft).

Toy makers jumped at the opportunity to make the new stuffed animal mascot of the current political administration.

By 1909 a number of firms touted the praises of this "astonishing little creature." He was a life-like looking animal with a sense of humor who could (unlike his chubby relative) hang by his tail and assume a variety of amusing poses.

H. Fisher & Co. (New York City) sold the first version of the inquisitive Billy in 1909, with Strobel and Wilken Company as their distributors. Shortly afterward, Hahn and Amberg, the Novelty Animal House (New York City) promoted a 13in (33cm) possum made from the skin of a *real* opossum. Fortunately, most of the company's smaller version (as well as those of other toy makers) predominantly used mohair plush cloth for Billy's coat.

Even Steiff climbed on the bandwagon with a Billy Possum of their own, complete with the ever present Steiff ear button.

Most possums were fully jointed with swivel heads and long felt tails. Many had squeakers. Billy Possum "hand motion" toys (today we call them puppets) were popular during this phase as well and were offered by E. I. Horsman of New York City. A 9in (22.9cm), 11in (27.9cm) and 13in (33cm) possum in light gray and silver brown were advertised in *Playthings* 1909 by Harman Manufacturing Company, New York City.

But no matter how many companies pushed the possum craze as "here to stay" the curious creature fell short of the magic of "the old reliable Teddy Bear."

Information regarding the political battle between Theodore Roosevelt and William Taft are well represented on postcards depicting the historical events of that era.

Today, Billy Possum toys and related political memorabilia are extremely rare and desirable collector's items.

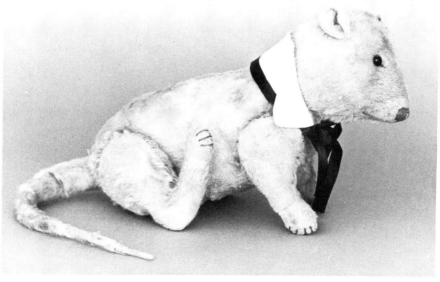

ABOVE: *Illustration 492.* Manufacturer unknown. c.1909. 11in (27.9cm) long; white mohair; blue faded stripes; shoe button eyes; jointed arms and legs; swivel head; felt tail and ears; excelsior stuffing. Condition: Good. Comments: Rare. Very long nose. *Author's collection.*

MIDDLE: *Illustration 493.* Manufacturer unknown. c.1909. 11in (27.9cm) long; gray mohair; shoe button eyes; jointed arms and legs; swivel head; beige felt tail; brown felt ears; excelsior stuffing. Condition: Excellent. Comments: Rare. *Author's collection.*

RIGHT: *Illustration 494.* Brass Billie Possum political clothes button. 1in (2.5cm) diameter; this button has also been found in a 3/4in (2cm) size. *Author's collection.*

OPPOSITE PAGE: *Illustration 491.* Steiff. c.1909. 12in (30.5cm) long; gray mohair; shoe button eyes; jointed arms and legs; swivel head; excelsior stuffing; light brown stitched nose, mouth and claws. Printed Steiff button. Condition: Excellent. Comments: Extremely rare. Note wonderfully big feet and good head shape, characteristics of Steiff. *Courtesy Volpp Collection.*

Illustration 495. Rare political postcard showing Billie Possum passing the Teddy Bear on his way to the White House. At the bottom of the card are the words "Good Bye Teddy." Photos of Theodore Roosevelt and William Taft can be seen in the corner of the card. This was one of a set. Copyright 1909, by Fred C. Lounsbury. *Author's collection.*

Illustration 496. Political postcard shows Billie Possum marching forth, suitcase in hand, as he moved into the White House after being elected President. *Author's collection.*

Illustration 497. A cute poem was written on this political postcard. Billie is patriotically dressed in red, white and blue. Series # E 243. B.B. London and New York. Printed in Germany. *Author's collection.*

Illustration 498. Billie Possum Spoon. c.1909. 5½in (14cm); markings read "Sterling, pat. applied for." Hallmarked Wallace. *Courtesy Mimi Hiscox.*

Chapter Eleven

Golliwogs — Teddy's Friend

One of Teddy's closest contemporaries in the world of soft, cuddly toys is the Golliwog. This "half-imaginary, half-human" looking creature is almost grotesque in appearance. In view of its strange look, the Golliwog's acceptance by children is rather odd. Yet, the Golliwog's parallel development and close association with the Teddy Bear remains consistent to this day.

Apparently, Golli's first public viewing seems to have been in Florence K. Upton's book *The Adventures of the Two Dutch Dolls,* published by Longmans, Green and Company, in London and New York, in 1895. The English artist's narrative told the story of the adventures and travels of two wooden dolls and a Golliwog.

Florence Upton was born of English parents in New York City (1873). She was only 16 years old when her father died. Later, the young artist and her mother returned to England. Her mother, Bertha Upton, first encouraged her to use her imagination to vividly illustrate children's books, while she herself would write the verses. Together they created almost a book a year from 1895 until 1909.

Upton based her drawings from the doll she found at a fair in America when she was a child. The artist sold the doll, along with some of her drawings, for charity during World War I. Enough funds were raised to purchase an ambulance with the inscription "Florence Upton and the Golliwogg gave this ambulance." The doll is now part of one of the Prime Minister of England's country homes. The Long Gallery, Chequers in Buckinghamshire.

The first Golliwog looks quite a bit like that of today's. His black untamed-looking hair comes straight out of his head. A major difference is the face of Miss Upton's doll, which appears to be made of a shiny leather with an applied nose and mouth.

Unfortunately, since the Uptons did not copyright their unusual doll, they failed to cash-in on lucrative royalties that could have made them a fortune.

The spelling of *Golliwogg* was later changed to Golliwog. The origin of this name however is still a mystery. Different theories have been offered. One is the name W.O.G. was the title given to a Western Oriental gentleman in Anglo-Indian times. Yet, the Golliwog with which we are familiar, has more resemblance to a southern minstrel with his wild fuzzy black hair, bright red smile and startling white outlined black eyes.

Another possible derivation was that it could have come from the Anglo Saxon word "polliwogg" (tadpole).

Still another theory surfaces from the late 1800s. At that time, British soldiers occupied Alexandria, Egypt. The native workmen wore armbands with the letters W.O.G.S. (working on government service). Thin and starving, they were dubbed "ghul," an Arabic word meaning desert ghost. The British troops are said to have anglicised the Arabic name "ghul" to "golly." Hence, the name "Golly-wogs."

Florence Upton's fantasy-being, the Golliwog, took the shape of an actual doll about 1912. Commercial and handmade versions were designed.

The majority were cloth or felt stuffed with Kapok. Early versions represented the Upton illustrations with formed three-dimensional noses, shoe button eyes and applied mouth dressed in smart jackets and trousers with a stand-up shirt collar and sporting a bow tie. Later on faces were also painted and embroidered. Not too many versions were jointed.

A beautiful jointed Golliwog is, however, advertised in the 1913 Steiff catalog. This toy is a higly prized collector's item today.

As with Teddy Bears, the unique little creatures found popularity with women as well as children. Early 1900s post cards and pictures show attractive young ladies affectionately holding Golliwogs.

The intriguing toy surprisingly served as a successful and long-running promotional symbol for England's largest marmalade manufacturer James Robertson and Son. In 1910, the Golliwog became their trademark. Robertson's incorporated the Golliwog into an advertising campaign in 1930. By exchanging the cut-out Golliwog logo for enamel broaches, Robertson's customers could exchange them for a wide variety of Golliwog pins (after the specified number of Golliwogs had been collected). As many as 12,000 children a week would send paper Golliwogs to exchange for pins. This costume jewelry was quite varied. Some showed Golli's holding musical instruments. Others, geared to the more sports minded, had Golli's holding golf clubs and cricket bats.

1934 saw the introduction of broaches shaped like berries, with the head of a Golli superimposed into the fruit. A Coronation Golli followed shortly afterward. His waistcoat patriotically carried the design of the Union Jack. Due to the shortage of metal during World War II, this campaign was discontinued until 1946 when it made a well-received come back.

An attractive pendant was produced for girls in 1956.

Later, a new design for the Golliwog came on the scene. His eyes were changed to look to the left. His smile was larger and his legs were now straight. The name *"Golden Shred"* was removed from his waistcoat and a whole series of different designs were now available.

A change from pins were the pottery Golliwogs introduced approximately in 1958. These were eventually discontinued due to inferior quality. The 2½in (6.4cm) colorful little figures consisted of eleven football players in different positions, and ten musicians playing different instruments.

Robertson's also used the stuffed cloth Golliwog for various incentive promotions.

English soft toy manufacturers, such as Dean's Rag, Merrythought and Chad Valley found Golliwogs a welcome addition to their toy lines. In fact, Dean's and Merrythought still manufacture these interesting toys today.

The climate in the collecting world seems to be readying itself for a Golliwog renaissance. Not only do Golliwogs and Teddies enjoy each other's company, the Golliwog deserves a special admiration all its own.

RIGHT: *Illustration 499.* Steiff Teddy Bear. c.1905. 30in (76.2cm); gold mohair; large shoe button eyes; jointed arms and legs; swivel head; excelsior stuffing. Condition: Excellent. Comments: Rare size. **Left:** Steiff Golliwog. c.1913. 12½in (31.8cm); black felt face with formed nose; shoe button eyes surrounded by white and red felt circles; red felt applied mouth; fuzzy black hair; black felt hands; jointed arms and legs; swivel head; excelsior stuffing; teal blue felt jacket; white shirt and vest; red felt molded trousers; clothes cannot be removed. Condition: Excellent. **Right:** Steiff Golliwog. c.1913. 19in (48.3cm); black felt face with formed nose; shoe button eyes surrounded by white and red felt circles; red felt applied mouth; fuzzy black hair; black felt hands; jointed arms and legs; swivel head; excelsior stuffing; bright non-removable blue felt jacket; white shirt and vest; red bow tie; loose fitting red trousers. Condition: Mint. Comments: Extremely rare. Beautiful examples of the early style of Golliwog. *Courtesy Barbara Fernando.*

Illustration 500. Collection of Merrythought Golliwogs. c.1950-1960. Range in size from the 9in (22.9cm) puppet on the left to the 22in (55.9cm) seated rare Girliwog. The mint condition minstrel is also rare. All dolls are made of felt with unjointed bodies stuffed with Kapok. *Author's collection.*

RIGHT: *Illustration 501.* Unknown English manufacturer. c.1920. 24in (61cm); black cloth face; shoe button eyes encircled with white cloth covered discs; embroidered mouth; unjointed body; dark blue wool jacket with wine colored velvet lapels; white shirt with wine satin bow; red wool trousers and black cloth hands and feet; clothes are not removable. *Author's collection.*

Illustration 502. Merrythought Golliwog. c.1950. 15in (38.1cm); black felt face, hands and shoes; plastic black and white eyes; red felt applied mouth; yellow shirt; bright red felt molded trousers and blue jacket; black wooly hair. Unjointed body; kapok stuffing; label on foot reads "Merrythought Ironbridge, Shropshire." Cardboard sign with Teddy and Golliwog colorfully advertising leather cleaner. Golliwog playing cards. Marked: "Publishers of the following were by Florence K. and Bertha Upton. Manufacturers to his majesty Thos. De La Rue and Co., Ltd., 110 Bunhill Row, London." *Courtesy Volpp Collection.*

Illustration 504. Florence K. Upton Golliwog Book. *The Golliwogg in War.* 11½in (29.2cm) x 8½in (21.6cm). The pictures were drawn by Florence K. Upton and the text was by her mother Bertha Upton. Copyright 1896 by Longmans, Green and Co., London, New York and Bombay. *Author's collection.*

Illustration 503. **TOP ROW:** James Robertson and Son Paper Golliwogs. c.1930. 2in (5.1cm); paper Golliwogs with black faces and hair; bright blue jackets, red trousers and yellow vest with the words "Robertson's Golden Shred" printed across his chest were given away with each jar of marmalade. Ten paper Golliwogs were collected by the children and mailed to the company to receive in return a little enameled Golliwog broach. **CENTER ROW:** James Robertson and Son Golliwog Fruit Broach. c.1934. 2in (5.1cm); enamel broach in the shape of berries with the face of a Golliwog superimposed into the fruit. **BOTTOM ROW:** James Robertson and Son Golliwog Broaches. c.1930. 2½in (6.4cm); an enamel Golliwog with black face and hair, bright blue jacket, red trousers and white vest with the words "Golden Shred" across his chest was mailed in return for the ten paper Golliwogs collected from the marmalade. *Author's collection.*

"GOLLIWOGG" IN FANCY DRESS.

Wishing you A Happy Christmas

Illustration 505. Postcards were made from Florence K. Upton's Golliwog book illustrations. This card shows the Dutch dolls dressing the Golliwog in fancy dress. Raphael Tuck and Sons' Christmas postcard N98096. Designed in England. Chromographed in Germany. By permission of Messrs. Longmans, Green and Co. *Author's collection.*

Illustration 506. Florence K. Upton's Golliwog and the Dutch doll were used for many colorful and amusing postcards. Postmarked 1907. Marked: "B.B. London." Printed in Saxony. *Author's collection.*

Illustration 507. Photographers used Golliwogs with portrait photos just as they did with Teddy Bears. Metropole Studios, Cardiff. *Author's collection.*

Chapter Twelve

Teddies Bearing A Driver's License: Juvenile Automobiles

Pedal cars, sometimes referred to as juvenile automobiles, are gathering momentum among collectors. Many Teddy Bears like to sit in the driver's seat of these miniature replicas of early cars. The growth of the recently popular collectible toy autos is linked to Teddy's particular affinity for cars that a small bear can feel proud to own. Lately, however, these tiny vehicles are gaining attention in and of themselves.

The juvenile auto, advertised as early as 1904, frequently came complete with bulb horns, emergency handbreaks, rear view mirrors and full instrument panels painted on their dashboards.

The early 1900s pedal cars had spoked wheels with solid tires. Some were propelled by pedals connected by a chain to toothed gears. Later the mechanism changed and flat steel rods connected the pedals to the rear axle.

Of course, the best of these intricate pedal cars were quite expensive. Children received them on special occasions such as birthdays and Christmas. Their parents paid between $8.00 and $35.00 for even the most basic models.

So popular were juvenile autos that complete sections in mail order catalogs were dedicated to them. Sizes were advertised to suit children from three to twelve years old.

The early, simple 1904 variety consisted of a steel frame, seat and steering wheel. Hammered sheet metal and steel suggested an engine and formed fenders. The whole chassis rolled along on childrens wagon or bicycle wheels.

In the beginning, the same manufacturers producing tricycles and scooters marketed the pedal cars.

More discriminating and affluent parents, paid high price for gas and steam powered vehicles.

As early as 1908, E. Huber of Birmingham, England, advertised in the *Toy Trader* with claims of originating the toy cars in England.

By 1920, companies such as Steelcraft Murray-Ohio, Garton and Gendron built the popular toys as part of their regular production. The American National Company of Toledo, Ohio, added a special extension to their factory for the exclusive manufature of juvenile autos.

Chryslers, Fords, Oldsmobiles, Chevrolets, Lincoln Hupmobiles, Packards, Stutz Studebakers — all the desirable full-size autos, came in scaled-down child-sized models.

The French even manufactured a pedal car in the early 1900s which resembled a Renault.

A replica of the 1927 Type 52 Bugatti, an almost perfect scale model, was designed to exhibit at a Milan Car Show.

In 1928 André Citroen created a child's size reproduction of the Citroen C6 Cabriolet for his own son. It was so well received, commercial manufacture was warranted. Powered by battery, it drove forward and in reverse. Accelerator pedals regulated the speed. The battery was even checked by a volt-meter on the dashboard.

Considering even the taste of little girls, light "feminine" colors brightened specially designated juvenile autos.

Wealthier children drove perfectly reduced models of luxury autos, generally propelled by electricity or gasoline.

Unfortunately, as with Teddy Bears, children didn't know their toy cars would one day be prized collector's items. So they rammed their vehicles into trees, bounced off of brick walls and collided with other cars. Washing, polishing and storing a toy pedal car was not common. More often, the juvenile auto was besieged with rain, snow and other destructive weather conditions. Therefore, discovering a pedal car in its original condition, one not battered and rusted, is not just *rare* — but nearly impossible.

Restoration of these cars, however, *is* possible. In fact, with the upswing in attention to Teddy's favorite toy, reproduction of small auto parts has begun.

So, if you find a car missing a headlight or windshield, don't despair. Parts are available.

My husband and I found our 1934 Pierce Arrow pedal car in pieces scattered all over the back of an old garage in northern California. Having restored and collected antique cars for years, Wally's expert eye knew that all the basics were there. I seriously doubted that pile of junk would ever be a car again.

Of course, Wally knew better. I'll never forget the thrill when that miniature automobile was restored to the proud, shiny bright red car it once was.

Our excitement probably equalled the emotion of the child who received that special birthday or Christmas present over fifty years ago.

My only regret was that I was too big to ride in it — but my Teddy Bear fit perfectly!

Continued on page 257

Gendron Whippet Roadster pedal car. 1928. 54in (137.2cm) long, 29in (73.7cm) high. One of the best quality built pedal cars. The pedal mechanism of this particular car is of a typical bearing variety found on the crankshaft of an automobile engine. This may have been a custom built feature. Original paint. Loren Tipton (Colleen Tipton's son) is the race driver. *Author's collection.*

BELOW: Gendron of Toledo Ohio Packard Roadster pedal car. 1927. 64in (162.6cm) long, 39in (98.1cm) high. This rare deluxe model is completely original, including features such as operating windshield wiper, original mud flaps on fenders, right-hand door opens, luggage rack, stop light (which can register either slow or stop), a fat man's steering wheel (which folds up), trunk opens and closes. Original condition. *Courtesy Carl Burnett.*

Steelcraft Lincoln pedal car. c.1932. 46in (116.8cm) long, 26in (66cm) high. Luggage rack. Restored by Tom Perez. *Author's collection.*

BELOW: Steelcraft Chrysler pedal car. 1931. 51in (129.5cm) long, 29in (73.7cm) high. A deluxe version with many accessories including electric lights (which are operated by a dry cell), emergency hand brake and bulb horn. Original condition. *Courtesy Carl Burnett.*

Steelcraft Gilmore pedal airplane. c.1920 Rare. Restored by Don Cooney. *Courtesy Cooney Collection.*

BELOW: American National Packard Coupe pedal car. 1925. 67in (170.2cm) long, 39in (99cm) high. Only six are known to exist. This extremely rare model is equipped with a high pressure lubrication system, pneumatic tires, and swing out windshield. Original condition. *Courtesy Carl Burnett.*

Gendron Packard pedal car. 1924. 52in (131.1cm) long. Weight 95 pounds. Fat man's steering wheel (which tilts up); spring suspension; deck lid; throttle and choke. Magnificently restored by owner. *Courtesy Dick McNab.*

BELOW: American National Packard Touring pedal car. 1929. 51in (129.5cm) long. 29in (73.7cm) high. This grand looking car in its original condition has a dual set of pedals, which is very rare. *Courtesy Carl Burnett.*

L.H. Mace and Co. "Dauntless."
Touring pedal car. c.1908. 68in
(171.2cm) long x 37in (93.9cm)
high. Extremely rare and desirable car from this era. Only one
that has so far been found to
exist in America. Body painted
green with red trim; "Dauntless"
originally painted on each side
of hood; side foot boards;
fenders; steel chassis; high speed
double chain and sprocket;
wheels have 5/8in (1.6cm) rubber tires; adjustable ball bearings
in axle bracket and wheels; brass
trim and side lamps (lamps burn
kerosene). *Courtesy Carl Burnett.*

BELOW: Casey Jones pedal car.
c.1950. American manufacturer.
41in (103.1cm) long, 24in (61cm)
high. Original condition. *Author's collection.*

OPPOSITE PAGE: This veteran Steiff Teddy Bear (24in [61cm]) is seated on an early drum, giving him much more character. *Author's collection.*

A group of rare c.1930 Schuco monkeys and Teddy Bears surround this cute bisque baby "Hilda" doll. 11in (27.9cm). *Author's collection.*

This original painting by Evelyn Gathings depicts the security a child receives from a Teddy Bear. Evelyn is known for her artwork depicting animals and children. Presently, she is at work designing a complete line of greeting cards.

OPPOSITE PAGE: J.P. Bartholmew Co. "Fire Patrol Wagon." Completely hand-made of American hardwoods and hand-painted. Flore Firemen were especially made to ride in this wagon. 22in (55.9cm) high; 21in (53.3cm) wide; 36in (91.4cm) long.

ABOVE: An old telephone looks so much more interesting when two bears decide to make a phone call. (Right) Steiff. 12in (30.5cm). c.1905. (Left) Musical bear. 19in (48.3cm). c.1920. *Author's collection.*

A group of English Golliwog's. c.1950-1960. *Author's collection.*

ABOVE: Two Pilgrim Flore Bears (14in [35.6cm]) gather dried corn to decorate for Thanksgiving. *Author's collection.*

Two rare Steiff Bears (c.1905-1907; 21in [38.1cm]) are affectionately posed as sweethearts. *Courtesy Sally Cain.*

SPECIAL
FOR
TO-DAY
ROAST
TEDDY BEAR
MOUNTAIN HOUSE
STYLE

GOOD EATING HERE!

COPYRIGHT BY L.GULICK·1909

William Howard Taft adopted the symbol of a "possum" to compete with Theodore Roosevelt's Teddy Bear. This rare 1909 political postcard by Crite shows Billie Possum about to devour the "Special meal for the day" — "Roast Teddy Bear." *Author's collection.*

"THE ICE BEARS BEAUTIFULLY."

"Little Bears." Raphael Tuck and Sons. Postcard series No. 118. Printed in Saxony. Postmarked 1907. *Author's collection.*

Portrait postcard. Postmarked 1917. The Hugh C. Leighton Co., Manufacturers, Portland, Maine. U.S.A. Made in Germany. *Author's collection.*

Roosevelt Bears celebrate the Fourth of July. No. 18. This postcard is from the rare second set of 16 (#17-#32). Copyright 1907. E. Stern and Co., Inc. *Author's collection.*

No. 18

" They put crackers all along the wire To prepare the field for an army fire."

The Three Bears, published by
Raphael Tuck and Sons, Co. Ltd.
New York, London, Paris. Soft
back cover. 8½in (21.6cm) x 6½in
(16.5cm). *Author's collection.*

The famous Roosevelt Bear books
created by Paul Piper under the pen
name Seymour Eaton. First book,
*The Roosevelt Bears, Their Travels
and Adventures*, published in 1905.
Three more books in this series
followed: *More About the Roose-
velt Bears* (1906), *The Roosevelt
Bears Abroad* (1907) and *The Bear
Detectives* (1907). Published by
Edward Stern and Company, Inc.,
Philadelphia. Hard back cover.
8¾in (22.3cm) x 11¼in (28.6cm).
Author's collection.

Continued from page 240

J.P. Bartholomew Co.

The revival of interest in early pedal cars also gave birth to some newer, 1984 models.

One of these classic creations is the "Bearcat," designed by Jeff an Karlene Neble, founders of the J.P. Bartholomew Co.

The Nebles first step into the collector's market was with Teddy Bear Wagons.

These completely handmade, beautifully painted toys were so appreciated and enjoyed by collectors, it gave Jeff the encouragement to design his version of a Teddy Bear's pedal car.

With his background in antiques and quality restoration, Jeff was able to produce his original version of a of a pedal car.

Modelled after the early style, Jeff's concept of his car was the perfect size for Teddy Bear passengers.

The "Bearcat" is built of wood and set on a steel under carriage. Painted with a rich dark maroon high gloss automotive finish, this modern "old-time" classic is a limited edition of two-hundred and is destined to be a collectors item of the future.

Illustration 508. Pedal car. c.1915. 36in (91.4cm) long, 20in (50.8cm) high; one of the early designs with wire wheels. Restored condition. *Author's collection.*

Illustration 509. J. P. Bartholomew Company. Jeff Neble enjoys putting the finishing touches to his "Bearcat" car which he designed especially for the Teddy Bear.

Illustration 510. The J. P. Bartholomew Company's "Bearcat" is a limited edition of 200. Painted in a dark maroon, it measures 31in (78.7cm) long; 15in (38.1cm) wide; 16in (40.6cm) high; a Flore Bear, outfitted for high speed touring, sits at the wheel.

Chapter Thirteen

Postcards

The early postcard era (in which the cards were called "Pioneer Cards") dates from 1869 to 1898. On May 19, 1898, Congress enacted "The Postal Act" calling for the words "Private Mailing Card" to be printed on the reverse side of any privately issued cards. In that Act, Congress also gave permission for private publishers to mail postcards at the same rate (1¢) as standard government cards. Prior to this ruling, private cards were charged 2¢ for postage.

Three years later, on December 24, 1901, the postal card law was further codified to order "post card" to be printed on all cards and to legalize divided back cards. Up until this time, only the address could appear on the back of a postcard. Now a dividing line could provide two sections, an address section on the right side and a message on the left. Postcards published before 1901 can be found with the message on the face of the card.

Already a popular European pastime at the turn-of-the-century, postcard collecting didn't reach comparable interest in America until 1905.

Collecting any kind of postcards can be fun and highly rewarding. But, when it comes to collecting Teddy Bear postcards, the advantages are even broader. Teddy Bear postcards offer similar satisfaction as collecting bears themselves. Yet, the cards require less of an investment, are easier to store, transport and display. Of course, with the increased interest in Teddy Bears the price of bear cards has risen accordingly. However, collecting these items can still be an affordable interesting and pleasurable avocation.

When purchasing a postcard, I suggest you consider the following guidelines: condition, rarity, detail, popularity, age, subject and publisher. Any tears, flakes, creases or soil considerably decreases the value of a postcard. Also, keep in mind, that a large percentage of postcards were published in sets of 2, 4, 6, 8, 10, 12 and so on up to 100.

Some of the most recognized and highly collectible sets of postcards are The Roosevelt Bears, published by Edward Stern of Philadelphia (1906-08). The Roosevelt Bears, Teddy B an Teddy G, were characters in Seymour Eaton's children's books. The cards were reproductions of the colored plates of the series of books. The rarest set of Teddy B and Teddy G cards are the second set of 16 postcards (#17-#32). These cards were produced from illustrations from *More About Teddy B and Teddy G, The Roosevelt Bears* (1907) by R. K. Culver. (See chapter on books.)

Another desirable and well-known series are the "Cracker Jack Bears" copyrighted in 1907 by B. E. Mooreland. These were large bruins colorfully advertising Cracker Jacks. Sixteen beautiful mailing postcards would be sent "Free" by mailing in ten sides of Cracker Jack boxes to Rueckheim Bros. and Eckstein, Chicago. This was advertised on the reverse side of the cards and on the Cracker Jack Boxes.

Another series of bear cards, the "Days of the Week" were produced in leather. Also William S. Heal manufactured a colorful embossed version in 1907. Seven in the set, the bears were engaged in weekday activities.

Postcards signed by the artist is a special collectible feature. Due to laws requiring royalties paid to artists, some publishers would not print the artist's signature.

Richard Felton Outcault was just one of the many famous postcard artists. Born in 1863 in Ohio, he gained recognition for his "Buster Brown and His Dog Tige" which appeared in many newspapers throughout the country. His son and daughter were models for Buster Brown and Mary Jane.

The series of the little girl and the bear (*Illustration 527*) drawn by Outcault were copyrighted by Raphael Tuck in 1903.

English artist Mabel Lucie Attwell often included Teddy Bears in her pictures of chubby children. Another English favorite is artist Angus Richardson.

Publishers developed trademarks that identified their cards. Raphael Tuck for instance, whose cards can be found in most collections, selected an English coat-of-arms as one of his trademarks.

The Raphael Tuck Company was formed in Germany in 1866. The patent used by Tuck during this period was "Art Publishers to the Queen Alexandra." When he moved to London, the patent was changed to "Art Publishers to their Majesties the King and Queen."

A notable brand name used by Tuck was "Oilette."

The "Little Bears" series No. 118 (*Illustration 76*) is just one of the many thousands of beautiful sets of postcards published by Tuck. They are embossed and vividly colored, showing some of the most detailed of all bear pictures.

Postcards come in many categories such as seasonal, political, advertising, greetings, views, souvenir, photocards, historical, novelty and comic to name a few. For example, the novelty category comes in different shapes or forms from the standard card. They can fold-out, contain squeakers or are made of different materials such as celluloid or leather.

Photocards are perhaps, from an historian's point of view, the most valuable type of card. But from a collector's standpoint, it is impossible to gauge the number that were developed.

Personally, when it comes to Teddy Bear postcards,

I'm not too selective in choosing a particular category. I'm just thrilled to find *any* bear related card.

Looking through my postcard album is unendingly entertaining. The fascinating stories of the past illustrated in the colorful cards is a precious window to history with which I find great and enduring pleasure.

ERCY GUTTENBERG MISS MAIDIE SCOTT MANCHESTER 710

This Side for the Address Only.

ABOVE LEFT: *Illustration 511.* This 1907 Teddy B embossed card not only depicts another version of Seymour Eaton's Roosevelt Bears, but we can also observe the message still written on the face of the card. The reverse of this card is in *Illustration 512.* It shows the undivided back card is still in existence. *Author's collection.*

LEFT: *Illustration 512.* The reverse of the 1907 Teddy B postcard in *Illustration 511.* This shows the undivided back card. The words in the right hand corner read "This side for the Address only."

ABOVE: *Illustration 513.* Portrait postcard. c.1910. A beautiful Steiff bear playfully stands on the shoulder of this pretty young lady while they pose for their photograph. Marked: "Guttenberg Photographer and Publisher, Manchester." Mailing date 1910. *Author's collection.*

Illustration 514. Portrait Postcard. c.1924. Black and white card with the message "To Dear Nana from Dicky with love. A year and 7 months. 1924." W. Pearce Photographer, Lewisham and Eltham, England. *Author's collection.*

BELOW: *Illustration 515.* Portrait Postcard. c.1907. A magnificent large white Steiff Teddy Bear is used as a companion to the little girl as she poses to have her photograph taken. A Steiff Teddy Bear of this type is an extremely rare collector's item today. *Author's collection.*

Illustration 516. Photo postcard. Two beautiful early white Steiff bears affectionately pose on a bench. Brown and white photo by W.D. Shipton, Glens Falls, NY. *Author's collection.*

BELOW: *Illustration 517.* The Thayer Publishing Co. Denver, Colorado, reproduced postcards from the *Mother Goose's Teddy Bears Book*, published by Bobbs Merrill Co. Copyright 1907 by Fred L. Cavally Jr. *Author's collection.*

As I went to Bonner
I met a Bear
With coal-black hair,
Upon my word and honor.

COPYRIGHT 1907 BY
FRED L. CAVALLY Jr

Illustration 518. Marked: "Copyright. Published by Langsdorff and Co., 19 City Road, London, E.C." *Author's collection.*

RIGHT: *Illustration 519.* The Cracker Jack Bears Series. Copyright 1907. B.E. Moreland. Rueckheim Bros. Eckstein, Chicago, U.S.A. *Author's collection.*

263

Ain't Babies Rough

A Happy Family.

Bassano.

BUSY BEARS GETTING IT IN THE USUAL PLACE.

Illustration 522. The Busy Bears Series. Published by J.I. Austen Co., Chicago - 436. *Author's collection.*

BELOW: *Illustration 523.* The Arrest. Marked: "Dep. Series 5001." Printed in Germany. *Author's collection.*

The Arrest

OPPOSITE PAGE TOP: *Illustration 520.* Published by Wildt and Kray London, E.C. Nr 1596. Printed in Saxony. *Author's collection.*

BOTTOM: *Illustration 521.* Bassano. National Series. Made in Great Britain. No. 411. *Author's collection.*

Illustration 524. Christmas greetings from the Valentine Series of postcards. Printed in Great Britain. Postmarked 1910. *Author's collection.*

Illustration 525. Little Teddy's Outing. Artchrom Depose. Copyright. Printed in Saxony. Postmarked 1908. *Author's collection.*

266

A
HAPPY
CHRISTMAS

I HOPE you'll have the happiest time,

. . . . You've ever had before .

With everything that you could wish

. . . From Yuletide's golden store. .

LEFT: *Illustration 526.* English artist Agnes Richardson incorporated Teddy Bears and Golliwogs in her childrens type postcard "Celesque Series." Published by the Photochrom Co. Ltd., London and Tunbridge Wells. Postmarked 1915. *Author's collection.*

BELOW LEFT: *Illustration 527.* Copyright 1903 by Raphael Tuck and Sons Co., Ltd., New York. Artist is R.F. Outcault. Note message written on face of card. *Author's collection.*

BELOW: *Illustration 528.* Novelty postcard. Opened by raising flap to pull out 12 black and white pictures of Boscombe, England. Valentine Series. Printed in Great Britain. *Author's collection.*

A " Bear "-er of Best Wishes from **BOSCOMBE**

BOSCOMBE

BEAR, BEAR, DONT GO AWAY
TO COME AGAIN SOME OTHER DAY
I WILL LOVE YOU IF YOU STAY
I WILL LOVE YOU ANY WAY

ABOVE: *Illustration 529.* Novelty postcard. Fold out three dimensional postcard. Made in Germany. Postmarked 1908. *Author's collection.*

Illustration 530. Squeeker type novelty card. Printed in Germany. *Author's collection.*

Chapter Fourteen

Books, Paper And Related Teddy Bear Items

With the amazing acceptance of the Teddy Bear, it is no wonder that books, songs and advertisements touted the wonders of these friendly toys. Teddies have been written and sung about since their inception. Their role as advertising spokesmen and personification of trademarks is seen even today.

According to historians, the most enduring and oldest juvenile bear story is *The Three Bears*. Its definite origin is unknown, but there are versions of the ancient tale in nearly every language from Russian to English.

Its English version seems to be most attributed to Robert Southey in his collection *The Doctor*, published somewhere between 1834-1847.

However, Eleanor Mure's 1831 manuscript of the fable is found in the Toronto Public Library's Osbourne Collection of Early Children's books. Her work, "The Celebrated Nursery Tale of the Three Bears" was in verse form, with roots in original oral tales in which Goldilocks was an old woman, not a little girl. Mrs. Mure's story and pictures were a birthday gift to Horace Broke on September 24, 1831. But very little else is known about her.

Another well-known character, prior to the advent of the Teddy Bear is Uncle Remus' Brer Bear, written about by American Joel Chandler Harris. Brer Bear, along with Brer Rabbit and other popular Uncle Remus characters, captivated the imagination of children in the Southern United States during the 19th century.

Of all Teddy Bear books, perhaps the most coveted series are the adventures of *The Roosevelt Bears* created by Paul Piper under the pen name Seymour Eaton. Teddy B and Teddy G looked more like real bears, than Teddies, and their influence on the toy bear market was tremendous. In fact, *Who's Who* credits Eaton with creating the Teddy Bear.

"Teddy B stands for black and Teddy G stands for gray — not bad and good as people sometimes think. However, with the wholesome mischief and hair-raising adventures of The Roosevelt Bears, the concept of bad and good seems more appropriate."

Eaton's first book (illustrated by Floyd Campbell) *The Roosevelt Bears — Their Travels and Adventures* was a collection of works copyrighted in 1905, since they originally were published in newspapers Sunday supplements and comic sections.

The series continued, compiling more of the syndicated adventures, in *More About The Roosevelt Bears*

(1906). Illustrated by R.K. Culver, Eaton's second book had Teddy B and Teddy G meeting their namesake along the way on their journeys.

Some say the 1907 *The Roosevelt Bears Abroad* was Eaton's best. Also illustrated by Culver, this third book was followed by *The Bear Detectives* (1908). This time Francis P. Wightman and William K. Sweeney did the illustrations. Although all four volumes are rare collectors' items, the last of the series seems to be the hardest to find.

Despite Eaton's commercial success, literary references give him little credit and many libraries of those days refused to stock his stories which he says were based on a mischief committed by children he actually knew.

Because critics treated Eaton with cold harshness, he fought back with defensive press releases and even one introduction to a book which justified his position: "President Roosevelt and his boys have been pleased," he explained in the preface to *The Travelling Bears*.

Eaton's follow-up books to his hard-to-find first four volumes were titled: *The Adventures of the Travelling Bears, The Travelling Bears in New York, The Travelling Bears in Out-Door Sports, The Travelling Bears Across the Sea* and *The Travelling Bears in England*. These books are easier to find, but still much sought after. They actually contain segments from the first four in the series.

Another prized possession by collectors of Teddy Bear books is the *Mother Goose's Teddy Bears*, illustrated and adapted to Mother Goose by Frederick L. Cavally, Jr., published in 1907 by Bobbs-Merrill Company, Indianapolis, Indiana. Famous nursery rhymes are illustrated with 32 wonderful color pictures.

Also, a well-known company which contributed so much in the form of early paper collectables is the McLouglin Bros. Founded in 1856 in New York City, the company started manufacturing paper toys. Their books are easily recognized by the beautiful colored picture on the cover and illustrations throughout the book. The company moved to Springfield, Massachusetts, in 1920.

It would be impossible to list all the Teddy Bear and juvenile bear books in which a Teddy is a prominent character. And, in addition to those books, Teddy Bears showed up in a variety of paper collectibles from Valentines to advertising booklets to toys and even games.

Teddy Bears were good salesmen, using younger

family members to influence their parents buying decisions. Teddy B and Teddy G proved the worth of Fleischmen's Yeast and Pettijohn's Bears made quite an impact with their breakfast food. Sauer's flavoring extract used a Bear Drawing Book as a premium item as did other manufacturers of the early 20th century.

Today, in my new hometown of San Diego, California, a firm called Classifinders uses a tuxedo-dressed Teddy Bear as its spokesperson. A telemarketing company (TEliDIrect) uses the initials T.E.D.I. and a logo of a Teddy Bear on the phone. So even today, advertisers are aware of the warm feelings a Teddy Bear envokes among clients and customers.

Between 1907 and 1911 more than 40 songs had the words Teddy Bear in their title. *Teddy Bear March, Teddy Bear Rag, Will You Be My Teddy Bear* and *The Big Brown Bear* are just a few. Even years later, Elvis Presley's *(I just want to be) Your Teddy Bear* was an instant hit.

But perhaps the most favorite tune is *The Teddy Bears' Picnic,* written by John W. Bratton. The instrumental tune alluded to Teddy Roosevelt's bear hunting picnic. In 1930, British songwriter Jimmy Kennedy put words to Bratton's melody. When the song aired on the B.B.C. it was an overwhelming success. By the 1960s, three million recordings of Kennedy's version had been sold.

The number of artists who've sung this song is nearly endless. One of the best known "If you go down in the woods today" crooners is Bing Crosby.

Collecting paper items related to Teddy Bears offers a wide range of beautiful and fascinating ways to appreciate our favorite star.

Books

Illustration 531. The Three Bears. Copyright 1904. Published by Altemus' Banbury Cross Series. Other stories included in the book are "Jack and The Bean Stalk" and "Little Red Riding Hood." Hard cover. 6¾in (17.2cm) x 5¼in (13.4cm). *Author's collection.*

Illustration 532. The Three Bears. Published by The Alfield Publishing Co., Akron, Ohio. Beautifully illustrated in color by Francis Brundage. Soft back cover. 10in (25.4cm) x 8in (20.3cm). *Author's collection.*

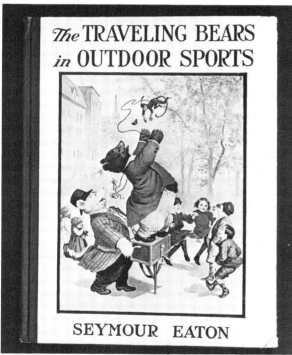

TOP LEFT: *Illustration 533. Two Little Bears* by Fredrika Grosvenor. A very small tale of two very small bears. Beautifully illustrated in color. Copyright 1905. McLoughlin Brothers, New York. 12½in (31.8cm) x 10in (25.4cm). *Author's collection.*

TOP RIGHT: *Illustration 534.* A page from the book *Two Little Bears* by Fredrika Grosvenor (Illustration 533).

LEFT: *Illustration 535.* The follow-up series to the first four volumes of the Roosevelt Bear books by Seymour Eaton were smaller editions with fewer colored plates. These books were taken from segments of the original volumes. Titles include *The Adventures of the Traveling Bears, The Traveling Bears in the East and West, The Traveling Bears in New York, The Traveling Bears in Outdoor Sports, The Traveling Bears at Play, The Traveling Bears in England, The Traveling Bears Across the Sea, The Traveling Bears in Fairyland, The Traveling Detectives, The Traveling Bears' Birthday.* Copyright 1905, 1906 by Seymour Eaton. Copyright 1906 by Edward Stern and Company Inc. Copyright 1915 by Barse and Hopkins, New York. Hard cover. 8½in (21.6cm) x 10¾in (27.4cm). *Author's collection.*

RIGHT: *Illustration 536. The Teddy Bears.* The book tells of the adventures of two children and the Teddy Bears. 14 full-page colored illustrations. Written by Clara Andrews Williams. Illustrated by George Alfred Williams. Copyright 1907. Frederick A. Stokes and Co. New York. Hard cover. 14in (35.6cm) x 10½in (26.7cm). *Author's collection.*

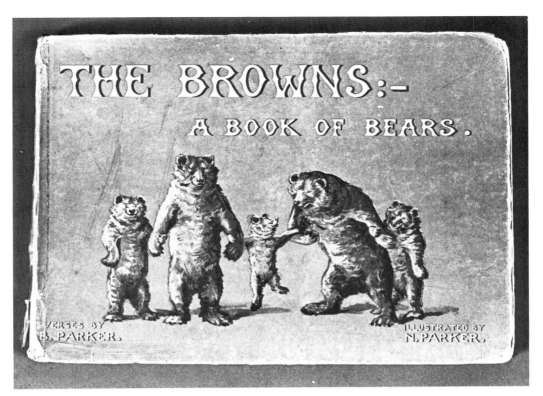

Illustration 537. The Browns. Fine drawings in black and white by N. Parker illustrate the 12 Teddy Bear stories. Written in verse by B. Parker. Printed by W & R Chambers, Ltd., Edinburgh and London. c.1907. Hard cover. 13in (33cm) x 9¼in (23.6cm). *Author's collection.*

Illustration 538. The Busy Bears. A story for little tots by Uncle Milton. Published by The Ullman Mfg. Co., New York. This series of Busy Bears tells of their weekday activities. Hard cover. 5¾in (14.7cm) x 4¼in (10.9cm). *Author's collection.*

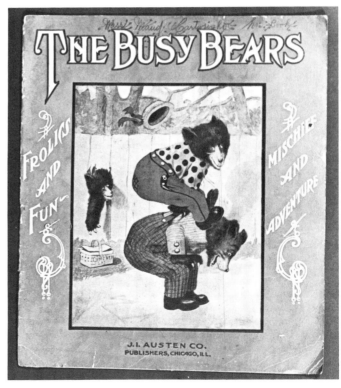

Illustration 539. The Busy Bears. J. I. Austen Co., Publishers, Chicago, Illinois. Copyright 1907. Verses by George W. Gunn. Events happening at school throughout the days of the week are colorfully illustrated. Soft cover. 9½in (24.2cm) x 7½in (19.1cm). *Author's collection.*

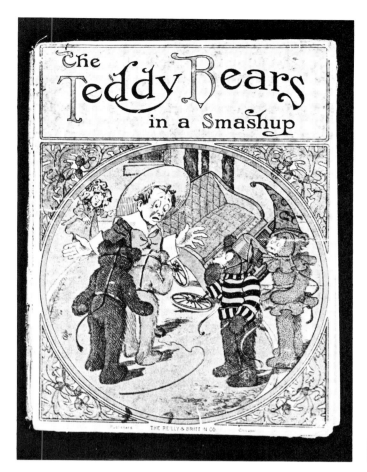

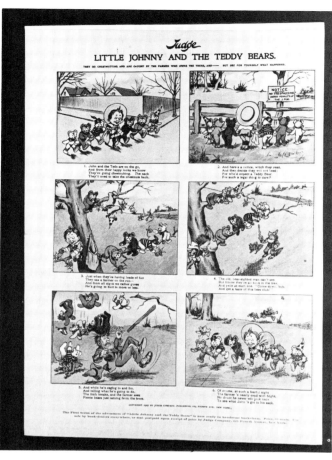

Illustration 540. The Teddy Bears in a Smashup. Published by The Reilly and Britton Co., Chicago. Copyright 1907. Hard back cover. 7in (17.8cm) x 5¼in (13.4cm). Eight books in the series included the following titles: *The Teddy Bears Come to Life, The Teddy Bears at the Circus, The Teddy Bears on a Lark, The Teddy Bears on a Toboggan, The Teddy Bears at School, The Teddy Bears Go Fishing, The Teddy Bears in Hot Water. Author's collection.*

Illustration 541. Little Johnny and The Teddy Bears. Printed by Judge Co.; published in their *Judge* magazine in 1907. Later the stories were converted into series of books. *Author's collection.*

Illustration 542. Little Johnny and The Teddy Bears. Comical adventures of six stuffed Teddy Bears and the mischievous Little Johnny. Rhymes by Robert D. Towne, Ed. Pictures by J. R. Bray. Copyright 1907. The Reilly and Britton Co., Publishers, Chicago. Published by permission of the Judge Company (originally a comic strip in the *Judge* magazine, see *Illustration 541). Author's collection.*

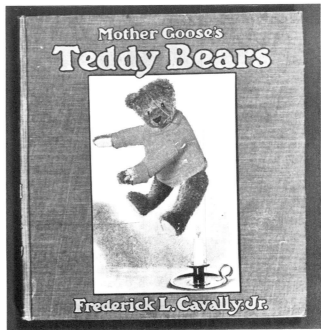

ABOVE LEFT: *Illustration 543.* Partial shape of a Teddy Bear is cut out for this cute 6in (15.2cm) book. Published by Valentine and Sons Ltd., Dundee, London and Montreal. *Author's collection.*

ABOVE RIGHT: *Illustration 544. Mother Goose's Teddy Bears.* Copyright 1907. Published by Bobbs and Merrill Company. Illustrated and adapted to Mother Goose by Frederick L. Cavally, Jr. 32 beautifully colored pictures illustrate this book. 11¼in (28.6cm) x 10in (25.4cm). Hard cover. *Author's collection.*

LEFT: *Illustration 545. The Roly Poly Cubbies.* The story of two furry little bear cubs who longed to see the world. Copyright 1916. Stecher Litho Co., Rochester, New York. Verses and Drawings by H. Brooke Levering. Soft cover. 7¾in (22.3cm) x 7½in (21.9cm). *Author's collection.*

ABOVE: *Illustration 546. Little Bear's Adventures.* Copyright 1928 by Rand McNally and Company, New York, Chicago, San Francisco. Author is Frances Margaret Fox. Pictures by Frances Beem and Warner Carr. Includes stories of a jolly little bear and all of his adventures. Hard cover. 7¾in (19.8cm) x 6¼in (15.9cm). Other books in this series include *Little Bear's Ins and Outs, Adventures of Sonny Bear, Doings of a Little Bear, Little Bear and his Friends, Little Bear at Work and Play, Little Bear's Laughing Times, Little Bear's Playtime, Little Bear's Ups and Downs. Author's collection.*

Sheet Music

ABOVE LEFT: *Illustration 547. The Lonely Doll Learns a Lesson.* The characters of this book are a Schuco Yes/No Bear, Steiff's "Jackie" and "Edith," a Lenci type doll. Author and Photographer is Dare Wright. Photographs in black and white. Copyright 1961. Published by Random House, Inc., New York. Hard cover. 12¾in (32.5cm) x 9¾in (24.9cm). *Author's collection.*

ABOVE: *Illustration 548. The Teddy Bear Pieces,* by J.S. Fearis. Published by McKinley Music Co., Chicago and New York. 10¼in (26.1cm) x 13½in (34.3cm). c.1907. *Author's collection.*

ABOVE RIGHT: *Illustration 549. Musical Echoes from Teddy Bear Land,* by R.G. Grady. Published by Gamble Hinged Music Co., Chicago 1910. 10in (25.4cm) x 13in (33cm). *Author's collection.*

RIGHT: *Illustration 550. It's Up to You. Would You Rather be a Tammany Tiger or a Teddy Bear.* Words by Jeff T. Branen. Music by W. R. Williams. Published by Will Rossiter, The Chicago Publisher, 10½in (29.2cm) x 14in (35.6cm). *Author's collection.*

Advertising

ABOVE LEFT: *Illustration 551. Sack Waltz.* By Metcalf. Published by DeLuxe Music Co., New York. 10½in (26.7cm) x 13½in (34.3cm). *Author's collection.*

LEFT: *Illustration 552.* Pettijohn's Cereal. c.1890. Large Bruins were used to advertise Pettijohn's Cereal. Most of these advertisements were in black and white. Shown here is one done in beautiful colors depicting the bear cooking cereal over an open fire in the woods for a little girl. The cubs play hide and seek in the background. *Private collection.*

ABOVE RIGHT: *Illustration 553.* Pettijohn's Breakfast Food. c.1890. Huge bruins were used to advertise this company's products. Their motto was "Bear In Mind our Trade Mark." *Author's collection.*

ABOVE: *Illustration 554.* Three handsome jointed Teddy Bears advertise this tailoring company's precise methods for the perfect fit. M. Born and Co., The Great Chicago Merchant Tailors. c.1907. 10½in (29.2cm) x 8in (20.3cm). *Author's collection.*

In the Teddy Bear Caves

of the exclusive Roosevelt Hotel,
New York City

In the Teddy Bear Caves, the famous playroom of the Roosevelt Hotel, the children guests enjoy the delights of a child's paradise. They often have their meals here—and "Horlick's" is always a treat for lunch. "All the children love it," says Miss O'Donoghue, dietitian in charge of the children's menu.

"We serve malted milk to the children regularly," says Miss O'Donoghue, dietitian, "—and of course it is 'Horlick's'"

At this magnificent hotel, where people of the great world come together, one expects nothing but the best of everything. Naturally, only "Horlick's" is ever served in the children of guests.

ABOVE LEFT: *Illustration 555.* A 1928 Horlicks malted milk advertisement pictures children riding huge bears on wheels through the Teddy Bear caves in the famous playroom of the Roosevelt Hotel in New York City. The reverse of the page shows children playing with a large jointed Teddy Bear while a group of smaller bears watch from the top of the cave. The caption below reads "Even Teddy Bears Stay With Us." Taken from *Woman's Home Companion,* November 1928. Note: Valuable information on dating bears can be found in old magazine advertisements in which Teddy Bears were used. *Author's collection.*

ABOVE: *Illustration 556.* Colorful dye-cut. 1923 calendar advertises John Bilodeau and Co., General Merchants in Groceries, Flour, etc. *Author's collection.*

ABOVE RIGHT: *Illustration 557.* Teddy Bears were used as promotional material for many companies. This 16in (40.6cm) Teddy Bear was mailed free with four subscriptions to *Needlecraft Magazine.* Note the American design of the bear. *Author's collection.*

RIGHT: *Illustration 558. The Lettie Lane Paper Family* by Sheila Young presents Lettie's grandmother who gives gifts to Lettie. *Author's collection.*

THE LETTIE LANE PAPER FAMILY
By Sheila Young
Presenting Lettie's Grandmother Who Brings Christmas Presents to Lettie

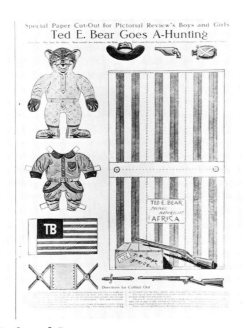

Bear Related Items

TOP LEFT: *Illustration 559. T.E. Bear Goes Hunting.* c.1909. Paper cut-out. A colorful picture of T.E. Bear, his clothes, tent and items required for his African hunting trip. "The Start for Africa" is the first of this series. The reverse of the page tells of his adventures. Also advertised is a cut-out T.E. Bear on muslin with clothes and a 20in (50.8cm) stuffed doll with Rough Rider hat and gaiters in durable cloth with a tissue pattern for his clothes. Taken from the *Pictorial Review* magazine. *Author's collection.*

BOTTOM LEFT: *Illustration 560.* English Teddy Bear Rattles. c.1900. **Left:** 1¾in (4.5cm). **Center:** 1½in (3.8cm). **Right:** 1in (2.5cm). Silver hallmarked. These bears were in all probability once attached and used to decorate larger rattles, such as the one in *Illustration 562. Author's collection.*

BOTTOM RIGHT: *Illustration 561.* **Left:** English Teddy Bear Seal. c.1910. 1¼in (3.2cm). Silver. **Right:** English Teddy Bear Perfume Bottle. 1½in (3.8cm). Silver hallmarked. Head is removable to fill body with perfume. *Author's collection.*

TOP RIGHT: *Illustration 562.* English Baby Rattle. c.1900. 7in (17.8cm). Silver hallmarked. Bone teething ring. Teddy Bears often decorated baby rattles. It is hard to imagine that a tiny baby was allowed to bite on something so easy to swallow. *Author's collection.*

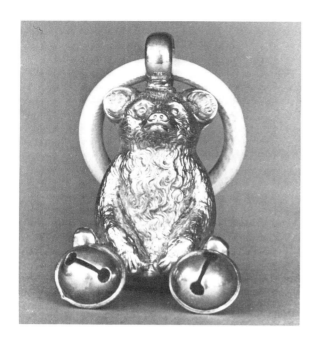

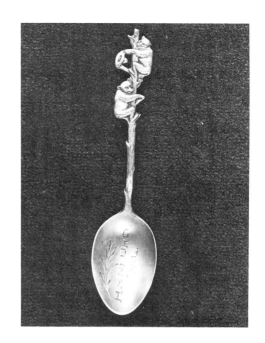

TOP LEFT: *Illustration 563.* English Baby Rattle. c.1910. 2in (5.1cm). Bone teething ring. Bear is silver hallmarked. Two silver bells are attached to the bear's feet. *Author's collection.*

TOP RIGHT: *Illustration 564.* Spoon. c.1907 5¼in (13.4cm). Sterling silver; marked on back "P & B" (Paye & Baker, North Attleboro, Massachusetts). Two Roosevelt-type bears are climbing the handle, which resembles a tree. *Author's collection.*

BOTTOM LEFT: *Illustration 565.* **Left:** Teddy Bear Bread Pin. c.1907. 3in (7.6cm) tall. The shape of a grey Roosevelt bear colorfully wearing a red jacket and yellow and red checked trousers and grey sweater is cut out of tin. The words "Teddy Bear Bread" is advertised in the center of the bear. **Right:** Teddy Bear Bread Pin. c.1907. 1¼in (3.2cm) in diameter. Blue background with a brown, jointed Teddy Bear. The words "Demand Teddy Bear Bread - Every Bite a Delight" surround the bear. Comments: Rare. Different colored jointed Steiff type Teddy Bears were used on various size pins by this company to advertise their product. *Author's collection.*

BOTTOM RIGHT: *Illustration 566.* Teddy Bears were also used to decorate buttons during the early 1900s. *Author's collection.*

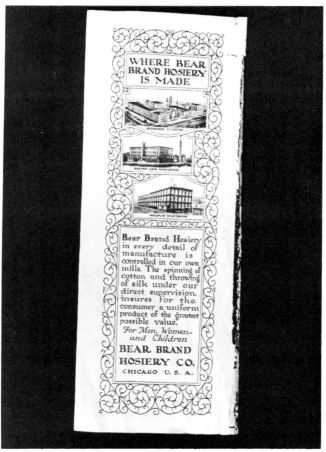

ABOVE LEFT: *Illustration 567.* Early 1900s version of The Three Bears is printed onto material and hand embroidered. 16in (40.6cm) x 13in (33cm). *Author's collection.*

ABOVE RIGHT: *Illustration 568.* Roosevelt Bear Toy. c.1907. 6¾in (17.2cm) long. A tin Roosevelt jointed bear rides a bike when string is threaded through the loop and the groove of the wheels. The hanging weight gives balance to the toy. *Author's collection.*

LEFT: *Illustration 569.* Leaflet taken from a box of Bear Brand Hosiery. The huge factories show how successful the company was, accounting for the number of varieties of advertising items appearing in collections.

ABOVE: *Illustration 570.* Bear Brand Hosiery. c.1920. 15½in (39.4cm). Brown hollow papier mâché bear advertises the merchandise by wearing a pair of the socks. Condition: excellent. *Author's collection.*

ABOVE LEFT: *Illustration 571.* A little paper bear was enclosed with a box of Bear Brand Hosiery and advertised that mailing him along with 10¢ would bring you a cloth bear in return. The bear in *Illustration 572* could possibly be this cloth bear. *Author's collection.*

ABOVE RIGHT: *Illustration 572.* Bear Brand Hosiery. c.1920. 10in (25.4cm). Oilcloth bear; stuffed with kapok; marked "Bear Brand Hosiery, Chicago, U.S.A." This bear appears to be the one that could be sent for in the advertisement in *Illustration 571. Author's collection.*

RIGHT: *Illustration 573.* Bear Brand Screen. c.1920. 36in (91.4cm) high, 29in (73.8cm) wide. This rare colorful advertising screen can be best enjoyed when the light shines through from the back of it. *Private collection.*

ABOVE: *Illustration 574.* Bear Brand Hosiery. c.1920. 20in (50.8cm) high, 36in (91.4cm) long. Rare papier mache bear painted black with gold lettering advertises Bear Brand Hosiery. *Private collection.*

ABOVE LEFT: *Illustration 575.* "Bears Inspection." c.1920. 28in (71.1cm) long, 18in (45.7cm) tall. Rare papier mâché advertising bear. Incised on base is "Bear's Inspection." Lyle's syrup tin is not original. *Private collection.*

LEFT: *Illustration 576.* English Cigarette Lighter. c.1900. 4½in (11.5cm). Silverplated bear with removable head. Fluid and wick are contained in body. Wick is threaded through cigarette, ready to ignite. *Author's collection.*

ABOVE RIGHT: *Illustration 577.* German Musical Stand. c.1900. 29in (73.7cm) high, 18in (45.7cm) wide. Beautifully carved wooden bear clings to the base of the stand. Three smaller carved bears are lids for compartments. When lids are raised, music plays. Comments: Rare. *Private collection.*

ABOVE: *Illustration 578.* German Hall Tree. c.1900. 8in (20.3cm). German wood carvings are displayed in this ornate hall tree. *Private collection.*

TOP LEFT: *Illustration 579*. Candy Container. c.1880. 8in (20.3cm). Brown flocked papier mâché rabbit, white painted papier mâché bear. Both animals have glass eyes. Head of rabbit is removable to fill body with candy. *Private collection.*

MIDDLE: *Illustration 580*. Heubach Bisque Figurines. c.1910. 2½in (6.4cm) long, 2in (5.1cm) tall. Bisque babies are dressed in brown bear skins. Comments: Rare. *Courtesy Joan Sickler.*

TOP RIGHT: *Illustration 581*. China Bowl. c.1920. 7½in (19.1cm) diameter. Cute early style Teddy Bears are colorfully shown riding on an airplane and rocking horse. Markings on base read "Hammersley and Co. Longton, Stoke-on-Trent, England." *Author's collection.*

BOTTOM: *Illustration 582*. **Left:** China Bears. 2in (5.1cm). Two Teddy Bears seated in front of a suitcase. Condition: Mint. Comments: These bears are part of a series. Each piece has the same Teddy Bear positioned next to different items. **Right:** China ashtray. 3½in (8.9cm). Two Teddy Bears are seated on the ashtray under an umbrella. Beside them is a match holder. *Author's collection.*

Chapter Fifteen

Famous Literary Bears

With all the Teddy Bears that appear in literature, there are a few that shine as stars. Winnie-the-Pooh, of course, is probably the most famous. Other famous literary bears of outstanding fame are Rupert Bear, Paddington Bear and Super Ted.

Winnie-the-Pooh

The true story of Winnie-the-Pooh is a living example of the powerful influence and relationship a Teddy Bear has on a young child's life. One of the secrets to the success of the famous author A.A. Milne was his ability to write his wonderful stories as seen through the eyes of his only son Christopher Robin.

Alan Alexander Milne was born January 18, 1882, at a prep school in Kilburn, London, England, where his father was proprietor and director. A shy child, Milne showed early talents in writing and founded the school's magazine. He matriculated to Trinity College, where he edited *Granta,* the university's journal. After contributing articles to a variety of newspapers and periodicals, Milne accepted a position with *Punch,* where he stayed from 1906 to 1941 as Assistant Editor.

In 1913 he married the wealthy Dorothy De Selincourt. After serving in World War I, he returned home to live in Mallord Street, Chelsea. There, on August 21, 1920, the now legendary Christopher Robin was born.

On his very first birthday, the little boy received a Teddy Bear nearly as big as he was. His parents purchased it for him from the elegant Harrod's Department store in London. They christened the Teddy Bear, Winnie-the-Pooh.

The name Winnie was taken from a real live bear which Christopher Robin loved to visit at the London Zoo. The bear was a mascot of a Canadian regiment and had been given to the Zoo in 1914 when the troops embarqued for France.

The "Pooh" part of Winnie's name was taken from another live friend of Christopher Robin's: a swan that swam on the lake near the Milne home in the country.

Living not too far away from Buckingham Palace, Christopher often walked there with his nannie, Olive Blackwell, who for some reason the family dubbed "Alice." There frequent viewing of the changing of the guards served as the base for one of Milne's most famous poems, written and popularized as a song during the 1920s and 1930s.

"They're changing the guard at Buckingham Palace,
Christopher Robin went down with Alice,
We looked for the King but he never came.
'Well, God take care of him all the same,' says Alice."
In need of friends, and shy like his father, Christopher

Robin and Winnie-the-Pooh became constant companions. He began to give life to his toy playmate in childish conversations, blaming poor Pooh for his own mischief.

One memorable incident happened when Christopher Robin's father was entertaining actor-manager Sir Nigel Playfair. The little boy came down the stairs, dragging Pooh behind him. "What a funny man. What a red face," said Christopher Robin. Milne questioned his son, asking why he had made such a rude comment. Christopher Robin protested his innocence, blaming it all on his toy bear.

Winnie-the-Pooh and other nursery animals Piglet and Eeyore became such an integral part of the Milne household that A.A. Milne began incorporating them into his stories.

His book entitled *When We Were Very Young* (1924) sold half a million copies.

Each daily adventure in their lives gave Milne more ideas and material for his precious stories. The books brought Winnie-the-Pooh to life, pleasing millions of children throughout the world. Milne continued to write other books and plays until he underwent brain surgery which left him an invalid.

Regarding the notoriety his father's fame brought him, Christopher Robin suffered mixed emotions. Strange as it may seem, Milne is known to have disliked children. Christopher Robin, sent away to school at the age of nine, was teased by his classmates over the image created in his father's famous poem "Christopher Robin is saying his Prayers." It caused him embarrassment and deep unhappiness.

Today Christopher Milne (who has dropped his middle name, Robin) has retired with his wife, Lesley, and lives a quiet life writing at his country home in Devon.

In 1981, at the age of sixty, Christopher Milne unveiled a statue of his childhood playmate, Winnie-the-Pooh, at the London Zoo. It was a memorial to A.A. Milne whose centennial was celebrated in 1982.

The famous artist responsible for immortalizing Milne's words pictorially was Ernest Howard Shepard. He is known throughout the world as "the man who drew Pooh." His fine drawings gained recognition in their own right.

His first sketches were in black and white, but when the books reached great popularity, the works were converted to color.

His original sketch "Poohsticks Bridge" sold in 1970 for 1700 pounds (approximately $4,000). At the age of ninety, Shepard generously donated 300 of his original Pooh drawings to the Victoria and Albert Museum.

Shepard is also famous for his work illustrating almost one hundred other books including the classic Kenneth Grahame's *The Wind in the Willows*. He died in 1976 at the age of 97.

Winnie-the-Pooh toys and related items are still as popular today as they have been through the past sixty years. Here in the United States, Sears, Roebuck and

Company holds the license for manufacturing the Disney Pooh items.

Late in 1984, Disney gave the rights to making replicas of the Winnie-the-Pooh animal characters to R. John Wright, an American doll artist, and member of N.I.A.D.A. (National Institute of American Doll Artists). The characters are faithful three-dimensional renditions of E. H. Shepard's original drawings.

Winnie-the-Pooh

Illustration 583. Winnie-the-Pooh. Late 1950s. 13in (33cm). Beige flannel; eyes are black beads; unjointed head and body; kapok stuffing. Possibly by Agnes Brush, Whitestone, Long Island, New York. Condition: Good. *Author's collection.*

Rupert Bear

Illustration 584. Tembro. c.1984. 25in (63.5cm). White acrylic fur; glass eyes; unjointed body polyester fiber filling; bright red sweater; yellow and black checked trousers and scarf. *Author's collection.*

Illustration 585. Page taken from a Rupert book. Copyright Beaverbook Newspaper Ltd., 1976. Printed in Great Britain. *Author's collection.*

Rupert Bear

Another popular bear character is a particular favorite of mine, since I grew up with him. "Rupert Bear" is the British equivalent of "Mickey Mouse." Almost every day since 1920, the London *Daily Express* has carried the stories of the Little Lost Bear on its center page.

Rupert Bear was originally created in 1920 by Mary Tourtel, the wife of the associate editor for the *Daily Express.* Rupert became a well-known character dressed in his red sweater and bright yellow checked trousers and scarf, when he appeared in the newspaper's cartoon series. Other than his bear like head, he resembled and acted more like a well mannered little boy than a bear. The stories in child-like rhyme, told of Rupert's adventures in the village of Nutwood along with his famous friends Bill Badger, Algy, and Edward Trunk the elephant. The cartoon characters were so popular "The Rupert League" was formed as sort of a fan club.

Due to failing eyesight, Mary Tourtel retired in 1935 when the hard task of continuing the famous artist's work was taken over by Alfred Bestall. He retired in 1965, but still drew the covers for the *Rupert Bear Annuals* until just a few years ago. Now the series is illustrated by a team of artists.

Ruperts' books, dolls, children's clothing and many more products have immortalized the little bear.

The Tembro Company in England is the only manufacturer currently licensed to make a stuffed Rupert Bear. They produce a 25in (63.5cm) tall unjointed version.

The ongoing popularity of the little bear has been shown by his record of only missing two publications of The *Daily Express* since his first appearance on its pages on November 8, 1920.

Paddington Bear

Another English contribution to bears in literature is Paddington Bear. He made his debut late in the history of Teddy Bears, but nevertheless seems to be following the popular pattern of Winnie-the-Pooh and Rupert.

Paddington Bear stories were written by Michael Bond. Bond conceived the idea from a bear he found sitting in the corner of a shelf in Selfridge's a large London store. Desparately searching for a last-minute Christmas gift for his wife, he took pity on the lonely bear and decided he would give it to his wife. On the way home, he christened it Paddington, after the train station close to his home.

Several days later, Bond was inspired to write a story about a stowaway bear that travelled from the darkest parts of Peru. He was a young, but confident bear that was discovered at Paddington Station with a label

Paddington Bear

Illustration 586. **Right:** English Paddington Bear. 18in (45.7cm). Unjointed body; wool felt duffle coat; felt rain hat; brim is fastened back with safety pin; Dunlop rubber boots. Due to the fact the English Paddingtons are unable to be exported to the U.S., Eden manufactured their own version. **Left:** Eden Paddington. 18in (45.7cm). Unjointed body; bonded flannel duffle coat; felt hat; rubber boots. Note: safety pin used in English bear is eliminated due to American safety laws. *Courtesy Lillian Rohaly.*

attached to him with the words: "Please look after this bear. Thank you."

Unfortunately, it wasn't until 1958, two years after the writing of the story, that Bond found a publisher that found his work meritous.

Unlike most furry, cuddly bears, Paddington's nose is all that can be seen peering beneath his wide brimmed oversized felt hat. He is ready for the worst of weather in his duffle coat and Wellington boots.

The original and favorite drawings of this unique bear were by Peggy Fortnum.

Paddington appeared on television in eight countries.

Super Ted

SuperTed is the modern day version of Superman. The bionic bear, wearing a zip-off fur coat, evolved in 1974 from bedtime stories told by Mike Read to his children. Read, who owned his own artifical flower business, fabricated stories of an ordinary forest bear developing magical powers when Mother Nature gave him a special word. His duty then was to be a guardian of small children. He was able to protect them from danger by changing himself into numerous disguises. The stories told by Read are now published and are popular children's books. His wife, Liz, designed "SuperTed" who is now a star, manufactured in a Welsh toy factory, run by Keith and Diana Jones.

In 1985, R. Dakin & Company, San Francisco, California, acquired the rights to produce SuperTed in a non-jointed version, complete with outer fur suit which can be "zipped" off to reveal SuperTed in his Superman-like outfit. Another version, also made by Dakin, is SuperTed dressed only in his flamboyant costume.

Chapter Sixteen

Bears And Their Original Owners

Discovering the personal history of a Teddy Bear and its owner(s) gives you a chance to really appreciate the priceless quality of these collectibles. Sometimes this awareness assists date and manufacturer documentation, but more frequently acts as another avenue to deeper understanding of Teddy Bears and their influence on people of all ages.

Loving memories of special times and fanciful dreams crop up in conversations with original bear owners. Each owner perceives his/her bear companions in a different light.

The following stories and photos offer a sample of the possibilities that exist in the field of "bear genealogy."

Three Generations of Love

The Steiff bears in *Illustration 592* shared love and affection with three generations of John Glass' family.

The first of the three bears was purchased in Breslau, Germany, by John Glass' grandmother Alice Hoff in 1907. Its characteristics are classically Steiff: shoe-button eyes, voice box and button in ear. Called *Brummbar* because of its brumm sound, the bear was loved first by Alice Hoff's daughter (and John's aunt) Ilse.

The bear was then stowed away in a trunk for twenty-three years. In 1937 it was given new life and a home with Ilse's nephew (John's brother Tom) and now lives with Ilse's sister (John's mother) Anni Hoff Glass in Southern California.

A second, smaller bear, whose Steiff button is missing, belonged to John Glass himself. Given to him by his grandmother Hoff, in 1936, John named his bear BIU (a childlike pronunciation of the German word *BÄR*/bear). Biu also stayed with John's mother (Anni Hoff Glass) when she emigrated to Southern California.

Now a third generation of bear lovers exists in this family. Aaron Glass (John's son), born in 1971, has a Steiff bear no more than a decade old. This last addition to the Steiff/Glass family lives in Los Angeles, California.

Through the Good and the Bad

These two bears reflect a heartwarming, yet sometimes sad, story of Jean Moore and her family.

The early American bear on the left in *Illustration 589* was given to Jean's older brother Fred in approximately 1909 in Nova Scotia.

By the time the family moved to California in 1922, Fred had outgrown his childhood toy. Jean's grandmother, meticulously saved and displayed her family's childhood treasures in a whitewashed cellar. Teddy sat in a high chair until it was adopted by Jean's younger sister. The young girl loved the bear, taking it everywhere until in 1927, at the young age of fourteen, she died.

Jean, being a kind loving person took Teddy in and he has been part of her life ever since.

Knowing the importance of the bear in a child's development, Jean gave her son Alan the bear pictured on the left of *Illustration 589* when he turned three. Alan loved the little bear. He played such a large part in his everyday life. He was even given presents at Christmas.

In 1938 Jean became ill and it was necessary to place Alan in a preventorium for a few months. He was the youngest resident.

As children are wont to do, several of the older boys teased young Alan. To make matters worse these thoughtless boys conspired against him and his furry friend and hid the bear.

When Alan returned home to his mother things were just not the same without his little companion. You can imagine the small boy's delight when one day the kind nurse appeared at the door of their house carrying the poor, wet and mildewed bear. She had organized a search party along with Alan's friends and the bear was discovered under an old building, right in the middle of a mud puddle.

Jean lovingly repaired and bathed the little survivor and hung him out to dry, until he was fit to go back to the arms of his rightful owner forever.

Foundling Bear

In the early 1900s unemployment forced many to leave home in search for work. Frankie Runzo's father found himself far away in Oakland, California, when his daughter was about to be born in Los Angeles.

Walking around Oakland's Lake Merrit, he consoled himself as he yearned to be with his pregnant wife. His thoughts were filled with both expectation and anguish.

A box appeared in front of his feet. Giving it a boylike kick, he noticed the box was not empty. When opened, it revealed its contents — a furry, gold Teddy Bear, peering out forlornly as if to say, "Please take me home!" And he did.

When Frankie's father was able to go back to Los Angeles he presented the foundling bear to his new daughter.

"Teddy and I were born on the same day," tells Frankie. "Needless to say, we've been constant companions ever since. Teddy would always go do the things *I* wanted to. Like climb trees and play in the garden instead of practicing the piano and violin. I'd always blame poor Ted to avoid a scolding for my tricks!"

Frankie's mother loved dolls. But Frankie just loved her bear. Her mother sewed the little bear an entire frilly wardrobe that ended-up stored away in a trunk. One birthday, she gave in to Frankie's wishes and made a pair of overalls for Ted. His initials were embroidered in bright red: TB. To this day, these remain Teddy's permanent clothes.

Teddy and Frankie loved to ride in her grandparents shiny, big 1930 Buick with its soft, rich-smelling leather seats and glass flower vases. They toured up and down the Pacific Coast Highway.

A favorite stop was Carlsbad by the Sea. 54 years later, Frankie and her husband Jim came back to that community. The couple transformed a single-story doctor's office to a fairy tale English Tudor style candy shop.

There, with Teddy supervising, the couple prepares mouth watering chocolate goodies. One of their most popular treats is — a chocolate Teddy Bear.

In and Out of Trouble

Margaret Bonis says her Teddy Bear keeps her memories alive. She and Ted were both born July 4, 1940, in Scotland. Throughout her travels Teddy has never left her side.

Her children love to hear Margaret recount myriad bear anecdotes. A favorite story is how Ted lost his fur early in life. Margaret's experiment with her dad's hand clippers was extremely successful and she recalls her exuberant joy watching the fur fall to the ground, leaving her once fuzzy playmate nearly naked.

In addition to Teddy's haircuts, Margaret aimed to take him abroad. With an aunt in the army in Africa, Margaret insisted on dressing up, putting her bear in a bright red wheelbarrow and marching off to join Auntie at War. She recalls they didn't get too far.

Ted forgave Margaret's mischievous antics and professes to still love her dearly.

Honored Bear

I'll always remember the evening I went by to visit Eve Westberry to be introduced to her Teddy. As I walked into the room, my eyes immediately focused on the bear. Sitting like a king on a throne, he had the position of honor in the center of the room. My heart skipped a beat as I picked him up. He gave me the dignified, yet warm look only a Steiff bear can. His silky fur was in remarkably fine condition, and through the years he still proudly displays his mark of quality, the Steiff button affixed firmly in his ear.

Just looking at the beautiful condition of this 24in (61cm) Steiff Teddy Bear shows the years of love and care he received.

Eve's first Teddy Bear was a dear little 9in (20.3cm) Steiff, presented to her on the day she was born, July 12, 1910. Although Eve loved her little bear she yearned for a large one which would offer her real companionship.

When she was six years old her dream came true. In 1916, her Aunt and Uncle did their Christmas shopping in Chicago's elegant Marshall Field's department store. There they purchased the largest bear in the store for their favorite little niece.

"When I opened the huge box I saw Teddy looking up at me. I couldn't believe my eyes!" said Eve. "I just knew we'd always be together — and we have."

Bright-Eyed Bear

S & H Green Stamps, diligently saved by Jane Olson's mother and grandmother, lead to the purchase of Jane Olson's Teddy Bear when she was two years old. It was 1915 when the women and toddler approached the store in Peoria, Illinois.

Jane halted when she saw a fascinating Teddy Bear sitting in the window. His name was Teddy Bright Eyes. A little switch on the side of his body lit up his eyes. Determined that Teddy was going home with her, Jane put up a fuss and wouldn't allow her mother and grandmother to look at anything else in the store. Finally, they gave in and traded in their stamps so the happy little girl could go home with her new friend.

Jane Olson and Teddy Bright Eyes have been inseparable ever since.

Illustration 587. Jim Runzo makes solid chocolate bears while Frankie and TB supervise. The chunks of chocolate are melted in a large metal bowl, heated below by four light bulbs. A chain continuously conveys the melted chocolate and takes it to the trough, where it is ready to be molded.

Illustration 588. Frankie and TB proudly stand behind the finished chocolate bears now removed from the mold. On the left is the rare c.1925 Teddy Bear mold, used to make the chocolate bears.

Illustration 589. Jean Moore holds her two treasured bears. On her right, an American style bear given to her brother in 1909. In her left arm is the "survivor," a 1930s American bear who belongs to Jean's son and has had a very eventful life.

ABOVE LEFT: *Illustration 590.* Margaret Bonis as a little girl lived in Scotland. Here she is holding her Teddy Bear before she discovered her father's hand clippers and gave him a hair cut.

ABOVE RIGHT: *Illustration 591.* Margaret Bonis holds her first and only Teddy Bear who still loves her despite her childish prank of shaving off all his hair.

RIGHT: *Illustration 592.* Three generations of Steiff Bears are shown here. They belong to the Glass family.

Illustration 593. Jane Olson loves to demonstrate how her childhood Teddy Bear's eyes still twinkle brightly after 69 years.

Illustration 595. Eve Westberry affectionately holds her lifelong companions: a magnificent 25in (63.5cm) Steiff Teddy Bear, a beautiful German bisque doll and a little 9in (22.9cm) Steiff Teddy Bear.

Illustration 594. Eve Westberry as a little girl. She proudly stands beside her best friend Teddy.

Chapter Seventeen

The Power Of The Teddy Bear

Teddy Bears have made life better for children throughout the years. A symbol of love and caring, they offer security, comfort and companionship.

Teddy Bear's nurturing attributes are especially important to unfortunate youngsters who've suffered mistreatment, parental desertion and/or illness. Frequently, the love provided by a little bear has been an abused or orphaned child's main source of emotional support.

If you love bears, you love children.

I'd like to inspire bear lovers to use our favorite toy to make life better for less fortunate children.

You may do this individually or through a group effort. For instance, you can take it upon yourself to offer a bear to a nearby hospital to make a scarey, strange experience more "bearable" for a frightened, sick child.

Or if you belong to a club, you may want to chose a children's organization to assist through projects and fundraisers.

For example, my twice a year Teddy Bear Show raises funds to donate to a particularly worthwhile charity. A local (Oceanside, California) residential treatment center for abused children provides an important specialized service and needs constant financial assistance. So at each show, the other collectors/exhibitors and I personally donate bears from our own collections to raise funds for the home. The profit from the sale of these particular bears goes directly to the home for abused children. The response has been wonderful. I'm proud to say our efforts have raised a considerable amount of money for the home.

It makes me feel so good to be able to help in this way and I know it will give you a feeling of satisfaction too.

I encourage you to reach out to those who need you through your bears.

FOLLOWING PAGE: *Illustration 596.* A 5 foot (152.4cm) mannequin of Theodore Roosevelt and the 3 foot (91.4cm) Teddy Bear tied to a tree depicting the historical event in 1902 when Teddy received his name, was created by Linda and Wally Mullins. To help raise money for the abused childrens' home and to commemorate "1985 as the year of the Teddy Bear," the Mullins donated these items for a silent auction at one of their 1985 Teddy Bear events.

Illustration 597. This charming c.1910 print is a beautiful example of the close relationship Teddy Bears have with their young companions and what a meaningful part they play in their lives. *Author's collection.*

Chapter Eighteen

Good Bears Of The World

The magic of the Teddy Bear is exemplified in The Good Bears of the World.

The non-profit organization, founded in 1973 by James T. Ownby, provides Teddy Bears to sick children and hospitalized adults, elderly people confined to nursing homes and abused children in shelters and foster homes.

The goal of the 10,000 international Good Bears of the World (GBW) members (and their local "dens") is to make the Teddy Bear a symbol of hope and faith and through his powers promote worldwide love, friendship and goodwill.

Jim Ownby, a journalist, conceived GBW in 1969 after reading Peter Bull's *Bear With Me*.

One episode, the story of "The Teddy Bear Man" captured Ownsby's imagination. Russell McClean earned the title of the Teddy Bear Man based on his personal experience as a child in Lima, Ohio. McClean never let go of his frightening memories of fear and terrifying loneliness as he lay in a strange hospital bed as a little boy.

As an adult, he figured that a Teddy Bear could dispel the negative emotions hospitalized children so often endure. In 1951, he began giving Teddy Bear's to children for that first scarey night in the hospital.

When Ownby read about McClean, he said: "It is patently obvious that this project should be taken up on a worldwide basis." Hence, Good Bears of the World.

The club was officially chartered and founded in 1973. Its two branches are in the United States and the United Kingdom. In the United Kingdom, Col. Bob Henderson heads up the organization. He is also the honorary historian for the group.

1985 was designated The Year of the Bear by Ownby, as a more hopeful follow-up to the doom-filled connotations (based on George Orwell's *1984*) of the year of 1984. During the year, Teddy will become a dominant factor in developing fellowship amongst all people, regardless of race, religion, age or sex.

The association also honors President Theodore Roosevelt on the Anniversary of his birth with "Good Bear Day" which is October 27. It was celebrated and officially proclaimed in 35 states in 1984. The GBW salutes Teddy Roosevelt and the legacy that he left and vows to continue to work in his memory providing love, understanding and goodwill to all people.

For information regarding the Good Bears of the World please contact: The Good Bears of the World, P.O. Box 8236, Honolulu, Hawaii 96815, U.S.A. (808) 946-2844.

LEFT: *Illustration 598.* The Official Good Bears of the World Teddy Bear. 11½in (29.2cm). Honey brown plush; brown eyes; unjointed body; polyester fiber filled. Label reads "© Ideal Toy Corp. 1981 Newark, N.J. 07105." Comes with application for membership to the "Good Bears of the World" and the story of the creation of the Teddy Bear.

BELOW: *Illustration 599.* Jim Ownby and Linda Mullins meeting at The Teddy Bear Boosters Luncheon to discuss The Good Bears of the World.

Chapter Nineteen

A Tribute To Peter Bull

Illustration 600. The late Peter Bull signs Bully Bear's Certificate of Authenticity.

This book would not be complete without a special tribute to the "King of the Teddy Bear" Collectors, the late Peter Bull.

Since Mr. Bull came from my homeland England, I was originally well familiar with his career as a famous actor (*Beau Brummel, Dr. Strangelove, Tom Jones, African Queen*), author and astrologer. Some years later,

I became thankful for his work in bringing the Teddy Bear collectors of the world together through his first monograph, *The Teddy Bear Book* (1969, Random House).

His story begins at the age of 16 when his mother donated Peter's childhood bear to a rummage sale. Not until thirty years later did he reveal the harbored deep resentment and poignant loss of security the incident caused.

A dinner party with friends surfaced the old feelings when Bull discovered he was not alone in his inhibitions. His companions confessed they, too, experienced trauma with the loss of their childhood toys.

Intrigued with his new found knowledge, Peter Bull began to research the relationships and encounters between people and their bears. His radio talks and newspaper publicity brought attention to Bull.

As a guest speaker on NBC's *Today* show, he requested Teddy Bear stories from the viewing audience. Within a week, 2000 letters poured in.

Bull did not consider himself a collector. The history of bears and the influence these toys had on men, women and children offered him more pleasure. His love of bears is shown in the numerous animals he rescued from neglect and those he adopted after they had been discarded. All but five of his 250 bears were given to him as gifts.

Bull was a one-man Teddy at heart. For more than 40 years his constant companion was a 3½in (6.3cm) Teddy Bear named Theodore, who fit perfectly in his pocket.

The most famous bear in Bull's collection is the hump-backed Aloysius, formerly called Delicatessen. The bear was a surprise gift from Euphemia Ladd, the owner of a dry goods store in Saco, Maine. Aloysius sat on a shelf in the elderly lady's store for 50 years. When producers of the TV series *Brideshead Revisited* sought to cast Sebastian Flyte's beloved Teddy Bear companion, Peter Bull produced Delicatessen. Renamed Aloysius, the bear was an overnight star.

Bull also had special affection for his own creations "Bully Bear," "Young Bear" and "Bully Minor." The bears were born with the assistance of Alison Wilson (nee Nisbet) of the House of Nisbet (Winscomber, England) and came with their own set of adventure books penned by Bull.

Peter Bulls' background and interest in astrology is well respected. On May 1, 1971, he opened "The Astrological Emporium" in a quaint old building off Kensington Church Street in London. Pauline McMillian was a gifted artist who painted gift items for the Emporium. With Peter's influence, it wasn't long before Teddy Bears cropped up in Pauline's work. It was Pauline's wonderful talent teamed with the insight of The House of Nisbet that brought life to the Zodiac Bears and book. Bull's twelve zodiac bears and book were one of the last contributions the King of the Teddy Bears made to the world. Mr. Bull's last book, *A Hug of Teddy Bears,* was published posthumously by E. P. Dutton, Inc., in 1984.

Peter Bull is responsible for uncovering the vast underground Teddy Bear movement. Arctophilists (bear lovers) the world over have him to thank for his revelation of the commonality of love and happiness individuals receive from their bears.

Peter Bull dreamt that Teddy Bears would some day be missionaries of this special understanding to people everywhere.

Peter Bull died May 21, 1984, in England, but he will long be remembered by Teddy Bear lovers throughout the world.

Directory of Teddy Bear Artists

(Note: Information was correct at time of publication. May be subject to change.)

Carriker, Pat. (619) 724-9074.

Emory, Flore. P.O. Box 1888, Fallbrook, CA 92028. (619) 728-3803.

Kinser, Charleen. 921 Boalsburg Road, Boalsburg, PA 16827. (814) 466-7846.

Kruse, Susan. 431 Wooden Drive, Placentia, CA 92670.

Kunkel, Dot. P.O. Box 691, Downey, CA 90241.

Lewis, Judy. 1128 Riviera Drive, Santa Ana, CA 92706.

Lindsay, Cheryl. 1366 Eldean Lane, Oceanside, CA 92054.

Neble, Jeff and Karlene. J.P. Bartholomew Co. 128 S. Cypress, Orange, CA 92666. (714) 532-4273/771-2436.

Port, Beverly. P.O. Box 711, Retsil, Washington 98378. (206) 377-9202.

Purpus, Joanne. 579 La Costa Ave., La Costa, CA 92024. (619) 942-5018.

Spiegal, Linda. 14776 Moran Street, Westminister, CA 92683. (714) 891-7089.

Tipton, Colleen. 1825 Forest Ave., Carlsbad, CA 92008.

West, Lynn. Lasting Endearments, P.O. Box 2040, Costa Mesa, CA 92626. (714) 650-2327.

Bibliography

Reference Works

Pollock's Dictionary of English Dolls. Ed. Mary Hillier, London, England: Robert Hale Limited, 1982.

Books

Bull, Peter. *The Teddy Bear Book.* New York: Random House, Inc., 1970.

Cieslik, Jürgen and Marianne. *German Doll Encyclopedia 1800-1939.* Cumberland, Maryland: Hobby House Press, Inc., 1985.

Coleman, Dorothy S., *et. al. The Collector's Encyclopedia of Dolls.* New York: Crown Publishers, Inc., 1968.

Fondin, Jean. *et. al. The Golden Age of Toys.* Greenwich, Connecticut: New York Graphic Society, Ltd., 1967.

Hutchings, Margaret. *Teddy Bears and How to Make Them.* New York: Dover Publications, 1964.

King, Constance E. *Antique Toys and Dolls.* London: Cassell Ltd., 1979.

King, Constance E. *The Encyclopedia of Toys.* New York: Crown Publishers, Inc., 1978.

Mondel, Margaret Fox. *Teddy Bears and Steiff Animals.* Kentucky: Collector Books, 1984.

Morrison, Ellen E. *The Guardian of the Forest.* New York: Vantage Press, 1976.

McCullough, David. *Mornings on Horseback.* New York: Simon and Schuster, 1981.

O'Brien, Richard. *The Fourth Edition of Collecting Toys.* Alabama: Book Americana Incorporated, 1985.

Ryan, Dorothy B. *Picture Postcards in the United States 1893-1918.* New York: Clarkson N. Potter, Inc., 1982.

Schoonmaker, Patricia N. *The Collector's History of the Teddy Bear.* Cumberland, Maryland: Hobby House Press, Inc., 1981.

Waring, Philippa and Peter. *In Praise of Teddy Bears.* Great Britain: Caledonian Graphics Ltd., 1980.

Wingate, Dr. Isabel B. *Fairchild's Dictionary of Textiles.* New York: Fairchild Publications, 1979.

Journals

Automobile Quarterly. Kutztown Publishing Co., Volume 12, Number 1. Pennsylvania: 1974.

Articles

Ackerman, Evelyn. "Schuco." *The Teddy Bear and friends*®. Hobby House Press, Inc., Spring 1985, pages 26-30.

Axe, John. "Merrythought." *The Teddy Bear and friends*®. Hobby House Press, Inc., Winter 1984, pages 17-24.

Gardener, Stephan. "Dakin." *The Teddy Bear and friends*®. Hobby House Press, Inc., Summer 1983, pages 10-11.

Methuen, A.B.P. "A.A. Milne." *This England.* Winter 1981, pages 21-24.

Schoonmaker, Patricia N. "Billie Possum." *The Teddy Bear and friends*®. Hobby House Press, Inc., Fall 1983, pages 20-22.

Sieverling, Helen. "Mechanical Bears." *The Teddy Bear and friends*®. Hobby House Press, Inc., Winter 1984, pages 38-41.

Stanton, Carol Ann. "Bear Facts." *Antiques and Art.* March 1978, pages 41-43.

Steiff, Alte. "Grisly." *The Boutonnier.* June 1984.

Index